Five Trophies and a Funeral

Five
Trophies
and a
Funeral

The Building and Rebuilding of
Durham County Cricket Club

S T U A R T   R A Y N E R

FOREWORD BY **PAUL COLLINGWOOD**

First published by Pitch Publishing, 2019

Pitch Publishing
A2 Yeoman Gate
Yeoman Way
Worthing
Sussex
BN13 3QZ
www.pitchpublishing.co.uk
info@pitchpublishing.co.uk

ISBN 978-1-78531-488-9

Typesetting and origination by Pitch Publishing
Printed and bound in India by Replika Press Pvt. Ltd.

Contents

In memory of Stephen Drury,

1945–2016

Foreword by Paul Collingwood

I'VE played cricket since I was a kid with my brother Peter in the back yard, but I've only ever had two clubs. Now I've called time on my professional career after 24 amazing seasons with Durham, the next time I fancy a game I'll be picking up the phone to Shotley Bridge Cricket Club asking if they'll have me!

Once I joined Durham County Cricket Club, I never wanted to leave – why would I? I got the same opportunities I could have had at Surrey, Middlesex or Lancashire. That was thanks to the vision and determination of men like Don Robson, Tom Moffat, Ian and Roy Caller, Mattie Roseberry, Bob Jackson and Geoff Cook to bring top-class professional cricket to a part of the world that had never had it.

Durham have become the blueprint for county cricket and represent everything our region is about. We might have different football teams and accents, but the north east of England is a family that looks after each other, and so is the cricket club that represents it at professional level. While I might have stopped playing for it, I will never leave it. When times allows, you'll see me in the stands at the Riverside, hopefully getting drinks bought for me!

I was approaching my 16th birthday when Durham played their first game of first-class cricket, and it was the perfect storm for me. I couldn't have imagined the brilliant career cricket has given me, playing for my home county and my country. Peter was four years older than me and working by then, so he didn't get the same opportunity.

Durham turning first class highlighted how many skilful players there were in north-east cricket, and you feel for those who missed the boat, like Stuart Wilkinson, a fast bowler I used to play against in the local leagues. Stuart took Geoffrey Boycott's wicket in the 1973 Gillette Cup but, because Durham were still a minor county, he didn't get the chance to test himself against top professionals on a daily basis as I did for 24 summers.

Clearly the club were always going to have to recruit players to set the ball rolling, but the people who set up the first-class club knew they had a blank canvas and had the vision to create something with longevity. They were all about talent identification and giving local lads like me opportunities. They looked beyond the County Durham border, also opening up parts of the country like Northumberland and Cumbria.

More than 20 years after it was set up, Durham's academy is still churning out international players. Add the quality of our coaching system and determination of north-east cricketers, and it's no surprise only Yorkshire, with all their resources, have produced more England Test players this century. It's a great combination that clearly works.

It was always going to take time for everything to bed down and for Durham to settle into the belief that we belonged in a first-class structure that had not changed for 71 years until we came along. My first few seasons were a real struggle, but my team-mates and I were shown the patience we needed to fulfil our potential as individuals and as a club. I'll always be grateful.

We couldn't do it on our own, and people like Dale Benkenstein, Michael Di Venuto and Mike Hussey played very important parts in the story – not just because of their skill but also their attitudes. Others, like Jon Lewis, Alan Walker, Gareth Breese and Callum Thorp, have been adopted into the Durham family, giving great service after their playing days.

While some counties have chased short-term success and others have maybe been happy at times to make up the numbers, Durham have got the balance totally right on the field. In the last couple of years, after our players and supporters were hit by a really harsh punishment for off-field mismanagement, there could have been a real temptation to fill the squad with Kolpak players and county journeymen who could get us back to where we once were much more quickly, but Durham have always looked at the bigger picture.

In doing things the way they set out to from the start, Britain's youngest first-class county has given itself a really strong identity, based on producing players in a relaxed environment and creating tough cricketers proud to represent our region and all it stands for. The longevity of some of our coaches has given everybody an understanding of what the club is about, driving behaviour. That identity kept us strong through the hard times and will bring the many good times also described in this book back.

When I was first starting to pick up a bat and ball, players staying at one club for 23 years was not so unusual, but now it is rare and getting rarer. The world is changing, and with the growth of franchise cricket players get used to different dressing rooms and moving club becomes more and more natural. But, even over the last few years as Durham have been hurt by departures, there were still people like me who wanted to stay, and others, like Ben Raine, Will Smith and Tom Latham, who wanted to come back. That's testament to that culture and identity.

Another part of Durham's identity is ambition, a constant theme of the story you are about to read. If anything, the difficulties the club have been through came from over-ambition, but I'd rather that than the other way.

It might take a few years, but I'm very confident Durham will get back to winning silverware and setting the standards for English cricket on the field as well as off it. The club is in a position to recruit again, which means it can add the extra ingredients so important to our past success. There is new leadership from a chairman, Sir

Ian Botham, and a director of cricket, Marcus North, who played for Durham and know what it is about, plus a chief executive, Tim Bostock, who can bring that outside perspective.

Some clubs have gone over 100 years without winning the County Championship, so for Durham to have done it in 16, and for me to have played a part, was incredible. Our first trophy, beating Hampshire at Lord's in the 2007 Friends Provident Trophy, was a fairy tale. We're not finished, though. No one at the club is content with what we have achieved, remarkable though it is. Right from the day it turned first class, Durham County Cricket Club has always wanted to be the best – not just the best team with the best players, but the best coaches and the best academy. If we didn't have that drive, we wouldn't be Durham.

There are many more chapters and many more trophies to come in this magnificent story. I am just proud to have played my part in getting things started.

Acknowledgements

FIRSTLY, an apology. There are probably a few former Durham players and/or administrators, some big figures in this story, put out that I did not interview them for this book. If you are one, I can only say sorry but easily the biggest challenge was cramming everything in. That so many people were so generous with their time left me with a huge amount of material, so I just tried to get a wide cross-section of experiences.

If you missed the cut, it was not personal. Besides, if you were at the club after 2005 there is every chance I did interview you along the way and even if you are not quoted, you probably helped inform me.

I did speak to David Boon, Tim Bostock, Sir Ian Botham, Gareth Breese, Jeff Brown, Paul Collingwood, Geoff Cook, Steve Coverdale, Andy Fothergill, David Harker, Stephen Harmison, Simon Henig, Gordon Hollins, Bob Jackson, Keaton Jennings, Neil Killeen, Jon Lewis, Chris Middleton, Tom Moffat, Phil Mustard, Marcus North, Graham Onions, Chris Rushworth, Will Smith, Mark Stoneman, James Welch, Dave Whitlock and John Windows specifically for the book, and I hope you enjoy reading their reminiscences as much as I enjoyed hearing them. Particular thanks go to Paul for writing the foreword, to Jeff for allowing me to pore over his old *Journal* cuttings, to Tom for showing me some valuable documents, and to Dave for also providing photographs of his historic trip to The Parks – I wish I had space to use more. Thanks also to Alison Sutherland for one of her pictures and my employers, NCJ Media, both for allowing me to write this book and to use some of their photos.

A massive thank you to Paul Cunningham and Chris Waugh for not only proofreading the book but in Chris's case acting as an invaluable sounding board too. I am also indebted to Pitch Publishing who, having taken the risk of publishing my first book, *The War of the White Roses*, were daft enough to let me write another. I hope I have repaid your faith. When it comes to the people who have shown me support or just taken an interest, there are too many to list but that does not mean I am not extremely grateful.

Most of all, thank you for reading. Without you, there would be no point. If you enjoy reading this book half as much as I enjoyed writing it, the whole exercise has been worthwhile.

Introduction

MONDAY, 3 October 2016 was the first time I set foot inside St Columba's Church in Scarborough. Despite being far bigger inside than it looks from the outside, and despite my dad and I arriving early, there was still barely a seat to be had at Stephen Drury's funeral.

The Rayners and the Drurys have been inextricably linked my whole life. Stephen was born and bred in Chesterfield but moved to Scarborough to practise law, which bizarrely was also my dad's backstory. My family lived in East Ayton, the Drurys across the river in the west half. Stephen used to run the Sunday school I attended with his son James at our village church, St John the Baptist's, where we were later confirmed together. He played the organ and, after retiring as a solicitor, became the vicar before moving to St Columba's.

James and I had gone to different primary schools but the same secondary school and sixth-form college. We had been swimming club mates and fellow cub scouts, and I had roped him into playing for our sixth-form hockey team. My dad drove us to school most mornings until James's mum Judith, a netball team-mate of my mum's, joined as a maths teacher for our second year. Twelve months later, my brother Jamie and James's younger sister Rachel joined the school run. By the time my youngest brother Ross did, James and I were at sixth-form college.

Those are the links I can think of off the top of my head, but there are probably more, so it was hard to take when James told me about Stephen's terminal cancer. He and his family had always been supportive of me so it was important to be at the funeral, even with a big story brewing at work. It was a day for perspective, after all.

Back home, Durham County Cricket Club's day of reckoning was looming. They had been living beyond their means for too long, and the authorities had decided to step in. Durham were saved from extinction, but at a high price. I took my pew not knowing what that would be, or when it would be revealed. I had been told to expect an announcement early that week. It was Monday morning.

When I got into my car after the service, I turned on the radio and waited for the sport bulletin. Nothing. I headed to the wake. I came away mid-afternoon to head to Sunderland where the football club's manager, David Moyes, would be pressing flesh with the media that evening. I ducked into my mum's house to pick up my things and change clothes, switching on my mobile phone. There was a voicemail message from work and, although it assumed I knew what had happened rather than telling me, it was obvious Durham's punishment had been handed down – and that it was severe. Even so, it was a surprise when I loaded up the internet: relegation from County Championship Division One and a 48-point deduction for the 2017 season the most eye-watering of a raft of sanctions. I would have to give Moyes a miss, get back to Newcastle and start writing.

Durham CCC had also come to play an important part in my life. From the wooden bench I used to sit on at Scarborough's North Marine Road cricket ground – from where I could not only see some of the world's best cricketers but also, in the background, St Columba's – I had become aware of their story. I started watching professional cricket in 1988 as Durham began harbouring serious ambitions to play at that level themselves.

The couple who sat behind me regularly travelled from County Durham because first-class cricket was not available to them at home, but that was about to change. In 1991 I watched Durham play for the first time at the Scarborough Cricket Festival, a glimpse of the club about to go from minor county to British first-class cricket's first addition since Glamorgan in 1921. The following summer they were back, transformed. Ian Botham was their star, smashing the ball over my head and into a washing line outside one of the B&Bs backing on to the ground. Over the next few summers they and I would be regular visitors.

After years of Durham coming to me, in 1996 I enrolled at Durham University, allowing me to see the team and its new Chester-le-Street ground develop. One wet day early in the 1997 season I was even able to interview their new captain, David Boon, for my student newspaper. After university I stayed in touch with my second team. My first job in journalism was as a sports sub-editor with the *Liverpool Echo*, and I moved to Aigburth in 1999. In 2001, with Old Trafford in use for a pop concert, Durham played Lancashire a few minutes' walk from my home in a one-day group game.

So perhaps it was inevitable that my first sports writing job would bring Durham back into my orbit. The timing could scarcely have been better. I joined *The Journal* in Newcastle early in 2005, the year Durham finally stopped being whipping boys and began establishing themselves as a major force in English cricket. Promotion in both forms of the game followed that season, then five major trophies between 2007 and 2014 as their academy churned out a steady flow of England players. When *The Journal*'s newsroom was merged with that of our sister newspapers, *The Chronicle* and the *Sunday Sun*, in 2009, I began covering the team away from home as well as at the Riverside.

It was therefore upsetting to see a county that had done so much to spread and enhance cricket treated so savagely. There were reasons for it – Durham's success had come while running up debts they could not afford, and the authorities were anxious to ensure others were not tempted down that path – but the punishment was widely seen as heavy-handed and disproportionate. Some in the north east suspected jealousy was at play too.

Having recently finished writing *The War of the White Roses*, it seemed inevitable I would pen another book about this situation. I decided not to jump in immediately, giving time for wounds to heal and perspective to be gained, but when *The Journal*, *The Chronicle* and the *Sunday Sun* decided in 2017 to stop staffing county cricket, it felt like a signal to get on with it.

The seeds of Durham's downfall were wrapped up in the way they passed into the first-class game, their subsequent success and how they tried to achieve it, so with the help of insights from key figures, this book will attempt to look at all of that, as well as asking what the future holds. The story is relevant to more than just those who support Durham or even cricket enthusiasts. Many sports clubs can learn from how they have produced and honed young players and from the more cautionary tale of how they overstretched. There are lessons too for the cricketing authorities if they want to avoid a repeat of the demise they contributed to.

I write at a time of great change for the English game, but hopefully some of the strengths which made Durham such a force in the early 21st century can soon return them to those heights. Their run to the Twenty20 quarter-finals in 2018 was encouraging, the form of their second XI even more so, and ambitious signings for that season and the next show the financial picture is improving under Sir Ian Botham's chairmanship. I hope you enjoy reading this story as much as I enjoyed researching, writing and occasionally living it. It would have been nice had Mr Drury been able to as well, but this book is dedicated to his memory.

1.

Upgrading to First Class

L OCAL sports writers Jeff Brown and Ian Murtagh were at Feethams to cover football on 4 March 1989, but Darlington's overdue first home win of the season was not at the front of either's mind. The previous day, Durham County Cricket Club's committee decided to write to the Test and County Cricket Board (TCCB) requesting a meeting to discuss a possible application for first-class status.

'It was something you knew was bubbling under the surface,' recalls Brown, a sports writer on *The Journal* since 1986. 'It was the biggest story I ever broke but it was one I did jointly with Ian Murtagh, who was with the *Northern Echo*. We'd been asked to keep it quiet until the whole bid was ready. We were covering a Darlington football match and there was a freelancer from *The Independent* there who said, "What's this about Durham bidding to become a first-class club?" We both feigned ignorance and then said to each other, "We've got to run this story because it's going to get out and if we're scooped on our own doorstep with a big story like this it won't look good," so we both broke it the following Monday.'

One of English cricket's most remarkable tales was about to unfold and the way Durham joined the first-class ranks shaped their successes and failures for more than a quarter of a century.

The impetus came from neighbouring Northumberland, when Newcastle City Council approached cricket-loving brothers Roy and Ian Caller to ask if they could organise a match as part of celebrations for the city's 900th anniversary. Their company, Callers Pegasus Travel, sponsored a sold-out Minor Counties versus the West Indies game in 1980 at Jesmond – a suburb of Newcastle – and from it came the 1981 Callers Pegasus Festival: back-to-back, one-day games between a combined Northumberland and Durham side and an International XI. The 6 August match was abandoned due to rain, but the following day saw a home win. The festival became an annual event, running until 1990 and attracting players of the calibre of Geoffrey Boycott, Mike Gatting, Graham Gooch, David Gower, Nasser Hussain, Allan Border, Dennis Lillee, Steve Waugh, Sunil Gavaskar, Kapil Dev, Imran Khan, Mike Procter, Clive Rice, Michael Holding, Clive Lloyd, Malcolm Marshall, Courtney Walsh, Dean Jones and Ian Botham.

Andy Fothergill kept wicket for Northumberland/Durham in 1983 and 1984. 'It was massive for north-east cricket because you'd have the best players in the world there,' he says. 'I played against Barry Richards and Graeme Pollock, which for a 21, 22-year-old was amazing. They were past their best by a long way but it was a fantastic experience. We stopped in a hotel the night before and you mingled with those people. It was a bit of a piss-up but you tried to keep yourself right because you wanted to experience the whole thing the next day.'

The festivals raised more than £170,000 for cricket, £65,000 of which went to Durham – 'absolutely critical to our existence', says Tom Moffat, who became treasurer in 1985 – and they showed their gratitude by making Ian Caller president in 1985. Northumberland did likewise with Roy in 1988.

Norman Graham, the Hexham-born former Kent bowler who was Northumberland's commercial manager, suggested Northumberland and Durham jointly bid for first-class status and move from amateur to professional county cricket. Nobody had joined British cricket's

County Championship since Glamorgan in 1921, so Durham chairman Arthur Austin and Northumberland secretary Ron Wood visited Lord's to take soundings. Austin had been one of Durham's finest wicketkeepers, playing in the 1936 victory over All India at Ashbrooke during the first season of a 60-game career which ran until 1954. By then he had been on the committee three years, becoming honorary secretary from 1969–75, then chairman. 'It didn't take us long to find out it was an impossible task,' he said.

'It was set up to fail because Northumberland just didn't want it but that would have been interesting because one of the problems with Durham was building a stadium,' says Bob Jackson, then Durham's joint-secretary. 'Jesmond's a very difficult parking area but there could have perhaps been some avenues there.' Moffat 'was told there was this antipathy between the two [clubs], and there were people at Northumberland you couldn't work with'.

A joint-committee set up to look into the possibility reported back in 1985: 'At least £500,000 would be needed to launch a side, and a guaranteed income of at least £300,000 per year would be required to maintain it. There is no possibility of this type of money being raised from spectator payments, and large and continuing sponsorship would be needed.' It warned 'some clubs might have to voluntarily go out of existence' to ensure grounds to play on, and there was resistance to leaving the Minor Counties Championship, the level below the first-class version. With even the climate cited as a reason, the report advised against a bid but said the counties would not stand in anyone else's way.

Some refused to take no for an answer. Mattie Roseberry and Mike Weston were Durham businessmen whose sons had been travelling to Lord's from the age of 12 for coaching. As well as captaining England's rugby union team and chairing its selection panel, leg-spinner Weston made 30 appearances for Durham from 1956–73. Roseberry's son Michael made his Minor Counties Championship debut for Durham in the 1984 final against Cheshire aged 17 but joined Middlesex the following year. Brown explains: 'Mattie Roseberry and Mike Weston said, "This is crazy, we should be providing first-class cricket up here for young lads to not have to leave the area."' At Marylebone Cricket Club head coach Don Wilson's suggestion, they built an indoor cricket school, the McEwans Centre, at Rainton Bridge near Houghton-le-Spring. It opened in 1986 with Wilson's former Yorkshire and England team-mate John Hampshire as head coach. Roseberry and Weston began floating the idea of Durham going first class alone.

Durham County Cricket Club had been formed at Durham City's Three Tuns Hotel on 23 May 1882, beating Northumberland by four wickets less than three weeks later. In 1895 they became founder members of the Minor Counties Cricket Association (MCCA), the body they would leave if Roseberry and Weston's dream came true. They won its Championship that year, jointly with Norfolk, and eight more times, equalling Buckinghamshire's record. Durham went unbeaten in 65 Championship games from August 1975 to August 1982 and in 1973 became the first minor county to defeat a first-class team, beating Yorkshire by five wickets at Harrogate in the Gillette Cup. Twelve years later they also became the first to do it twice, passing Derbyshire's 171 all out with seven wickets and 4.2 overs to spare in the 60-over NatWest Trophy at Derby.

'I went down not expecting to play but Richard Mercer had a back injury,' says Fothergill. 'Because Darlington was my club and [Durham skipper] Neil Riddell was captain there, for things like that I would go down and just be 12th man because I just loved being around it. When we were fielding we felt like a first-class side, but when Michael Holding was charging in he hit David Jackson on the helmet and David came off. When he went back on, he was out first ball. Holding slowed down after that and started to pitch the ball up. If he'd have bowled to his full potential we wouldn't have got anywhere near it. I was due to be the next-but-one in, but I was thinking, "Oh my God, if I have to bat, I'm going to be killed!" Merce was fit for the game against Kent in the next round so they picked their strongest side, which was fine. They got absolutely hammered [by 79 runs].'

Fothergill had caught Derbyshire's eye and was invited to a trial second-team game against Lancashire, but his attitude showed why Roseberry and Weston were so determined to establish a first-class north-east side. 'I was almost press-ganged into going by Neil Riddell, who was my mentor,' he admits. 'I didn't really want to but he told me to go down for the experience. I'd borrowed Neil's bat, and stuff from everybody else, but I didn't have a helmet. Playing at Darlington on such a slow, low wicket, I didn't need one. John Stanworth, the Lancashire captain, saw me walking out to bat and knew I was a trialist. He asked me, "What are you doing? Where's your helmet?" When I said I didn't have one, he stopped the game and lent me his, which was amazing. I didn't keep in the second innings because Derbyshire's first-team wicketkeeper [Bernard Maher] had broken a finger, so Chris Marples wanted a game. I fielded second slip and gully, and got two catches off Devon Malcolm, which was another surreal experience not having gloves on.'

Fothergill was not bothered when the trial came to nothing. 'I was playing football for Bishop Auckland, cricket for Durham as a minor county, and I had a decent job, so life was quite nice,' he explains. 'With Bishop Auckland I was playing to a good standard, and FA Cup football. I loved that time. When Durham went first class it was my home county, all your mates were playing – you knew everybody, you knew the area and it was a lot more comfortable. I knew it was a once-in-a-lifetime opportunity so I was really pleased to grasp it. The money wasn't any good but it wasn't for the money.'

Burnopfield had produced Colin Milburn, the explosive 18-stone batsman whose Test career was cut short when he lost his left eye in a 1969 car crash, as well as Glamorgan off-spinner Jim McConnon, capped twice by England in 1954. Stockton's Richard Spooner, Norton's David Townsend and Eaglescliffe's Cecil Parkin also wore the Three Lions, but 19th-century England cricket and rugby union captain Andrew Stoddart, Peter Willey and Bob Willis were the only Durham-born players with more than ten caps – and claiming Willis was a stretch. He lived there for six weeks before his dad left the

Sunderland Echo and moved to Manchester. Considering the Durham Cricket Association Arthur Austin chaired and Bob Jackson had been secretary of since it was revived in 1970 had 114 affiliated clubs – twice as many as Northamptonshire or Leicestershire – there was a lot of untapped talent.

In the autumn of 1988, Roseberry spoke to committee member Riddell – Durham's captain since 1980 – about his idea. The left-hander from Staindrop made his debut in 1972, a week after turning 15, and his List A (professional-level one-day) debut at Harrogate in 1973, taking the team to within 15 runs of their historic victory. When he retired in 1990 it was as Durham's leading appearance- and run-maker. Riddell, who ran his family's roofing company, saw minor-counties cricket as a platform for those who could not play full time. 'We would be closing a door to all the good amateurs, many of whom could have played first-class cricket but were precluded from doing so because they had jobs, responsibilities, families, aspiration,' admits Tom Moffat. 'They couldn't afford the time, the commitment and the money to take on a tenuous link into first-class cricket. Had I ever got the chance I would never have been able to take the risk because I was a chief colliery engineer with three children at 27, which would have been the peak of a first-class career.' Riddell, assistant secretary Sam Stoker and president Ian Caller told Roseberry they could not support him.

His plan was to stage games at Sunderland's Ashbrooke, which attracted 18,000 spectators for Durham versus Australia in 1948. Durham would use it for around 30 days a year, staging five first-class matches and three or four Sunday League games, while 'compatible' clubs hosted the rest. They would meet the expense, and Sunderland Cricket Club could make money from refreshments. Sunderland's committee approved this in principle in November 1988 but, while wishing him well, leader Don Robson – also a Durham committee member – said the county council would be unable to help develop Ashbrooke. Chester-le-Street Council's Labour Group secretary Malcolm Pratt told Roseberry it was out of their jurisdiction, and a meeting with South Shields Council officials also drew a blank. When Roseberry, Weston and Hampshire met John Hall at his Wynyard Hall estate, the Metrocentre developer would only support them if games were played there. Lord Lambton's agent discussed Lambton Castle, but shooting rights made that unworkable. Roseberry also asked Pratt about a Chester-le-Street ground.

In October 1988, Roseberry approached Austin, who showed him the 1985 Northumberland/Durham report and suggested he speak to Moffat. 'Mattie was always trying to do it as a business thing because he was a businessman,' Moffat says. 'I said, "It cannot work like that, Mattie. You've got to go through Durham." He was so intense, and I do give him and Jack Hampshire credit. It's sad he gets so little recognition, because he did spark us off again, but he was going down the wrong road.'

Moffat supported the principle though, and spoke up for it when he, Austin, Stoker and secretary Jack Iley met Roseberry, Weston and Hampshire at the Rainton Lodge Hotel on 15 November 1988. Durham's committee was told about the meeting on 5 December, when Austin asked Moffat to pick up Roseberry's groundwork and produce a report.

A working party of Austin, Iley, Moffat, Stoker, Robson and Jackson would liaise with Roseberry and his supporters. Iley shared Riddell's concerns about abandoning minor-counties cricket, but Moffat saw his job as convincing the doubters. Like Iley and Austin, he was a former Durham wicketkeeper, making 52 in the first of seven appearances between 1966 and 1968. Now 58, he ran his own publishing company and had formed the Durham Small Businesses Club.

'When Glamorgan went first-class in 1921, all they had to do was put a fixture list up!' he says. 'There were 28 real doubting Thomases on our committee, people including the treasurer, who said it was impossible. They didn't want to be little fish in a big pond. I've always been a real positive Jonny. As a wicketkeeper, it was my role to make things happen. When I walked on to the field with my gloves on, I would say to myself, "I'm the best wicketkeeper here today," and 90-odd times out of 100 I was.

'A lot of people were very important to it, but I always believe that without my drive and vision Durham wouldn't have been a first-class county. Some people might think I'm being too arrogant but you cannot do what I've done without having an ego. When I was chairman of the business club, I had a chief exec who used to say, "My biggest problem with you is picking up your ideas and putting them into practice because you're such an ideas man they cannot always be right." I said, "Yeah, but a lot of them are." I'd done so many outlandish things that worked. I believed there was no reason why we couldn't [go first-class].'

Two days after Brown and Murtagh broke their story, Moffat posted a letter to TCCB secretary Alan Smith asking for 'an early indication of your positive support for an application – provided we meet the criteria necessary.' Smith replied: 'I could not give a direct answer.'

Moffat's report, presented to Durham's committee at the McEwans Centre on 21 March 1989, looked at the 1987 balance sheets of non-Test-match counties Derbyshire, Glamorgan and Somerset – all of whom made losses – with expenditure ranging from the former's £456,187 to the latter's £637,454. Durham were one of the wealthiest minor counties with more than £28,000 in the bank in late 1988, but Moffat reckoned running a first-class county would cost £750,000 annually. Durham would receive around £200,000 a year from the TCCB and anticipated taking £50,000 at the gate, leaving £500,000 to be raised for each of the first three years, plus the cost of a new ground, which would become self-financing. Floating as a public limited company was suggested.

An application should include cricket structures at school, under-13, under-15, under-19, under-25, second XI and minor counties levels, as Moffat over-optimistically advocated minor counties and first-class teams in parallel. Durham had no offices, ground, paid staff or full-time professional players, and a secretary, financial director and commercial director were essential. There were formidable hurdles, but Moffat wrote, 'we owe it to the people of the north east to try our very best to do this'. The meeting was so secretive that copies of his report were collected in afterwards.

The ambitious plans chimed with the zeitgeist of north-east sport. The 1990s would see Sunderland and Middlesbrough build new football stadia, which had to be quickly extended to 48,000 and 35,000 all-seater capacities respectively to meet demand. Even with Newcastle United's St James' Park expanding towards a capacity of 52,000 by the end of the millennium, it became difficult to get a seat to watch the region's star-studded Premier League teams. Newcastle and the now Sir John Hall started the boom by appointing former England captain Kevin Keegan as manager in 1992 and in 1996 made Alan Shearer world football's most expensive player. Hall's ambitions for the Magpies were not limited to football. He bought Durham Wasps ice hockey side and Newcastle Comets basketball team to join a continental-style sporting club. Newcastle Gosforth were acquired too and became the Falcons, winning rugby union's Premiership under ex-England fly-half Rob Andrew in 1998.

That can-do attitude prevailed at Durham's committee meeting, Riddell having been won over, if not Iley. The day after Moffat presented his report, Durham produced a press release revealing the committee had agreed to request a meeting with the TCCB and set up a feasibility study to examine when they could expect to join first-class cricket, the cost and support available, and to look at potential sites for a 'super stadium'. 'The sad part has been the demise of Northumberland,' Jackson reflects. 'It would have been better if they'd got on board, but once they decided it wasn't to be it just made us more enthusiastic.' Moffat, Robson and Ian Caller formed a working party to operate on the board's behalf, reporting back when necessary. 'We had carte blanche but there were tensions with the board,' admits Moffat. Durham asked Smith if the TCCB could set up their own to assist them.

'The way TCCB board meetings worked back then was that the executive committee would meet in the morning, the rest of us would join in the afternoon, we'd have dinner in the evening and the rest of the meeting would take place the next morning,' explains then-Derbyshire chairman Chris Middleton. 'I went to the dinner at the MCC banqueting suite, and at about half 12 or one o'clock I came out to catch a taxi back to my hotel. On the way out, AC Smith said there had been a request from Durham to become a first-class county. That was fairly amazing news.

'I couldn't quite work out why he was telling me this at that time of night, and then he told me they were forming a working party, so I said I thought that was a good idea. Then he asked me to chair it, which fairly floored me! AC told me he thought I was the ideal man for the job – he was very good at using the old oil. He said he couldn't talk to me about it there and then, and we'd speak tomorrow. So the next day we all gathered in the Long Room at Lord's before the meeting. I went up to Alan and said I had a hazy recollection that he'd told me Durham were applying for first-class status and that he'd asked me to chair a working party. He said that was right – and I'd agreed. I was pretty sure I hadn't, but that was how AC did things!

'He said I'd better have [Lancashire chairman] Bob Bennett on the committee because that was who Don Robson had gone to initially, and I realised it was Bob who'd dropped me in it. [TCCB assistant secretary] Tony Brown was the secretary and he was very useful. I wanted someone young and fairly clued-up so I suggested [Northamptonshire chief executive] Steve Coverdale. It was important to get the southern counties on board because some of them probably weren't too precise about where Durham was! I thought you can't get much further south than Kent so I asked [chief executive] Jim Woodhouse and he said it sounded very interesting. There was also [TCCB finance officer] Cliff Baker. The first meeting was at Old Trafford [in September 1989] because Derbyshire were playing [against Lancashire] and Bob Bennett would be there. Over the next year and a half we had various meetings around the country and we really couldn't see anything against it.'

The working party's brief was to make a recommendation to the TCCB but, like Moffat, they were not coming at it from a neutral perspective. 'I think it's fair to say Chris's attitude was, "We're going to get these guys in," although he never said it to me in so many words,' Coverdale concedes. 'He liked rubbing people up the wrong way, so when some of the southern counties objected it probably made him more determined. The Callers entertained us wonderfully at a couple of lovely stays at Linden Hall [which they owned]. If we'd been put up in a pokey hotel we may not have been so inclined to support them. We were probably not as totally objective from the very start as we perhaps could have been.

'All sorts of promises were made in terms of sponsors and so on. We were led to believe quite fervently that the support had already been granted. There was a feeling the playing strength of the squad was such that the team would be fairly competitive from the start. There was a lot of naivety, a starry-eyed innocence. They didn't realise how big an exercise it was to run a first-class county. We did talk in detail about what was involved in setting up and staging matches and the expectations of various stakeholders and asked if they were sure about the revenue streams. They talked about how, within 90 minutes of Chester-le-Street, they had I think it was six million people to draw on. We wondered how strong the support base really was.'

Naïve is a word Moffat often uses. 'They had no practical experience,' reasons Middleton, 'and we were there partly to try and guide them. We pulled people in from other bits of the game or directed them to people they needed to talk to. They were naïve, but I can't imagine a situation where they would not be. They thought they could do it and they could. We couldn't look 25 years into the future and they couldn't either.'

In Robson, Durham had a dynamic and determined force. In 1973, aged 39, he became Durham County Council's youngest leader. A former Doncaster Rovers and Gateshead footballer, cricket was his big passion and he was chairman of Greenside Cricket Club, the Tyneside Senior League (TSL), and the National Cricket Association, in charge of the recreational game. 'This was Don Robson's crusade and it would wither without him,' insists Coverdale. 'He knew everybody and opened every door. He was a huge political animal and people didn't want to let him down because they knew that as well as being able to open doors for them he could also close them. He was an amazing, amazing man and the power he wielded in County Durham was remarkable.'

Jackson says: 'The working party of Robson, Caller and Moffat did a bloody fantastic job and, when the reports were coming back, it just inspired you to be part of it. Don could be brusque and there was always the element of who thought of it first, but I looked forward to their report each time when it was very delicate awaiting their decision. It couldn't have happened without Don – his drive, his enthusiasm, his knowledge and his connections.'

Jackson had first-hand experience of Robson's arm-twisting when he stayed on as secretary of the North West Durham League after his club Lintz joined the TSL. Robson wanted Jackson as its secretary. 'I said no at first,' smiles Jackson, 'then the next day there was a sentence in the *[Newcastle Evening] Chronicle*'s local cricket section saying Bob Jackson was expected to become the secretary of the TSL. That's how he worked.'

Moffat says: 'There were times when we had every department in County Hall working for us. Having said that, [future cricket club director] Ken Frankish was the director of economic development at Durham County Council then, and he always said the money put into developing first-class cricket in Durham was the most productive money they'd ever used.'

Told by Smith they 'would be entirely free to decide whether to concentrate your efforts on a purpose-built headquarters ground or whether you would "wander!" around the county', Durham were convinced that to be financially viable they needed their own home and aimed to have it built by their second or third first-class season. 'We were very, very lucky,' Robson told me in 2012. 'We were talking about the university ground in Durham. Durham City planners did not want it there because it was a built-up area and a conservation area, which was fair enough. Newton Aycliffe offered us a site near the Yorkshire border but we wanted somewhere more central in the county. We were offered a site in Houghton-le-Spring for £1. When we got there the contamination was incredible. It would have taken us three or four years to level it and build the ground.

'Then we were approached by a farmer in Chester-le-Street who said he wanted to stop his lease because it was too wet for him. Whoever is up there was looking after us. We had a huge piece of land and we could feed into it and protect the castle. I was quite convinced [nearby] Lumley Castle would be the focal point.' Its location just off the A1(M) was a riposte to those complaining about Durham's remoteness.

On their first visit, the TCCB working party toured the various club grounds Durham hoped to play on initially. They returned in November 1990. 'After watching Sunderland draw with Manchester City, we were shown around various possible venues for the headquarters,' Coverdale recalls. 'We had a long walk by the side of the River Wear in Chester-le-Street. We'd been to Lumley Castle on the first trip and seen the view and got the history. It was absolutely freezing and grey and it took an eternity to walk the two and a half/ three miles. I don't think any of us had the vision of what it would become – certainly I didn't. It was just a vast, bleak expanse. By the time we had walked around you were frozen to every crevice of your body!'

Coverdale was not the only one struggling to get his head around Durham's plans. 'The only thing on this big open field was the caravan they were working out of,' Middleton explains. 'We said we thought it could be a decent county ground and they said, "Oh no, we want a Test match." That was the first time I'd heard that and it came as quite a shock. We were sceptical.'

It is an important statement. When the Riverside became a financial millstone it was widely reported the TCCB insisted on an international-standard ground as a condition of first-class status, but they only asked for a 'showpiece stadium'. 'We weren't really told we had to build an international stadium but we had to build a quality stadium,' Moffat confirms. 'Our intention – Don, Ian Caller and I – was to build the best stadium we could. There were things we did which were obviously designed to welcome top-class games over and above county games. All we had done lent itself to the idea [of hosting Tests].' Jackson says: 'As far as I was concerned, a "showpiece stadium" meant a top, top ground. What I had in mind was a ground to seat 14,000 or 15,000.'

David Harker, who became financial controller in 1991, admits: 'There was a view at the time that the criteria the TCCB had set in terms of money in the bank and developing a "showpiece stadium" was done to dissuade Durham almost, but the guys involved took that challenge on. If they took that as something over and above what was intended, no one really appreciated the longer-term implications. With the benefit of hindsight, was it overly ambitious? I'm loath to criticise anyone with ambition, particularly in this part of the world, because they were certainly honourably motivated.' Durham's initial plan, which included 100 executive homes, a hotel, business park, all-weather nursery ground, football pitches and parking for 3,000 cars, plus a 10,000-seater ground, was approved the day before the TCCB working party's first meeting. It would be the first purpose-built cricket stadium since World War Two.

The 107-acre site was council-owned and, according to the county's structure plan, not supposed to be developed. It was home to rare fauna and flora, and nature-lover Stan Hornsby told the *Northern Echo* 44 species of bird could be lost. Durham had the county and district councils – with Robson staying out of negotiations – batting for them, arguing this was a project of regional significance. The business park was dropped and a conservation area and river walkway incorporated.

Retired civil servant John Minto, who lived opposite Moffat in Chester-le-Street, went to a public meeting to support the plan but, after hearing it, ended up becoming chairman of 'Save Our Riverside'.

They enlisted David Bellamy and gathered 18,000 signatures on a petition, with claims some signed ten times. There was a counter-petition too. 'I had to take it around the school,' Paul Collingwood recalls. 'Mrs Hodges, my French teacher, wouldn't sign it because she walked her dogs around the park. I was really hurt!'

It was an emotive issue, as shown by the June 1990 resignation of Labour councillor Maureen Pattison, yet when the plans went on display at Chester-le-Street's civic centre, the *Sunderland Echo* reported fewer than 600 people saw them and only 206 commented – 57 for, 116 against. 'Malcolm Pratt [chairman of Chester-le-Street District Council's environment and parks committee] had the courage, with his chief exec, to deal with his objectors, and one of the reasons he became president [of the club in 2002] was because of the work he did for us,' Moffat explains. Environment secretary Michael Heseltine decided a public enquiry was unnecessary.

When Glamorgan turned first class, Sir Sidney Byass pledged £1,000 over ten years, but Durham's application alone cost £21,216.30 – and for it to succeed the TCCB wanted them to have £1m in the bank. Whilst Price Waterhouse spent 18 months writing a 70-page business plan, Durham's working group set the ball rolling. 'I knocked on so many doors and wrote so many letters,' says Moffat. Robson told me: 'I used to go every Saturday morning to get my fruit at a shop in Ludgate. A rag-and-bone man used to go around with a wheelbarrow collecting. I was in the shop and I spoke to this fella. He said, "Are you Don Robson?" I said I was. "Are you going to bring the cricket to Chester-le-Street?" I said I hoped so. He disappeared and two minutes later he came back and gave me a ten-pound note, two fivers and some coins. Tommy Young, who owned the shop, said, "That bugger, he owes me £82.50!" It was a reaction to a vacuum.'

Brendan Foster's Nova International public relations firm was commissioned to produce a 12-minute video – narrated by Northumberland-born England batsman-turned-BBC commentator Tom Graveney and featuring Riddell – to attract sponsors. Newcastle Building Society, Co-Operative Bank and British Gas responded.

'I wasn't surprised Durham were able to raise so much money so quickly because Don was one of those people who could do things, and it was very much his pet project,' says Middleton. 'As far as he was concerned, there was no way it was going to fail. He knew every lever to pull and every arm to twist.' Durham raised £1,218,750 in sponsorship. 'Our biggest problem was stopping companies giving us the bulk because we wanted it phased over a period for tax reasons,' Moffat reveals. 'A box [at the Riverside] for ten years was £100,000 but we didn't want that up front.'

Nevertheless, the road was not without bumps. Told by Smith they would be unable to join until 1991 at the earliest, that was still talked of as the target in autumn 1989 – until Durham were persuaded to slow down and aim for 1992. The idea to join the 1992 Second XI Championship, then the first-team competition 12 months later, was rejected for fears the delay might deter sponsors. The day after outline plans for the Riverside were approved, in September 1989, the *Northern Echo* reported Durham had the support of ten counties but they needed a two-thirds majority from the 17 first-class counties, MCC and MCCA.

'There was a fair degree of antipathy from a number of counties, particularly in the south,' Coverdale acknowledges. 'Their attitude was that Durham was nearly the North Pole and it would take a three-day expedition to get up there, as well as diluting the distribution of TCCB money. When we first started, the vibes I was picking up from my colleagues around the country was that this wasn't a goer, we would just pay it lip service. My concern as chief executive of Northamptonshire was that Durham was a very fertile source of players for us. My sense was that it was very nice being shown around but that they did not know what was involved in running a first-class county club.'

As secretary of the Professional Cricketers' Association, Geoff Cook felt the mood in dressing rooms change. He says: 'A lot of people were warming to Durham over a two- or three-year period and, although there was still a lot of opposition from various quarters through all sorts of emotions – a bit of jealousy, a bit of protecting the game as it was – it was gaining momentum and the people within Durham were becoming more and more bullish in their approach, which they had to be.'

'One or two players understandably thought there wasn't room for an 18th county. Even at that stage a lot of the players thought there was too much cricket, and an 18th county would just mean more. Even within Durham there was a lot of resentment from the older minor-county players who were quite rightly massively proud of their achievements and history, and slightly resented dispensing with the minor-county team; these big lads were coming in and showing off and trying to be a first-class county.'

Coverdale remembers a moment of doubt in June 1990. 'We were at The Oval where Derbyshire were playing Surrey,' he says. 'We went along to see the business plan. We were told Price Waterhouse had done some quite detailed work on it and the meeting started with a bit of a presentation from them. I'm not sure why, but it came to a bit of a halt and Don and Chris had a chat, while the rest of the working party were asked if we would withdraw. While we took the opportunity to see Waqar Younis bowl at the speed of light, we speculated what was going on and our view was they were going to pull [out of the bid]. We were maybe away for an hour, an hour and a half.'

Robson died in 2016 so the only person to ask is Middleton. He has no recollection but insists: 'If that had been the case I would have told them.' Moffat is unequivocal: 'There was never one degree of doubt that we would go ahead [at that stage].'

By the time Durham officials and the media gathered at Callers Pegasus's Newcastle office to await the decision on 6 December, the doubts had gone. Austin and Robson were at Lord's, and the phone call came at around 4pm. Durham would receive first-class status on 1 January 1992 (and be invited to all relevant TCCB meetings in 1991), provided 'all planning permissions and financial detail with regard to your new ground is delivered unequivocally by 1 February 1991', when a chief executive or professional secretary, plus a central head groundsman, should be in place. Durham were to give a full progress report at the 5/6 March 1991 TCCB board meeting. Moffat wrote back to formally accept on 20 December. 'We are keener than anyone to have these three posts [Durham also wanted a director of cricket] filled as early as we can,' he wrote, but warned 1 February might be too soon to advertise, interview and install candidates.

There had been no votes against, and TCCB cricket secretary Tim Lamb said: 'One of the most exciting things about Durham's arrival on the first-class scene is it gives cricket access to 4.2 million people.' Durham, though, were already thinking bigger. Ian Caller in Newcastle echoed Robson's sentiments in London when he told the media: 'My dream now is to see a boy from Burnopfield, Blackhall or Billingham play for Durham, and then England, as Colin Milburn did.'

2.

Cooking Up a Team

IT is six years and two trophies since I put the question to the late Don Robson but, speaking to another of the pioneers who took Durham into first-class cricket, I am expecting the same answer. Tom Moffat duly delivers. 'The best signing Durham made was the director of cricket,' he says, without pause for thought.

Stephen Harmison is just as quick to praise the man Robson described as 'a real icon of the club'. 'The ground should be named after Geoff Cook,' he insists. 'I'm all for naming a stand after Paul Collingwood after what he's done for Durham – and there are other people like Dale Benkenstein, Simon Brown and myself who've had a big influence – but what Geoff Cook's done, and the way he is, I'd name the whole ground after him. If it wasn't for him, hardly any of the people who brought success to Durham would have been there.'

By the time their first-class status was approved in December 1990, Durham's greatest signing had already been made. Cook became an 'adviser' to the bid in September on the understanding he would be the county's first director of cricket if it was rubber-stamped, and he stayed until retirement in September 2018. There were also spells as a player, coach and captain of both first and second teams, as well as running the academy, and even being an 'executive director' when they were between chief executives. Cook is not just a legend of Durham cricket, but, given the number of county, international and world-class players indebted to him for their careers, the wider English game.

Cook won seven Test caps and captained Northamptonshire between 1981 and 1988, but by the time Durham approached the Middlesbrough-born opener his 20-year Wantage Road career was coming to an end. He had been offered a job by a sports promotion firm in Cambridge and was not set on staying in cricket. 'Alongside Durham making some initial chats, Nottinghamshire came along and spoke a bit as well because they were changing their director of cricket, or whatever he was at the time,' he recalls. 'But I hadn't really buckled down when the Durham thing started to gain momentum. It was an exciting prospect from a professional sense and also an emotional sense being a north-eastern lad.'

John Hampshire, head coach at the McEwans Centre, and David Graveney were keen on the job but, in July 1990, Robson and Moffat went to Trent Bridge to talk to Cook, who was not part of Northamptonshire's team to play Nottinghamshire. Robson, Moffat and Ian Caller were so convinced they had the right man they did not even run it past the committee before offering Cook a small salary as adviser. 'He was a north-east lad who'd just announced his retirement from first-class cricket and it just seemed to all fit,' says Moffat. 'He had a good reputation; he'd been a steady batsman who played for England.'

Then-Northamptonshire chief executive Steve Coverdale was helping Durham's bid as part of the TCCB working party, but insists: 'The interest in Geoff came from the Durham end, certainly not me. Geoff is one of my son's godfathers and I didn't want him to go. But much as I would have liked to have kept him at Northamptonshire, he and Judith [Cook's wife] wanted to go back home.'

Durham's division of labour was clear. 'He was responsible for the cricket side while we looked after the rest. [The board] had to accept there was a professional area we were unable to participate in, so we left him to it,' Robson told me. Fellow director Bob Jackson says:

'Nobody challenged Geoff because Don gave him enormous scope to progress it as he saw it. They talked often. Don had a knack of choosing people to do specific tasks, and Geoff was one.'

The blank canvas offered an opportunity no other county could. 'I was so fortunate,' Cook says. 'I had this picture of Durham-born players occupying some really meaningful positions within the team for a long time. It took a lot of patience from everybody and a lot of understanding and generosity. I had to have massive belief in what we were trying to achieve.'

Cook's coaching trademark was encouraging players to think for themselves. 'He let you learn from your mistakes. If you succeed, great, but if you failed, that was fine as well,' Graham Onions explains. Paul Collingwood 'always found him very encouraging, which is what you want as a young kid. He made you work hard but enjoy what you were doing.' Not that Cook could have achieved what he did by being a soft touch. 'He's very tough on the young players, he challenges them all the time and turns them into young adults on the cricket field,' Harmison explains.

Before Cook could coach, he needed a team. The board thought the one he had would do. 'Durham had been such a successful minor county – almost unbeatable for a long period in the 1970s and '80s – so there was a bit of arrogance that they were bound to be able to go first class,' then-*Journal* cricket writer Jeff Brown explains. Heavy NatWest Trophy defeats in 1989, 1990 and 1991 told the story more accurately. Jackson admits: 'It was decided very early on to have the local talent come through, and I was expecting we'd be able to keep more or less the same team, but the difficulty for some of the players in their late 20s and early 30s was taking up a new career at that age.'

Moffat's feasibility study had been clear: 'We probably have not one player currently in the county side who could now play in the first-class game… We will always have to "buy" a side, whether local players or not. Initially, our full staff would probably be all "bought" imports. However, we would always be aiming for increasing numbers of local-born players.'

Durham used 42 players in 1991. As well as their final Minor Counties Championship season, they played Sheffield Shield champions Victoria, Yorkshire, a Local League Professionals XI and Sri Lanka, appeared at the Harrogate and Scarborough festivals, and faced Glamorgan and Denmark in the 60-over NatWest Trophy. 'It was a never-ending series of trialists, people who'd dropped out of other counties and youngsters hoping to make their way,' Brown recalls. 'Geoff Cook played a lot [averaging 49.64 in 27 matches] and I think there was an assumption he'd be opening the batting, but he always said he wanted to step aside and be behind the scenes. All the minor counties wanted to bring them down. I think there'd always been a bit of animosity because they'd been so good for so long.

'There were players who came in and you thought, "He will never be a cricketer!" and others where you thought, "Wow!" But it was difficult to judge because I'd only ever seen first-class cricket on the telly. I didn't envy Geoff Cook trying to put together a team when so many people wanted to chance their arm. The one I felt most disappointed for was Paul Burn, a prolific minor counties run-scorer and a policeman. A lot of these guys were going to have to take a leap into the unknown and give up a lot, but Paul just didn't make it and for guys like Steve Atkinson, another prolific batsman, it just came too late.'

Newcastle-born wicketkeeper Andy Fothergill was willing to take a chance. 'It was a case of, "I'm not sure if I can compete at this level," because I was 30,' he admits. 'Batting-wise, the game had passed me by. It's all right doing it in a one-off NatWest game and having a bit of a go for a 20- or 30-run cameo, but when you have to knuckle down and build an innings facing different bowlers in different environments on different wickets – I would watch some of the players I played against and think, "How do they do that?"

'Everybody was really, really excited about the whole thing. Paul Burn and Ian Conn were unlucky to miss out, they're probably the only other two who you'd say were good enough and they always performed in the NatWest. I was selling shop fittings, and I was thinking it was only six months of the year and the guys kept my job open if I wanted it for the next six months. You were playing with and against your heroes, people you'd seen on television.'

Averaging 45 with the bat in the Minor Counties Championship, Fothergill was Durham's 1991 player of the year. 'Hmm… was I?' he says. 'I don't know whether it was more, "Well done Fothers, you've made the transition." It might have been more clubman of the year because I did like to keep the enthusiasm going and keep everyone buoyant. Geoff was trying different wicketkeepers all the time, but I generally performed when I needed to.

'Neil Riddell had already spoken to Geoff, who'd asked, "Is he a bit lazy?" Neil said I definitely wasn't, but Geoff was just a bit concerned that I didn't always come up to the stumps when the ball was in the field. In club cricket you didn't do that all of the time because it didn't always come into you. In first-class cricket it nearly always comes into the wicketkeeper, so I just thought, "If that's what I have to do, that's what I'll do." I was fit through my football, so I wasn't lazy. Geoff needed players who would fit into this squad because you only needed one bad apple. Anyone who came in and was arrogant soon got shot down by the local lads – and not in a nice way.'

Cook quickly found a sounding board. 'We were playing three or four new players each game and, even at that stage, people were coming on to the romantic side of things, trying their luck and seeing how it went,' he recalls. 'To an extent it was always going to be a subjective thing and Phil Bainbridge was a great help. He played in that last year as a minor county so being able to bounce impressions of players off him was useful.' Released by Gloucestershire at the end of 1990, all-rounder Bainbridge made his debut at the Harrogate Festival and combined playing with working for the marketing department.

In 1991 Guisborough's Stewart Hutton broke John Glendenen's record for the most runs in a North Yorkshire South Durham League season by an amateur and was persuaded to take a pay cut and leave his job as an accounts clerk at ICI Wilton to play alongside him.

Eppleton's Jimmy Daley and Bishop Auckland's Gary Wigham were released from the Lord's groundstaff to play when needed. Durham saw off Yorkshire interest to sign Stockton-born England Under-15s all-rounder Paul Henderson and John Wood, whose Bradford League bowling impressed ex-Durham player Peter Kippax. Darren Blenkiron, son of Warwickshire bowler Bill, joined too.

Batsman Gary Brown made his first-class debut for Middlesex in 1986 but had been playing for Durham since 1989 and working at the McEwans Centre. Mark Briers had played for Leicestershire and Worcestershire's second XIs, but the leg-spinning all-rounder came to Durham's attention taking 5-75 against them for Bedfordshire in 1990. Ian Smith – a 25-year-old from Chopwell, near Blaydon – had been released by Glamorgan after nine seasons, hampered by back injuries.

Easington's Middlesbrough-born professional Glendenen played for Yorkshire's second XI between 1983 and 1986 and had trials with Somerset and Gloucestershire. Not only was his double-century against Victoria at the Racecourse Ground in September 1991 Durham's first since England rugby union international Edgar Elliott's in 1903 and 1906, but he also became the first to pass 1,000 runs in a season for them. The Portakabin salesman had only been awarded a contract the previous week on the back of a NatWest Trophy century against Glamorgan.

Making his debut alongside Bainbridge at Harrogate in 1991 was one of Durham's most-inspired signings. Simon Brown was linked as soon as they turned first class. Now playing for his local club Boldon in the Durham Senior League, the 21-year-old left-arm seamer had been a team-mate of Cook's at Northamptonshire but had fallen out of love with the professional game. He was released after one first-class appearance in 1990 and, while the likes of Fothergill, Glendenen, Briers and Henderson were being made to earn theirs, he signed a two-year contract at Durham. 'It was perfect timing,' he told me in 2012. 'Without sounding conceited, when I was at Northants I always thought I had enough ability to make a career out of cricket, and

Durham was a good chance to do that. I probably had the opportunity to bowl more for Durham than if I'd gone somewhere else.'

Brown took 20 wickets in eight minor counties matches while qualifying as an electrician, and it soon became clear he had a future in the game. Many feel he deserved better than one England cap, dismissing Pakistan's Saeed Anwar in his first Test over at Lord's in July 1996 – only for the umpire to call no-ball. Brown kept his feet behind the crease when trapping Aamir Sohail lbw from his tenth delivery but, in an era of revolving-door selections, match figures of 2-138 saw him dropped for the second Test. Stephen Harmison has a sense of 'what might have been' about Brown's career too, often playing through injury as he carried the attack through Durham's difficult growing spell. 'Had "Chubby" come along a few years later it would have been great for Durham to have him in that group of myself, [Liam] Plunkett and [Graham] Onions,' he argues. 'With his left-arm variation, Durham would have been even more forceful.' Most people, though, would settle for 518 first-class wickets for their county – a Durham record only surpassed by Onions in 2017 – in a career that ran until 2002.

Nine of the 1992 squad were north-east born, with Quentin Hughes and Robin Weston on part-time contracts while continuing their studies. Bringing in players from other counties was more difficult. 'We didn't really have an idea how to do it and we honestly had not approached anyone [before December 1990] because we knew it could lose their county's vote,' insists Moffat. As secretary of the Professional Cricketers' Association, Cook was well connected and recruited its treasurer as Durham's first first-class captain.

David Graveney spent 19 seasons at Gloucestershire, where he followed an unfortunate family tradition by getting the sack in 1988, in his case as captain. The end of his eight-year captaincy was announced on the day he completed a Championship-best 14-wicket haul against Worcestershire. Graveney's uncle Tom suffered the same fate 28 years earlier, while his dad Ken lost his job as chairman in 1982. 'He's a very sensitive, understanding fella who'd done a good job as captain of Gloucestershire,' Cook says. 'He knew what it was all about and he always has been an outstanding diplomat with media, players and authorities, so he brought all those things into play. He became more involved in the last year as a minor county and, although he didn't play for us, he was still heavily involved in the discussions.'

Graveney had been sounded out by committeemen Robson, Ian Caller and Riddell about the director of cricket role in January 1990, but Durham were warned against appointing someone on an International Cricket Council blacklist – Graveney had been player-manager of a rebel England tour of South Africa that year – so took heed instead of his glowing words about Cook, who pulled out of the first such tour in 1982. Graveney continued playing first-class cricket in 1991 but joined Somerset on the understanding he could leave if a position of responsibility came up.

Durham held a romantic appeal for a player based in the south west all his life. 'My family originated from Riding Mill [near Hexham in Northumberland] but the links went beyond that because Geoff Cook was probably my best friend in cricket, so there were lots of things that made the idea of captaining Durham attractive,' he told me. 'My family were in Bristol and my children were at school so we had to make a decision about how that would work, but we did, and I ended up living near the Metrocentre for three years.'

A club with Durham's ambitions needed stardust. 'People wanted sexy players, high-profile international players,' Cook explains. There was no more high-profile cricketer in England than Ian Botham. The country's greatest all-rounder was reaching the end of a legendary career. He had not scored a Test century or taken a five-wicket haul since the 1986/87 Ashes but still had the appetite for the big occasion. He opened the batting as England reached the 1992 World Cup Final and was behind only Pakistan's Wasim Akram in the tournament bowling averages and wicket-takers. As usual, he reserved his best for Australia, taking 4-31 then contributing 53 to a 107-run opening partnership as England won by eight wickets. Having also made his

100th Test appearance that winter, it provided an opportunity to bow out at the top, which Botham ignored.

'Chris Middleton made a throw-away comment as a joke about signing Botham and you could see the seeds planting in Don's mind. You could see it registering in his head. Durham had to have someone like that,' says Steve Coverdale, part of the TCCB's working party assisting and assessing Durham. 'It was the sort of daft thing I'd say!' his chairman responds. Botham had won six trophies in five years with Worcestershire, and his 1991 first-class averages of 43 with the bat and 24 with the ball were his best since 1986 and 1982 respectively, yet with his family home being in nearby North Yorkshire he felt like a natural fit.

In April 1991 Scottish and Newcastle Breweries announced a three-year sponsorship deal with Durham which, at £325,000, was worth £25,000 more than the one Yorkshire struck with Tetley Bitter three days earlier. When Scottish and Newcastle began sponsoring Newcastle United they were instrumental in bringing a figurehead player to St James' Park, and in 1992 they lured Kevin Keegan back again, this time as manager. Botham's Worcestershire contract ran until the end of 1992, but he was such an obvious cricketing equivalent that when the brewery tie-up was announced he had to put out a statement denying any contact with them about sponsorship or promotional work, or with Durham. Scottish and Newcastle managing director David Stephenson corroborated that, but added: 'If he were to become available and the club felt he would lead them into the Promised Land, naturally we would be pleased.'

Durham's board were split over Botham. As Bob Jackson put it, 'The difficulty was that Ian was a player who'd had his better years,' and his colourful personality sometimes attracted controversy. Moffat was adamant: 'It was far from unanimous but I stood up and said, "Mr Chairman, all the arguments against Ian Botham fall to the ground. We cannot afford not to take him." We needed someone to give us credibility and put bums on seats. He might have had baggage but he had a reputation which would do that and, as the treasurer, I said we could not afford to not do it. Signing him was one of the better things we did. I was definitely the loudest voice in the boardroom speaking up for him as the then-treasurer but he did all I hoped for. He gave us credibility.' Robson explained: 'In a week we got 3,500 members. Suddenly we went from being a newspaper article to something concrete.'

On 26 July the board decided only Robson would be allowed to speak to the media about Botham and, when Worcestershire released him the next day, the chairman announced: 'We will be putting in an official offer as soon as we can. We are certainly not going to allow the grass to grow under our feet.' On 28 September Botham signed a two-year contract thought to be worth £100,000. He spoke of his desire to play for five years, by which time he hoped his 14-year-old son Liam might be a Durham team-mate. 'I was quite happy to come home because I'd been down in Somerset and Worcester,' he explains. 'I've lived for 30-odd years where I am now [in Ravensworth] and just a little bit further south before that, so it was nice to come home to play. I knew my career was coming to an end and I thought it would be a nice way to get involved with a brand-new club that had been waiting for its opportunity; to be part of that was a wonderful experience.'

One of those lukewarm about Botham's arrival was Cook. The pair toured together twice with England but were very different characters. In his 1994 autobiography, Botham wrote that: 'If [Cook] had his way we would have stood up before the start of each match and belted out a chorus of "The Red Flag"', whereas Simon Hughes described Botham as being 'further right than Genghis Khan'. Rumours Cook had threatened to resign if Botham was recruited reached the ears of the latter, who claimed he had been offered the captaincy. Graveney volunteered to join the ranks if it meant the difference between signing the all-rounder or not.

'Ian's never quite explained to me in any detail what he'd been party to in terms of discussions with the board, but he was still involved with the England set-up and I just felt if he was given a reasonable sort of licence then, knowing him as I did, I knew there would be occasions where he'd get turned on by what was in front of him and turn in the performances,' Cook argues. 'I was with the second team most of the time in that first [1992] season so I didn't attend that many first-team games but Ian was renowned for his larger-than-life approach and still is – even more so then. There was always a worry that the young guys in the team would come rapidly under his wing, that was almost inevitable. It was very much a question of not combatting that, but riding it. He'd had a wonderful career and brought into Durham exactly what the committee had hoped for. He'd increased an already massive public swell of interest and enthusiasm.'

Tyne Tees Television agreed to sponsor Durham's overseas player for the first four seasons, and it initially looked like they would be paying a fast bowler in 1992, possibly Craig McDermott, Merv Hughes or Patrick Patterson. Unsuccessful moves were made for West Indians Courtney Walsh (who played for Northumberland in 1983) and Joey Benjamin, plus Redcar-born Paul Jarvis. Durham University-educated Paul Allott agreed terms, only to change his mind late in the day. Richie Richardson, star of the West Indies' tour of England in 1991, had played club cricket for Burnmoor the previous summer and later admitted: 'I would have loved to play for Durham. There was a lot of talk about me playing for them – but it just didn't work out.' According to Graveney, 'There was not much enthusiasm for him from club officials.' Instead the job fell to the world's best one-day batsman. Dean Jones made 144 for Victoria against Durham in 1991, then signed a contract reputedly worth £50,000 a year.

'I just wanted to be really tested,' he told me. 'The Australians who'd been over never had a bad word to say about English cricket. You have all the spinning tracks in the south and it tests the bottom half of your body. Then you'd come up to places like Derby with their four quicks and the top half gets a workout. I was contemplating going to Yorkshire and other places, but I decided to go to Durham. Botham had signed by then and there's no doubt that got me across the line.' That Jones's mother-in-law was from South Shields added to the appeal.

Other signings were less glamorous. Counties were only able to recruit two category A players – those looking to leave their counties at the end of contracts despite being offered extensions – over three years. 'It was really restrictive,' says Cook, 'although the counties were helpful. Sometimes it suited them if they had a player on their books who was going to retire in a year or two and Durham was an alternative, they were almost glad to get them off their hands.

'It was exciting and great fun. We used lots of players in 1991 and there were all sorts of rumours going on, but the balance was always to try and get a team that would reflect the ambitions of the board, give a little bit of entertainment and excitement to the north-eastern people, justify all the efforts that had gone into gaining first-class status, and try to mix in a bit of local blood. That last point was important to us, it was the history we were moving into. The crossovers were Glendenen, Fothergill, Henderson, John Wood, Hutton and Daley, as well as Mark Briers, who wasn't a Durham lad but played in the minor counties.

'A lot of it was pragmatic but Ian and Graveney were massive figures in the English game at that stage – in the world game [in Botham's case]. They were great recruits for all sorts of reasons but we were never going to be able to recruit a Graham Gooch, who was outstandingly good for England at that time and at the pinnacle of his career, because the counties just wouldn't let them go.' Gooch's contribution would be as a batting consultant from 1998–2001.

No official allowances were made for Durham's unique circumstances. 'They said they didn't want any favours and we didn't offer them any,' says Chris Middleton. 'But it was the beginning of the era where players were starting to move around. Now it's got to the stage where players move clubs almost as often as they change their socks. I'm from a county [Derbyshire] where we'd been used to having players for 20 years but that was starting to change. Ten years earlier it would have been much more difficult.'

Inevitably, though, the majority of those available to Durham fitted a certain profile. 'We were virtually forced to sign a lot of players who were past their sell-by date,' Moffat admits. 'That sounds critical of them but really it was a compliment that they came to do a job for us, maybe some of them knowing they were past their best. We were never going to be able to get any of the real high-fliers – I think a lot of them would be frightened to jeopardise their careers.'

Wicketkeeper Chris Scott made his Durham debut against Victoria, having been released by Nottinghamshire after ten years and, with Cook identifying a lack of local slow bowlers, Redcar-born Phil Berry was released by Yorkshire a year early to join. He had taken 60 second-team wickets in 1991 but still not got a look-in. Cook's former opening partner Wayne Larkins joined from Northamptonshire and was an entertaining and productive presence in his three seasons. Paul Parker's solitary Test cap came in the final game of the 'Botham's Ashes' series of 1981, but his 15-year relationship with Sussex was far more enduring. When he was asked to stand down as captain after four seasons, Durham moved in. Simon Hughes was released by Middlesex at the end of the 1991 campaign and, although he claimed to have been offered '£20,000 more than I'd ever earned before', the main attractions of his two-year contract were returning to the county where he studied at university and playing alongside Botham. It was not just spectators he had pulling power over.

'One of the advantages Durham had was they weren't hidebound by decades of doing it one way and they set out to do it properly,' says Jeff Brown. 'I think there was a little bit of jealousy from clubs who were stuck with rigid structures.' The TCCB working party suggested Durham become a limited company, and it was based along similar lines to Moffat's Durham Small Businesses Club. The old club was dissolved on 21 March 1991, when the committee voted itself out of existence. In its place was a board of six 'A directors', two of whom would stand for re-election each year. They, in turn, could select up to five 'B directors', elected on two-year terms to do specific jobs. The committee agreed to automatically select Moffat and Robson for continuity, and, with Mike Weston choosing not to stand, Roseberry, Jackson, Neil Riddell and Bob Milner were voted in. Jack Iley became a vice-president, Arthur Austin the UK patron and Sir Donald Bradman his overseas equivalent. Ian Caller was re-elected president while his London-based brother became a B director. Solicitor Ian Mills was the secretary, Price Waterhouse the auditors, and Co-Op the bankers.

'I thought Northamptonshire had as good a committee as any in the country, pretty much, because they were wonderfully supportive people working for the benefit of the club, but they let the small executive team we had at that time get on with it,' says Steve Coverdale. 'But you had other counties dominated by huge committees, with people elected according to what region they came from. My sense was that it was a fairly small group of people driving everything at Durham.' As Middleton says: 'They didn't have any problems with meetings running on long past midnight – I had a few of them in my time! – but it was clear Don was going to run things anyway.'

There were occasional tensions. 'I've met a lot of people on the committees of other counties since and a lot were kind enough to say we blazed a trail,' Moffat comments. 'There were only two times where there was an election [to the board] and both times it was me because Don put candidates up against me but I didn't beat them, I slaughtered them. I was the only one who used to challenge him – and to challenge Don Robson was the kiss of death – but after we both retired he was my best friend. I think he thought I was up for being chairman. We used to go head-to-head quite a lot but it wouldn't have been the story it was without him.'

Coverdale recalls: 'The last time we [the TCCB working party] went up to the north east I spent a lot of time with Don Robson, being driven around by him, and I wonder if he was sounding me out for the job of chief executive because he kept talking about the importance of it. I was actually suggesting Chris Hassell, who had left Lancashire [and would join Yorkshire] but in the end they went with Mike Gear.' Moffat says: 'It's the kind of thing Don would do. He was a total unilateralist.'

Gear had played for Surrey and Essex's second XIs, but what most attracted Durham was his time as TCCB assistant secretary, and he signed a four-year contract in April, although he only got halfway through it. Financial controller David Harker's secondment from Price Waterhouse became permanent in August.

In keeping with union man Cook and Labour councillor Robson's principles, there was an egalitarian feel about Durham. Initially caps were awarded when players signed first-team contracts and, although they fell in line with the tradition of awarding them on merit from 1998–2005, after that they were handed out on debut. The second XI was called Durham A. Physio Sheila Job's six-month secondment from Newcastle Sports Injuries Clinic caused problems at chauvinistic Lord's, while 45-year-old Brian Hunt was the first-class circuit's youngest scorer, even though he had been doing the job since 1975. He continued until his health left him no choice in 2016.

'The game was starting to change a little bit,' Cook reflects. 'One or two counties were starting to take a more innovative approach to one-day cricket or their structure, employing cricket managers and coaches and playing in a much more aggressive way, a much more skilful way. Surrey were a really successful team and they were introducing new methods and new thinking. I felt Durham's requirements then were to try and combat that from a more mature standpoint with the players that we had, and the education [of young players] was always going to start underneath that, really.

'From an administrative sense we weren't hamstrung by people's egos. Don was obviously an extraordinarily powerful and capable chairman with lots and lots of influence and he ran a formidable show. In cricketing terms, we tried to avoid a traditional county cricket structure with caps and so on so that people would feel they were all developing together. It was idealistic in many ways.'

Hampshire's Tom Flintoft, formerly of Middlesbrough's Acklam Park and 1990's groundsman of the year, was given the job of overseeing Durham's club grounds plus the new Riverside square once he laid it in September 1992. Ashbrooke was rejected, partly because of a ridge on the ground and concerns about car parking, but Darlington's Feethams, Stockton, Hartlepool, Gateshead Fell, Durham University's Racecourse and Chester-le-Street's Ropery Lane were approved by TCCB pitch adviser Harry Brind, and a 1992 Benson and Hedges Cup tie was played at Jesmond to maintain links with Northumberland. Nineteen clubs expressed an interest in hosting Durham A. Staging first-class cricket was expensive – upgrading Gateshead Fell and Feethams cost around £22,000 each.

By the mid-noughties, Durham were leaving the likes of Middleton's Derbyshire behind. 'I suppose I was surprised at how quickly they started winning trophies and bringing players through, but they had a circle of very determined people and a new broom sweeps all clean,' he reflects. 'There were no mixed feelings. I wished them well and welcomed them to Derbyshire whenever they came. There was some pride when I saw them doing well but it wasn't me that did it, we just gave them some advice along the way. Having said that, I wouldn't want to do it again. I was working full-time as a solicitor so it was a lot of extra work.'

With the ambitious groundwork laid, it was finally time to play cricket.

3.

A Good Scriptwriter

A S 1992's opening round of Sunday League matches reached a conclusion, the man *The Guardian* called 'Durham's own Messiah' had not done much by his own melodramatic standards.

In the words of *Journal* reporter Jeff Brown, Durham were 'in danger of losing a match they appeared to have long sewn up'. Chasing 247 in 40 overs to win, Lancashire were 140/5 after 30 but, as Simon Hughes ran in to bowl the final over, the target was down to ten with one wicket remaining. When Danny Morrison looked for a quick single from the opening delivery, the throw from short midwicket hit the stumps, with Warren Hegg stranded. The fielder, inevitably, was Ian Botham. 'The crowd erupted,' says Durham wicketkeeper Andy Fothergill.

Until their televised victory in front of a sold-out Racecourse Ground, Durham's entry into professional cricket had been low-key. Botham and Dean Jones were preparing for the World Cup when their new team-mates headed to Zimbabwe for a four-week pre-season tour, Hughes was also in Australia and New Zealand working and playing, Darren Blenkiron was touring Pakistan with England Under-19s, and Steve McEwan was on an accountancy course. Paul Henderson was given leave from college to make the trip and, when

John Wood damaged back muscles in the final training session before departure, England Under-15 international Neil Killeen was pulled out of school. 'I'd never been out of the country and I didn't have a passport so my dad had to drive to Glasgow to get me one,' explains Killeen, due to sit his GCSEs at Greencroft Comprehensive in May. 'I had to ask my headmaster for permission to go and he didn't want me to.'

Brown went too, as did the *Northern Echo*'s correspondent, former Durham University, Tynemouth, Darlington, Sedgefield and Aldbrough bowler Tim Wellock. '[Sister newspapers] *The Journal*, *The [Newcastle Evening] Chronicle* and the *Sunday Sun* had separate staff but, because the cricket was going to be so important, they decided there had to be someone there and they couldn't afford to send two or three different people so I got the job,' Brown explains. 'I was at all the events, I got invited to the parties, I travelled with the players, sometimes drove them around.'

Zimbabwe used their matches for World Cup preparation. In the first, played 4,000ft above sea level at Harare South Country Club on 3 February, they made 274/4 in 50 overs – including 90 for Andy Flower – before restricting the tourists to 151/8. The second game was much tighter but Zimbabwe triumphed by two wickets. Durham won six of their 11 games, with Graveney the leading wicket-taker and Wayne Larkins, Paul Parker, Stewart Hutton and Mark Briers making centuries, but the tour's importance went beyond runs and wickets.

'It was hard for the kids – Paul Henderson, Gary Wigham, Jimmy Daley – because they were only 17, 18,' Fothergill explains. 'They were away from home for a month – that's hard on anybody and there was a bit of homesickness but it forced you to get to know people and we had a good laugh. Me and John Glendenen would fine people for stupid things. Jimmy Daley got up for breakfast before the first game, which was on a Monday. His orientation was all over the place and he didn't realise it was 6pm on Sunday! But he was only 17 from Eppleton, a pit village in Sunderland – he'd probably hardly ever been out of

Sunderland, never mind the country.' Fines were 10Z$ (about £1), and whoever was responsible for the day's biggest laugh had to wear a maroon bow tie for the rest of the evening. Musical entertainment came from Parker. 'He was a very good guitarist,' Brown recalls. 'He was singing along to "American Pie" and the Kinks.'

The Cambridge University classics graduate's impact was such that Geoff Cook broke his promise to wait until the whole squad assembled before choosing Durham's vice-captain. It can hardly have helped Cook's relationship with Botham, but Fothergill felt it was a good choice. 'Paul Parker was the nicest man you'll ever meet – and the most intelligent,' he says. 'He was a lovely man to talk to, especially for the kids if they needed support.'

Durham had a six-week wait between their return and two limited-overs friendlies in Essex, both lost in front of healthy crowds. As none of the tour matches had first-class status, history was made at The Parks on 14 April 1992. 'There was no real sense of occasion, except for cricket nerds like me,' says David Whitlock. 'It really felt like a normal Oxford University-versus-county game with just a few more press and fans. If I say there were 150 spectators there, that would probably be a major exaggeration.' Even director Bob Jackson was missing, not something you could often say over the next quarter of a century. The historic date was not printed on the scorecard, which had the game taking place on '15, 15 and 16 April 1992' – ironic because snow and sleet prevented play on the 15th.

'I decided there probably wasn't going to be another first first-class game in my lifetime, so I should get along,' says Whitlock, a Warwickshire member living in Coventry. 'There were one or two film crews, Patrick Eagar and one or two other cricket photographers. Alan Lee was there to write about it for *The Times,* along with some other reporters I wouldn't have recognised. *The Times* made a big deal of it and gave it a full colour picture in their sports section but generally it was very low-key. I didn't come back for the next two days but I was really pleased to have gone along and taken a picture of the toss and the first ball, because not many other people did.'

McEwan was also desperate not to miss it, at wife Debbie's bedside in Durham at 2am before heading to Oxford after the birth of daughter Amber Rahne.

'I'm not sure why it got such small coverage, really, but in a way that was good, it turned out to be a practice match,' says Cook. 'Prior to the game we were scratching around for somewhere to train because it was quite wet that April, and Boldon were kind enough to provide us with a pitch on the end of their square. There were some pretty fearsome players batting that day and if we started with 20 balls we must have finished with zero!'

Hughes tweaked a thigh muscle in the warm-up in Oxford and mugs of tea, not water bottles, came out at the drinks break. 'It was a typical early-season game where you got the impression most people would rather be doing something else,' Whitlock recalls. 'I wandered around beforehand and had a few Durham players looking at me quizzically. I wandered up to the square to take a picture of the toss and nobody seemed too bothered about that. The only other person who took a picture was Simon Hughes and he obviously had a better eye for a picture than me because he stood on the opposite side, getting the pavilion in the background.'

Graveney called incorrectly but it said something about the fixture's competitiveness that opposite number Geoff Lovell granted his wish to bat first anyway. Parker faced the first delivery and, along with 26-year-old Glendenen, the only Durham player making his first-class debut, took the score to 119/0 at lunch. Hartlepool's George Sharp was the other north-easterner making his first-class bow – as an umpire, alongside Chris Balderstone. Resuming after five sessions of bad weather, Glendenen became the first first-class debutant since Essex's Jon Lewis in 1990 to score a century. Parker, 98 not out at the time, followed him five minutes later and, when their 222-run stand ended, Jones, then Phil Bainbridge, batted until Graveney's declaration and 65 overs in the field.

Bainbridge marked his 34th birthday with Durham's maiden wicket and Wood dismissed Jason Gallian before shaking hands on a draw. It meant when Ryan Pringle was born in Sunderland the following day, it was with a clear route into first-class cricket he took 22 years later, but the real stuff started when Botham arrived from his safari in Northern Transvaal ahead of Lancashire's Easter Sunday visit. At Durham's media day, the *Sunderland Echo*'s Tim Rich asked if he thought the circus surrounding him might die down now he had come north. Looking at the clamouring cameras and microphones, Botham replied: 'Jeez, where do you come from? Never-Never Land?'

Hughes approved of Graveney's policy of telling his players to report an hour before the start (2.05pm in this case). 'Most county teams are obliged to arrive much earlier, then just sit around doing crosswords or reading porn,' he wrote, but it did little to ease the captain's anxiety. 'It was my first experience, although it was going to be repeated quite a lot at Durham, of wondering what the chances were of all my players turning up on time!' Graveney chuckled 25 years later. 'The layout of the Racecourse means there's only a narrow road and one gate to get in.

'I remember getting there early and there was an older man who didn't have a ticket [the game was a 5,500 sell-out] with a very young boy. He asked if he could walk his grandson around the ground just so he would be able to remember the day and that absolutely underlined its importance to me. The players eventually turned up but there were all sorts of little incidents. The programmes were locked away in a Portakabin and someone had lost the key, so that had to be broken into!'

Overlooked as wicketkeeper at The Parks, Andy Fothergill played in the Sunday League game. He definitely got the better deal. 'It was amazing, even just driving to the ground,' he says. 'Because I lived in Darlington and Beefy [Botham] lived in Ravensworth, he used to pick me up. I'd bring my bag down from the flat and the boot would be open – and Beefy sat inside the car. I would be looking around hoping everybody's seen me. He didn't talk about cricket, really, we'd have the music on and chat. One day he asked me to pass his diary from the back seat and look someone's name up, so I was flicking past

Mick Jagger, Elton John and the rest. I remember driving down the bank at the Racecourse and it was packed an hour and a half before the game, even though the weather was bloody freezing.'

Waiting for Botham was Neil Killeen. 'I wasn't playing so I was basically there to help out with the big boys,' he recalls. 'Ian Botham and Dean Jones had just played at the World Cup and it was quite a surreal experience. The nets were across the far side of the ground and the ball kept disappearing into the river! When I finished bowling I went to sit on the bank to watch with the rest of the fans.'

Winners of the 1989 Sunday League and both one-day finals in 1990, Lancashire were suitably glamorous opponents, even without Wasim Akram. 'When I was a kid they were my team. In one-day cricket in 1992 they were the kiddies,' Fothergill remarks. Cook says: 'I'm sure the fixture was organised by the influential people.' Lancashire included Graeme Fowler who, like team-mate Paul Allott and opponent Hughes, played for Durham University while at Hild Bede College. 'I hadn't been back to the Racecourse since I left and I don't think Paul had either, so we were both looking forward to seeing what it was like,' he said. 'It wasn't the Racecourse that we knew because there were temporary stands up and you couldn't move for people. When it came to the pavilion, though, nothing much had changed – they hadn't renovated it, although they might have painted it.'

Neil Fairbrother won the toss and fielded, bringing opener Botham into the game immediately. 'It was five overs before he attempted to light the blue touchpaper with a straight driven four, blasted back over Allott's head,' Brown wrote. 'And with only 14 to his name he charged so far down the track to Allott that wicketkeeper [Warren] Hegg could even afford to drop the ball and scoop it up again, before completing a slow-motion stumping.'

If Botham failed to spark on the slow pitch, his replacement at the crease did not. 'There was pressure on me, all right. I was nervous as hell,' Dean Jones told me in 2012. 'I knew it could be a bit hard on those pitches early in the season. I was well aware if you don't get some runs early they [the supporters] will fall away.' He reached his century off just 80 deliveries, his second fifty coming from 34, and was only out to the final ball of Durham's 246/4. 'He was a master craftsman,' Fothergill gushes. 'Bains [Bainbridge] got 37, "Ned" [Wayne Larkins] got a fifty but it was totally different to Dean Jones – he was ones and twos, bad balls went for four, and even-worse balls six. He just ran the field ragged.'

Future Durham captain Nick Speak top-scored for Lancashire with 58, but for a long time it seemed the spectators would get the result they wanted. Botham removed England team-mate Fairbrother with a brilliant one-handed catch in the covers and Mike Watkinson was starting to look dangerous until playing on to the all-rounder, but a 35-ball knock and 1-57 bowling second change were hardly *Roy of the Rovers* stuff. Hegg, Ian Austin and most explosively Phil DeFreitas, with 33 from 11 deliveries, brought Lancashire's target into sight. After Botham's 15-run final over, Simon Brown removed Allott but conceded 12.

'If Beefy fancied it and wanted to win, we always competed and a lot of the time we won,' argues Fothergill. 'If he couldn't be bothered, we might as well have not turned up.' He fancied this. 'I remember certain members of the committee saying, "Just go out and have a good day and enjoy yourselves boys,"' Botham recalls. 'We all sat in the dressing room and said, "Pig's arse – we're here to do a job." We made a point of telling them that negativity was not for our dressing room. I don't know who wrote the script, but it worked out well. I think we all chipped in, actually. I remember a couple of good catches behind the stumps and some excellent fielding by Dean Jones.'

Cook says: 'The result and how it was attained was fantastic. Both were fully deserved. The win took a little bit of pressure off and it put us on the map a little bit. It was important.' Jones joked: 'If all games are as tense as that I'm going home!' His century kicked off a mutual love affair with the Durham cricketing public. 'When people ask me who was Durham's best player, I always say Dean Jones,' comments Bob Jackson. Hughes called him 'the most electrifying person I'd ever played with'; Fothergill labels him 'a god, really'.

Jones told me: 'I captained Derby for two seasons and we nearly won the Championship in 1996, but I had more fun with Durham. I knew the people in that part of the world were really friendly but I felt like I was their best mate. I was living in Durham and they were dropping off cakes and cards and made my family feel absolutely fantastic. My daughter [Phoebe] was nine months old and we just felt like one of their own.'

Even Lancashire caught the mood. 'In a weird way we almost celebrated the fact that they won their first game,' said Fowler. 'There was opposition to Durham being given first-class status but not from us, so we were almost delighted for them. If you get off to a good start it makes such a difference. To win the first game like that would have sent a huge buzz through the club.' Fothergill admits: 'I got lashed because you were just on such a high. The game had everything. The crowd erupted when [Botham] hit the wickets. We cracked open a few beers in the dressing room afterwards and Paul Parker got his guitar out again. The Lancashire players could hear the music from their dressing room.'

Glamorgan reduced Durham to 18/3 in the Benson and Hedges Cup at the same ground two days later, only for Botham to take control. Batting at five in the 55-over game, he made 86 from 196/9 before being caught by Viv Richards. Botham had already removed Hugh Morris with the new ball when he found his old Somerset team-mate Richards's leading edge. If big occasions coaxed the best out of Botham, so did taking on friends. 'I'll never forget the sound of it hitting his hand and the fact he wanted to get it so much,' Jones recalled. 'It went from 5,500 people to 25,000 in terms of the noise. I felt like I'd won the World Cup. Those two games helped people get right behind us because now they had their own team and their own legends.' Although Glamorgan wriggled away from 8/3 to win by four wickets, Botham was man of the match.

Next came a century described by *Wisden* as 'a glorious display of controlled aggression' at home to Leicestershire in Durham's Championship opener. Despite giving Parker a 53-run headstart on the final day, Botham beat the shining light of Durham's first innings to three figures. Even their 178-run fifth-wicket stand could not overcome being bowled out for 164 on day one, however, and the visitors won by seven wickets.

Botham passed 50 in four of his first six games. The last of them, the 55-over Benson and Hedges Cup group game against the Combined Universities, was his first wicketless match for Durham – and his first without a catch – but his 72 was important to the victory. Not only did he top-score at Gateshead Fell in Durham's second Sunday League game, but his direct hit denied Leicestershire's Tim Boon the match's only other half-century as the hosts won by eight runs. Parker responded to his first first-class failure for Durham – at Kent in May – with his third century, at Glamorgan. He was averaging 54.4 by the end of June, which tailed off to a still-commendable end-of-season 40.3. Called 'far and away our best fielder during the season' by Graveney, Parker was Durham's player of 1992.

Glamorgan witnessed Durham's first Championship win and another stunning Botham catch off Richards. 'As always, he was stood about two yards in front of everyone else [at slip], Viv went for a drive and nicked it so it went off like a shell and he just took a dive and caught it one-handed,' says Fothergill. 'That's when you go, "He's a genius."'

The bowler was 17-year-old debutant Paul Henderson, who also removed England internationals Morris and Matthew Maynard, but did not bowl in the second innings because of sore shins. They were scanned, but too early, and it was only two years later Henderson learnt he had suffered a stress fracture of his left leg. He made four further first-class appearances and three in one-day cricket, all in 1992, before being released in 1994. 'Young lads like Paul Henderson were always going to find it tough,' Cook reflects. 'That was why it was important we got the academy off the ground and established in the fairly tight structure of north-east cricket.'

Fothergill experienced cricket's highs and lows in the two-day win. 'I dropped a catch when Glamorgan were nine down, although they still needed another 100,' he says. 'Steven Bastien skied it and I ran underneath it and dropped it. I was gutted. I'd kept really well and that was the only mistake I made. He was out three balls later or whatever it was and all the lads were taking the piss, but when I walked back to the changing room Viv Richards was at the door and he just put his arm around me and said, "Don't worry about that, you've had a good game, we all do it." That was Viv Richards! I'd never met him before in my life! That was the sort of camaraderie from some of the teams we played – Lancashire were another but some of the southern teams I didn't quite get along with.' Steve James was less gracious, arguing: 'It was us playing particularly badly rather than them playing well.'

John Wood, then 20, dismissed the country's in-form batsman Tony Middleton with his first Championship delivery and David Gower his sixth at Hampshire in May on his way to 5-68, and 18-year-old Jimmy Daley made 88 on his debut in the competition, a hotchpotch of 16 three- and six four-day games. Stewart Hutton started with 43 and 40 when Glendenen was dropped after four ducks in five innings. 'Glendo was a fantastic character, one of the funniest guys I've come across,' says Jeff Brown. 'He loved everything about cricket except playing it. I think he just found it a bit overwhelming.'

Durham's maiden Championship home win came by eight wickets with three overs to spare against Somerset at Darlington in June. 'I hit a ball to [Richard] Snell,' recalled Jones, who made 78 opening the second innings after Glendenen suffered breathing problems. 'My wife Jane sat in the members' area yelling "Drop it!" which he did. Durham's chaplain [Brian Rice] tapped her on the shoulder and said, "I prayed too, but I did it quietly!" What blew me was we had to travel to Derbyshire to play the next day, so we didn't have a chance to celebrate properly. I didn't fully understand how much travelling I would have to do. I didn't know if they were ripping up the A1 or putting it down!'

The county treadmill was always likely to be tough on a squad with plenty of old-stagers and novices, but little in between. 'Paul

Parker and I were probably the two fittest people in the team, but mentally it was so hard,' Fothergill admits. 'If you're keeping wicket for Durham and we're generally getting bowled out for 180, 200 then the opposition are making 600, you were in the field a long time. Anyone will tell you my concentration levels aren't the best anyway.'

Fothergill was not the only one feeling the strain. 'The run-ins I had with Don Robson were because the team struggled in the first season,' Jeff Brown recalls. 'I got summoned to a meeting at Stockton and I knew what it was about so I took in all my cuttings. Don said, "When I go to pick up my morning paper my newsagent says, I see your lot lost again, it's all over *The Journal*!" I said, "What am I supposed to do when you're losing?" I put a load of cuttings on the table, the ones saying the team was losing and the ones saying isn't this fantastic, which was ten times as high. He very grudgingly accepted it. We did eventually come to see each other's views.'

Considering his flying start, Botham's end-of-season first-class averages were unremarkable, fifth in Durham's batting, seventh for bowling. 'When the big games came around he set the examples,' explains Cook. 'Getting him on a day-to-day basis was always going to be tough. The heights he reached in the 1980s, not just his achievements in the cricketing sense but his charity walks, were amazing and it was very much a case of giving him a lot of licence at Durham.'

Fothergill reflects: 'We only saw glimpses of what he could do and he couldn't bowl like he used to because of injuries, but he still swung it and when the ball came down the seam was still perpendicular. I think his body had absolutely given up by the end. I remember talking to him about the Lancashire game and he said the atmosphere was absolutely amazing. That probably kept his desire going a little bit more.' Botham was fired by being involved in something new. 'It was great,' he comments. 'We had a great bunch of guys – a lot of us in the same boat coming to the end of our careers. It was an adventure, none of us knew where we were going to go.'

His Lancashire heroics apart, Jones got off to a slow start but picked up to become the first Durham batsman to 1,000 first-class runs. Third in the national averages and top in the Sunday League after passing 50 in six consecutive games, his influence extended beyond the scorebook. 'Just talking to him was brilliant to understand how you would win a game, but you couldn't always execute it because you weren't Dean Jones!' says Fothergill. 'I remember playing at Stockton against Northants [in May 1992, a last-ball away win] and in the second innings we were 75/5. I came out to bat with Dean and we got through to lunch. At lunchtime Dean said, "You know Curtly [Ambrose] will be coming back on just after lunch?" I said, "Do me a favour Dean, because I've never faced anyone like that…" I'd faced bowlers that quick, but not 9ft 7in! Dean took the first few balls and he was ducking and diving, getting hit. I thought, "I'm going to die if he's doing that to Dean Jones on a slow, low wicket!" I was slamming the shit out of David Capel at the other end and ended up not facing Curtly. I wasn't scared but I hadn't got the tools to deal with that.'

The Somerset win was Durham's last in the 1992 Championship but they reached the NatWest Trophy quarter-finals and, despite not making it out of their Benson and Hedges group, Steve McEwan saw them over the line against holders Worcestershire. Picked for Australia's tour of Sri Lanka, Jones was due to leave after the Grace Road quarter-final. However, three days after consecutive centuries against Pakistan at Ropery Lane, Jones broke his finger at Trent Bridge. With Graveney suffering ligament trouble in the knuckle of his spinning finger and an infected knee, second-team captain and coach Cook, now 40, was drafted in, prompting Tim Wellock to write in the *Northern Echo*: 'Desperation time has arrived for Durham.' Cook made 16 as Durham lost to a Leicestershire side beaten in their previous 11 one-day home games.

Not only did Jones miss Durham's big match, it was wrongly assumed he would be selected for Australia's 1993 Ashes tour. He returned, but only to coach the second XI. 'It was bloody awful,' he said. 'By the time I found out I wasn't in the Ashes squad the deal was already done with Anderson Cummins [to be Durham's overseas player].'

Wellock wrote Jones's absence 'appears to have inflicted severe psychological damage' as Durham were bowled out for under 150 four times in the first three Championship games without him. Third in the Championship in mid-June, they did not win any game after 9 July, yet supporter enthusiasm and team spirit remained good. 'The itinerant nature of the club just made it really exciting, we had lots and lots of full houses,' says Cook, though it made finding practice facilities difficult. 'It was a crazy couple of years with some great stories and the cameras following us around all the time. We had players who quite enjoyed the attention and took it all in their stride, but it did overwhelm some of the younger players like Jimmy Daley because they didn't have the coping strategies young players have now.' Capped at 6,000 in June (about 1,600 more than in 2018, and 2,000 more than the business plan anticipated), Durham's membership was second only to Essex of the non-Test counties, occasionally causing supporters to be turned away.

Fothergill says players 'mixed very well. There was no drinking culture, everyone was always fit and raring to go the next day but we just liked to enjoy ourselves and relax. We were a really well-bonded unit, we just weren't good enough. It was a very eclectic changing room. When you played against other first-class counties they all seemed to be the same person. They didn't like to play against us because of the characters we had.'

Graveney knitted it together. 'I wish I could have come earlier because a lot of us weren't in the autumn of our careers, we were in the winter,' joked the captain, who was 39. 'We were seven guys from all parts of the country thrown together with some local players. Geoff had nurtured these players in the minor counties, and I saw it more as my job to manage the expectations of the membership, and to try and educate the media. The dressing rooms on the outgrounds we played on weren't big enough to accommodate 11 first-class cricketers, so I spent a lot of time with the members and the media.' Not that it was always by choice. Having given up smoking, Graveney was pacing the floor so much he was sent to watch Durham's Benson and Hedges Cup game at New Road from his car. 'Grav cared a lot about how people thought about the club,' says Jeff Brown. 'He would explain decisions in the bar afterwards and speak to anyone. It was important to be visible when the team was losing.'

Botham was more or less allowed to prepare as he saw fit, and other allowances had to be made too. 'He couldn't do what other cricketers did,' Brown explains. 'In pre-season we'd get a list of all the hotels Durham were staying in so we would book into the same ones and you'd meet up the night before the game. Everyone would be in the bar with Beefy upstairs with a bottle of claret because if he was in public he'd get hassled by someone who either wanted a photo, wanted his autograph or wanted to swing a punch at him. We were all a bit in awe of him – media and players, who found it a bit overwhelming for such a big personality to be in the dressing room, especially kids who'd been playing Durham Senior League the previous year.

'Towards the end of the season Durham were playing at Taunton and Beefy was off the field, injured. I took a punt and went to the dressing room and asked if I could have a chat. It was like I was his long-lost best mate – I couldn't get away. I think he just needed someone to talk to and I came away thinking, "Blimey, it must be a solitary existence when you're so much in the public eye." That was before selfies and people taking videos of you.'

Durham finished 36 points adrift at the bottom of the one-division Championship but ninth in the Sunday League. 'We scared a few teams but the problem was keeping everyone fit,' Botham explains. 'We had some great moments for a fledgling side but we were just treading water until the new players came through. Some good talent emerged, like Simon Brown, big John [Wood] – who was quick, but not the fittest man on the planet – and Dean Jones added a lot to the party.' Graveney admitted, 'It soon became very evident that the club was recruiting all-rounders to cover two bases at once, but once

Dean Jones got injured it left us with a lack of batting depth and not enough runs to work with.'

Cook argues, 'The 1992 season really started in 1990. It was a huge build-up with a lot of emotions wasted. Once the romance of early season started to fade away, the players were going to have to rely on their own motivation. I thought we'd win more games but I suspected it would be a heck of a struggle. Simon [Brown] carried the bowling virtually single-handedly in those early years.' That was the thinking behind signing West Indies fast bowler Cummins for 1993, although batsman Martin Crowe had been teed up until dissuaded by New Zealand. Chris Broad was also linked after being released by Nottinghamshire, but instead Graeme Fowler became Larkins's opening partner.

If Durham's 1992 media day had been a bun-fight, 12 months on things were different. 'We were standing around – me, Tim Wellock, Doug Weatherall [of the *Daily Mail*] and Tim Rich – saying, "Who should we chat to?", and we decided Beefy because you didn't get much of a chance,' Jeff Brown recalls. 'Someone asked him how he thought the season would go, and he said, "I'm hoping for a big one this year because it will probably be my last one in cricket." He kept on talking and I think all four of us stopped writing and were open-mouthed. We asked him, "Hang on, this will probably be..." and he said, "Yeah, I'm going to retire this year." There are few occasions in a journalist's career where you think, "Wow, we've got a story here!" so we all went scurrying off to find the nearest phonebox and it was the front-page lead in the next edition of *The Chronicle*.'

In *A Lot of Hard Yakka*, Hughes recounted a conversation between Botham and umpire Peter Willey after an April Benson and Hedges Cup match: '"When have we got you again then, Will?" Botham asked. "Oh, June, Gateshead Fell against Middlesex. But you'll have lost interest by then, Beefy."' Botham played – making nought and one not out, and not bowling – but Willey was not far off.

Botham's England career was over. Picked for the opening two one-day internationals against Pakistan in 1992, he batted at seven and did not take the new ball. He carried a groin strain into the Test series, which sat in the middle of the 55-over matches, and did not take a wicket or bat at Edgbaston. His first-innings contribution to the second Test, at Lord's, was two runs and five wicketless overs before Waqar Younis broke his toe as he made six in the second. Botham returned to finish the one-day series and ended it wicketless at Old Trafford before watching the top six reach their target. His final Durham wicket of 1992 came on 6 August but Graveney sensed his enthusiasm had been on the wane since England left him out after Lord's.

Botham being Botham, he had not given up on a swansong in the 1993 Ashes, particularly after two wickets for the Duke of Norfolk's XI against Australia. England lost their three one-day internationals and first two Tests while Botham scored 101 and bowled 51 overs against Worcestershire, but gave debuts to Mark Lathwell, Graham Thorpe, Martin McCague and Mark Ilott instead. Botham played against Surrey, taking no wickets and facing only eight balls across two second-day innings. Chairman of selectors Ted Dexter asked him to captain England A on what Botham called 'a clog-dancing mission' in Holland. He refused.

Without the carrot of international cricket, Botham was tiring of life at Durham. 'It had nothing to do with the playing, just the backroom politics,' he insists. 'There was a bit of a power struggle going on.' In early July 1993, two days after Durham were knocked out of the NatWest Trophy, Botham climbed out of bed. 'It took me five minutes,' he recalled in his autobiography. 'My left hip had been playing up all season, and my left knee and shoulder ached as well, but to be honest it was difficult to distinguish one pain from another.'

Jeff Brown recalls: 'I was staying at my mother-in-law's and it just so happened they got the *Mail on Sunday* delivered. On the third day of the tour game with Australia I got a cup of tea and my breakfast, got a chair out, went to the bottom of the garden, put my feet on the fence, took a sip of tea, opened the paper and the back-page story was "Botham quits" by Peter Hayter, his ghostwriter. I dropped my tea, dashed in, got changed and went to Beefy's farewell.'

Even with rain delaying play until 2.30pm, there were 3,000 spectators at the Racecourse. The previous day Durham enforced the follow-on for the first time in first-class cricket against a strong Australian side preparing for the fourth Test. Botham finished the game running through his bowling impressions and bowled for the last time in professional cricket with his tackle out, before keeping wicket without pads or gloves. *Wisden* called it an 'unbecoming, flippant performance'.

Botham had only told Jones, Cook and Graveney about his retirement, swearing them to secrecy until the newspaper got its exclusive. He offered to stay on in limited-overs cricket – Durham declined – but reasoned that since the county were doomed to finish bottom, it was better to give Championship opportunities to others. Don Robson was upset to find out the way everyone else did, and there was a petty stand-off over what came first, Botham's final pay cheque or the return of his sponsored car. Botham said he ignored a request from Mattie Roseberry to front a 'coup' to oust Robson but his bitterness was undisguised. In his 1994 autobiography he described joining Durham as 'one of the worst mistakes I ever made'. Less than a week after it was published, the club gave him life membership.

'The game after Australia, Durham went to Essex and won [for the first time in the Championship for almost 14 months] and I think we all wrote, "Who needs Ian Botham?"' says Brown. 'It was good for the first year, for both sides. He got back in the England team briefly, but once he realised his international career was over I think he was just ticking off the days.'

Durham won six of their final seven Sunday League games to finish seventh but the Championship victory at Essex was only repeated against Warwickshire at Feethams, and there were five innings defeats. It was time for a new script.

4.

Nice Stadium, Shame About the Team

'I THINK our ground is one of the finest county grounds in the country, if you exclude the great ones like Lord's,' Tom Moffat says proudly. 'Nancy [his wife] and I have been on Test-match grounds in the West Indies, South Africa, Zimbabwe, Australia, all over the world, and not many first-class grounds are better than Riverside.

'When we built it we had a fine manager, Joe Sherrington. Joe oversaw all of the construction and, if you look at it today, there's still elements that look good because we went for the quality – stainless steel, good quality plastics and not a lot of wood – that deteriorates. If you get that right, the rest follows.'

When the Chester-le-Street ground hosted its maiden first-class match in May 1995, the team was lagging way behind, as the 111-run margin of defeat to Warwickshire showed. Durham had finished 16th in the 1994 County Championship but were a place lower in 1995, and bottom for the third time in their first five seasons the year after.

It had been similar for the last new first-class county. Glamorgan finished bottom twice in their opening five Championship campaigns, and only once outside the bottom two. In 1925 they lost 13 games on the trot.

When Durham began the 1994 season at Oxford University, David Graveney, John Wood, Chris Scott and Phil Bainbridge were their only survivors from the corresponding game two years earlier. John Glendenen and Mark Briers had been released in the winter, the former not playing again after being struck on the elbow by Waqar Younis during Ian Botham's final Championship game. Paul Parker offered to play part-time after taking a job at Tonbridge School in Kent, but Durham signed Mark Saxelby from Nottinghamshire instead. Even Graveney was only playing because of a back injury to Alan Walker, signed from Northamptonshire to replace the retired Simon Hughes. Graveney had been sacked as captain after consecutive wooden-spoon seasons.

'There were lots of difficult decisions at that time,' stresses Geoff Cook. 'Ian Botham retired but he'd fallen out of love with Durham at that stage. Wayne Larkins was coming to the end of his career and he was a popular figure. These were friends of mine who had been friends for 20 years within the game, so they were all tricky decisions. Once the novelty had worn off and the Bainbridges, Parkers and Graveneys had gone, the next tranche of players were always going to find life pretty tough because the County Championship was starting to get competitive, and when teams had a chance of winning they were a lot more ruthless. Durham were giving them a chance to win because of the callowness of the team. Switching to four-day cricket provided more opportunities to win too.'

Jeff Brown, ghost-writer of Graveney's *Journal* column, felt he was hard done by. 'It was a bit harsh to blame him for the fact Durham had struggled for two years,' he argues. 'They gave it to Phil Bainbridge on the basis that he was a great guy and a really solid performer with bat and ball and the captaincy virtually destroyed him because it was a huge task trying to make a team out of such disparate parts. It was almost impossible. Players were just being catapulted into the first-class game.'

Bainbridge was Durham's player of the year in 1993 after heading their batting and bowling averages. One of *Wisden*'s cricketers of 1985, the Almanack partly put his success down to Gloucestershire's 'wise, psychological touch' in making him Graveney's vice-captain. 'It was good for me,' Bainbridge said. 'I thrive on responsibility.' Now Bainbridge was in charge, Graveney was diplomatic as ever. 'I can't deny I'm disappointed to lose the captaincy, but what's past is past,' he said.

Bainbridge's successor had already been anointed though, as often when that happens, things did not pan out as planned. Durham fought off Somerset and Hampshire to sign John Morris on a six-year deal described as the 'longest and most lucrative contract yet offered to an English county cricketer', despite the fact he was 30 when the season started and had won the last of his three England caps in 1990. Winter coaching and promotional work were included to justify the largesse. Stephen Harmison calls Morris, on the losing Derbyshire team against Durham in 1985, 'one of the best players of quick bowling I've ever played with', but then, as now, he was better known for an ill-judged moment on the 1990/91 Ashes tour. Morris and David Gower flew a Tiger Moth aeroplane overhead as Robin Smith and Allan Lamb batted in a warm-up game against Queensland. They might have got away with it but for the long lens of a pesky photographer.

His £1,000 fine – the most England were allowed to take from his £15,000 tour pay – was the least of Morris's punishments. Despite having earlier made 130 in England's only first-class victory of the tour, and despite a half-century in the post-Ashes one-day series, he never played Test cricket again. 'All I hope is that the side is picked on ability, and not silly things like flying aeroplanes,' Morris said on his arrival at Durham. He would be disappointed.

Durham further reinforced their batting by signing Jon Longley from Kent. Saxelby made 181, Morris 90 and Longley an unbeaten century as they opened their Championship campaign with 625/6 declared at Chesterfield en route to a seven-wicket win over Derbyshire. In May, Gloucestershire were beaten by 108 runs at

Gateshead Fell. Morris became Durham's maiden first-class double-centurion in the next game but, like his Queensland hundred, it was completely overshadowed.

Before the match at Edgbaston, Anderson Cummins warned: 'We can't afford to worry about Brian Lara. It's a team game, and there are ten other guys we've got to bowl at as well.' It was pretty rotten advice because Warwickshire's Lara was in the form of his, and just about anyone else's, life. A run which started with Test cricket's then-highest score – 375 against England in Antigua in April – had him averaging 175 in first-class cricket. So when Morris made 204 not out in Durham's 556/8 declared, Lara responded with an innings that completely put it into the shade.

Perhaps most astonishing is that when he started it, he did not bat that well. 'He rarely timed a shot in his first hour,' Brown reported, and it was not just his view. 'I wasn't really myself out there,' Lara commented. 'I felt I was struggling.' Cummins bowled his international team-mate for ten, but overstepped the crease and was no-balled. 'On 18, he flashed at Simon Brown and offered a faint edge, which wicketkeeper Chris Scott would normally accept 99 times out of 100,' wrote Jeff Brown. 'This, however, was the 100th.' Lara was 111 not out on Friday night, his seventh century in eight first-class innings.

Saturday's play was rained off, Sunday handed over to 40-over cricket (Lara made just six in Warwickshire's 84-run win), so, when bad blood between opposing captains Bainbridge and Dermot Reeve put paid to a contrived finish, Lara decided to just bat, and bat, and bat. With Graveney injured during the match, debutant spinner David Cox endured figures of 0-163 despite claiming: 'I only bowled about ten bad balls.' Larkins took the opposite approach. 'I deliberately set out to bowl a pile of garbage,' he said. 'Ian Botham got wickets like that for years.' Neither could stop Lara reaching a world-record first-class score of 501 not out from 427 deliveries.

'When it [Lara's edge] went down the first thing I thought was, "That could be costly,"' Scott said. 'You think someone might go on to get a hundred – but not 500.' Jeff Brown had changed his tune by then, calling it: 'Arguably the greatest innings the game has yet seen.' Not that Durham could claim it derailed them, beating Northamptonshire by an innings and 87 runs at Hartlepool later that week. Morris top-scored with 186 before his form briefly deserted him, 46 in nine first-class innings dropping his end-of-season average to 45.

Bainbridge was very consistent – unfortunately. After starting the season with just 68 runs and two wickets from Durham's opening five first-class games, he played for the second team during a pre-Edgbaston break in the schedule and made five and 73 against Warwickshire seconds at South Shields. Following it with 67 against their seniors might have raised hopes but had no long-term effect. It was the first of only three Championship half-centuries in 1994, and despite playing another two seasons Bainbridge never scored another first-class hundred. He averaged 77 with the ball and although his one-day numbers were better – scoring his runs at 29 (one fifty) and taking wickets at 38 – they were nothing special. Even his fielding suffered. During a 116-run defeat to Yorkshire at the Racecourse he dropped his fourth catch in five days. He was stubbornly refusing to resign, but Brown wrote, 'It might now be kinder to relieve Bainbridge of the burden of leadership and let him get on with what he does best… You feel for the bloke.'

Carrying an injury to his right knee cannot have helped, and by the end of the campaign Bainbridge needed a shoulder operation too, but what made things much worse was the team's dreadful Championship form. Fourth in June, Durham's final game against Glamorgan at Hartlepool was a wooden-spoon decider, with the hosts in danger of an eighth straight defeat. They won by three wickets, led home by Morris's 123 not out after Simon Brown's nine-wicket match haul. Bainbridge's contribution was 20 runs across two innings, one wicket and three catches. 'If we hadn't won, I would have seriously thought about asking the club if they felt anyone else could do a better job, because it was vitally important we weren't last for the third successive season,' Bainbridge revealed afterwards. Durham reached that conclusion anyway. The arrival of Indian Manoj Prabhakar, another medium-pace all-rounder, delayed Bainbridge's next first-team appearance until late June, and he spent most of 1995 captaining the second team. Graveney retired at the end of the 1994 campaign, aged 41, to be replaced by new recruit James Boiling.

Fowler and Andy Fothergill had also been eased out, released with Phil Berry, Gary Wigham, Paul Henderson and Ian Smith, as the squad was cut from 28 to 21. Fowler had joined on a two-year contract hoping to coach the second XI afterwards but, as he put it: 'Once I'd had a domestic change of arrangements and run off with the marketing manager [his now-wife Sarah], I think that chance disappeared.' Martin Robinson became second-team coach and youth development officer, freeing Geoff Cook to spend more time with the seniors.

Saxelby was preferred against Oxford University and Fowler saw the writing was on the wall when Cook said he did not see the point in him playing for the seconds. Sixties in his opening three first-class innings of 1994, the latter pair against a South Africa attack led by Allan Donald and Fanie de Villiers, made little difference, and he only played two further first-class games all season. His silver lining was making Durham history in the second team. On 2 August 1994, in front of around 3,000 spectators, Durham's second XI played Middlesex in the Riverside's first game. 'Like everyone, I had some lows and some extreme highs in my career, and memories that probably don't mean a lot to other people, but they do to me,' Fowler told me in 2016. 'To captain Durham's second team in the first game at the Riverside was one – particularly as our first daughter, Katherine, was born on the evening of the third day, and the fourth was rained off. I even remember the first ball, bowled by Franklyn Rose.'

Kevin Thomson, not Durham trialist Rose, took the first wicket with the aid of a Fothergill catch – not that the wicketkeeper remembered. 'Geoff asked if I wanted to play in the three-day game or the one-dayer, and I said if it was going to be my last game I'd like to have the full three days,' Fothergill says. 'The wicket was a bit up and down but the seats around the outside were all full, with the pavilion getting built in the background. We changed in the scorebox. It was great to be involved with. I got the first fifty – and I only scored four for Durham [in the first-class era].'

Neither Fowler nor Fothergill are bitter. 'There was no money in the game when our generation of cricketers, the elder statesmen of that early Durham squad, played, so we played because we loved it and we made damn sure we enjoyed it off the field as well as on,' said Fowler, who set up and ran Durham University's ground-breaking and prolific centre of excellence in 1996. 'It was a privilege to be a professional sportsman.'

Fothergill's replacement, David Ligertwood, followed Boiling from Surrey. 'Geoff asked me at the end of my two-year contract [in 1993] what I thought,' Fothergill reveals. 'When he said they were thinking about giving me another year I said, "Fine." I knew then I wasn't going to go any further – I didn't play [for the first team] in the third year but it was nice to be a part of it. There was no animosity between me and Chris Scott. We practised and socialised together because in that first year Scotty, Bains [Bainbridge] and Paul Parker had a house in Darlington, where I lived, so when there wasn't a game on we all socialised together. I don't think I could have played every game. Looking back, it's 100 per cent pride. I used to play for Durham. I was part of history, even from 1982 and my first game at Carlisle, Cumbria away – rained off. It was pride then and it's pride now.'

Durham were again wrong-footed over their overseas player, assuming Cummins would tour with the West Indies in 1995. A verbal agreement to sign Shane Warne was vetoed by the Australian Cricket Board. They saw off interest from Yorkshire to agree terms with Craig Matthews, the player Warwickshire signed for 1994 until injury forced them to turn to Lara. But as Matthews awaited Cricket South Africa's approval he had a change of heart, staying in Cape Town for business reasons. Durham, therefore, turned to

Prabhakar, who had his nose broken by Courtney Walsh at Christmas but recovered in time for the English season. Cummins, who had taken 109 first-class wickets in two seasons with Durham, spent the summer playing for Bromley.

If being Durham's overseas player was beginning to feel like a poisoned chalice, the captaincy was even more so. Mattie Roseberry's son Mike looked a sensible as well as romantic choice as their first Durham-born first-class captain. He had spent ten seasons at Middlesex, during which time he plundered his home county. Roseberry made 173 in their first-class bow at Lord's in the 1992 Championship, and 152 the next time he faced them there, two years later. He was England's leading first-class scorer in 1992, with 2,044 runs. There were winner's medals too, in the NatWest Trophy, Benson and Hedges Cup, and Championship.

The Penshaw-born batsman's two years in charge of Durham were riddled with bad luck, bad results and very bad form. Things had not started promisingly, needing stitches and a nerve removed after an edge hit him in the mouth when fielding in the slips on a pre-season tour of South Africa. His BMW was dented by a Saxelby six as Durham beat Leicestershire by 50 runs in his opening Benson and Hedges Cup game. Durham's run of eight lost Championship tosses only ended when Peter Hartley twice hit Roseberry on the hand at Harrogate, forcing him to miss the game at Northamptonshire. Morris deputised, and called correctly. Roseberry returned for three of the final five Championship matches of 1994 and lost the toss in all of them.

In June, Roseberry colluded with Mark Benson to set Durham 201 to beat Kent and end their four-match Championship losing streak. They were bowled out for 85. Alan Walker took a club record 14-177 against Essex at Chelmsford in the next match, yet still his side lost by 179 runs to go bottom. It at least went a long way towards keeping Walker at the club, which would be important in the long run. The sequence ended with back-to-back victories over Derbyshire and Glamorgan, but again Durham went into the season's final match staring down the barrel of eight straight defeats. Again they won, by an innings and 114 runs. 'Despite what the Championship table shows', Jeff Brown wrote, 'few would have quibbled if Durham had picked up their third wooden spoon in four years.' The most glaring problem was the batting, with only 20 Championship bonus points for it – comfortably the lowest and half that of Glamorgan and Kent, who sandwiched them in the table. 'Mike Roseberry was supposed to be the catalyst for turning things around,' Brown explains, 'but the problem was they built this ground at the Riverside and they played on it before the pitch had settled down. It was unpredictable.'

Even with Allan Donald, Gladstone Small and Tim Munton injured and Lara touring with the West Indies, treble-winners Warwickshire were fitting opponents for the Riverside's maiden first-class game, which started on 22 May 1995. The initial capacity was around 8,000, leaving only 1,000 seats available to non-members, but bitterly cold weather kept the first-day attendance below 4,000. Life members Graveney, Parker and Simon Hughes were there, but not Ian Botham. As at The Parks in 1992, Chris Balderstone umpired – this time alongside John Hampshire.

Roseberry won the toss twice but obviously lost the one that mattered. 'I had to throw it four times so the photographers could get their pictures,' he revealed. Even though Nick Knight and Andy Moles put on 172 for the first wicket as Warwickshire posted 424, Morris's 128 was the ground's first century. Jimmy Daley was unable to bat in the second innings after the first of seven broken hands for him, suffered as Durham won the Riverside's opening Sunday League game by two runs. Simon Brown's 11-192 could not stop Warwickshire taking revenge the next day in the Championship.

Daley returned from his broken knuckle in a 50-over friendly against Denmark and promptly injured it again, ruling him out of 12th man duty at the fourth England versus West Indies Test. The county received a ten-point deduction, suspended for 12 months, when umpires David Constant and Jackie Bond marked the pitch Somerset won by 286 runs on in August as 'poor'. Days earlier, Mike

Gatting commented: 'I was quite happy to get away from here being the only one of our lot who was injured. If you expect your team to do well you have to give them decent pitches to play on and, talking to other teams, they've not had that.' Gatting and Roseberry had been hit on the hands, and Walker broke his toe in Middlesex's 386-run triumph.

'I remember speaking to Davie Houghton when he was coach at Middlesex about how we kept batters here believing because even a few years ago the pitches were still bowler-friendly,' says Jon Lewis, whose 21-year association with Durham began in 1997. 'We had to use the indoor nets to give them a surface every now and again where they could trust themselves. Starting here at 26 [as Lewis did] was certainly easier than being 18, 19. Playing regularly on flatter pitches, Jimmy Daley may have had a different outcome to his career. Jimmy just looked a good player but he kept breaking his fingers and that affected his confidence. He probably never got the numbers most people thought he would.'

Gatting and Brown were by no means alone in believing Durham played on the Riverside square too soon. 'We had no alternative,' then-director Tom Moffat insists. 'It was never as bad as it was made out. One particular captain made a big issue about it simply because we beat them in the first one-dayer there. It was petty. I used to think Dermot Reeve wasn't a bad all-rounder but I lost all admiration for him when he used the pitch as an excuse. If you get beat, you get beat.'

The tension Roseberry was feeling spilled out as he headed to the pavilion after his second duck in eight days in the Somerset defeat, having gloved the first delivery he attempted to play. He did not take kindly to a comment as he passed Stan Ross of Tudhoe. 'He went in the dressing room, chucked his bat down, then stomped back out with his gloves and pads still on and started having a bit of a row with this guy,' recalls Jeff Brown, watching through his binoculars. 'We went over to see him afterwards and said, "It was in full view of the public, we can't ignore this, what did you say to him?" And he told us. He said, "I wanted to punch him," so we said, "We're going to leave that bit out because that won't do you any good.'" Roseberry apologised to Ross, but wrote in *The Journal* column Brown ghosted: 'Can you imagine how much it hurts me that I'm not getting any runs? It's so simple from the boundary.'

Injuries did at least mean more opportunities for youngsters as Durham used 24 players in first-class cricket in 1995. With John Wood and Steve Lugsden missing through stress fractures of the back and Walker suffering hamstring trouble, 19-year-old Neil Killeen finally made his competitive debut at Leicestershire in the Sunday League. A little over two months later, he took Durham's first five-wicket haul in the competition, at Northampton, following his Championship debut. Killeen had trialled at Lancashire the previous winter but held off joining in the hope of getting his chance at Durham.

'It was tough,' he admits. 'I came back from Zimbabwe, played quite a bit of second-team cricket and did well, but the contract never really came. I remember Geoff [Cook] ringing me asking would I play at Leicester in a one-day game and I said I'd love to but I wanted a contract until the end of the season. That was the start of my journey. I didn't want to play anywhere else. I had opportunities throughout my career to move away but there's something infectious about this place and it's the same now.' Killeen's three-year sports science degree at Teesside University was put on hold. Paul Collingwood made his debut in a friendly against Denmark – though all I get is incredulity when I inform him he was at the non-striker's end when victory was secured. Mike Weston's son Robin made a golden duck and four at home to Somerset on his Championship bow. Despite plugging holes in the first team, Durham's second XI finished third in the 1995 Championship.

Wayne Larkins made way, released at the end of the season along with Saxelby. The latter went voluntarily after 194 runs in ten Championship innings, having been pushed down the order by Roseberry's arrival. Larkins signed off with 121, completing the set of centuries against all 17 other first-class counties on his old Wantage Road patch. But at 42, and with opener Sherwin Campbell

– averaging 45.4 against England that summer – lined up as the 1996 overseas player, he was jettisoned despite being third in Durham's 1995 run charts and averages.

Again Durham wrongly thought their overseas player would tour England the following year, though this time they probably did not shed many tears. Cummins believed he had a verbal agreement to return, but Cook thought otherwise, and was looking for a top-order batsman to replace Prabhakar. Desmond Haynes and promising Australian Ricky Ponting were talked about, as were the world's top-ranked batsmen Michael Slater – scorer of three centuries in the previous Ashes series – and Steve Waugh, until Australia organised a tour of Sri Lanka during the 1996 English season. Shivnarine Chanderpaul was mentioned in dispatches, as were Andy and Grant Flower. Chris Lewis was sounded out as an English recruit but joined Surrey instead. The dream ticket, though, was to finally bring back Dean Jones.

Durham claimed Jones had agreed terms, only to sign a two-year contract to captain Derbyshire at the 11th hour. Despite thinking big about their overseas options, they hinted money was the stumbling block. 'We also have to spend money in other areas,' Cook stressed. Durham life member Jones responded: 'I'd like to think I'm a loyal kind of guy, but when it comes down to it, cricket is my job. The captaincy swung it. Durham didn't offer it – although I didn't ask – but Derbyshire gave me the chance out of the blue.' They also appointed Jones's Victoria coach Les Stillman. Inevitably, Jones's first competitive game for Derbyshire was against Durham, and he made 67 in a 104-run Benson and Hedges Cup win.

Durham faced the age-old problem for sports clubs – attracting money would be more difficult without a winning team, and building one would be tougher without investment. 'We had 12 boxes at the Riverside which were all sold in the first season, but you're still in the north east of England and people don't have that much money to fill the boxes every day for maybe 20 days of cricket – or the customers,' says Fothergill, who spent two years in the marketing department after retiring. 'You only tend to fill them for internationals, as with most grounds. You'd probably got the biggest businesses in the north east there anyway at that time, it was just difficult to keep that momentum going. The first year was great, the second year, "I might," then the third year...'

Jones was clear where the issue lay: 'Even when I was there I felt one of the problems was they were concentrating everything on the new ground.' By the time the Queen officially opened the Riverside in October 1995, £9.8m had been spent on it. There had been plans to begin work on a new grandstand, members' lounge, pub and indoor school before the end of 1996, but when Durham raised half the £2m needed the Sports Council did not supply the rest as hoped. Even Graveney had doubts when work began on the Riverside in 1992. 'I dug the first hole,' he recalled. 'I'd spoken to Don [Robson] and everyone about how they'd managed to collect all the players and money they did and their enthusiasm was incredible. But I genuinely thought it was one step too far building the ground on what was just wasteland.'

Moffat is adamant that, 'if you get your infrastructure right, the rest will come. The infrastructure's more important than the team because the team might be successful today and down tomorrow. Your infrastructure's there forever. If your infrastructure's right and you start to win, the rest follows. We proved that.' Cook adds: 'I'm not sure how they could have become more concerned with the cricket. They were all concerned with the results and when we were losing there was massive panic within the club saying, "Oh, we've got to sign this and sign that," but I felt it was important we held firm and had a strong nucleus towards the end of the '90s for the academy products to come into. I think deep down there was an understanding but there was an awful lot of disappointment when results weren't going well. These people had put a lot of effort in to get Durham into first-class cricket. They came in with a romantic vision and suffered lots of disappointments. A lot of them committed their own finance to it. All that had to be respected.'

The 1996 season would be yet another disappointment. The mid-July Costcutter Cup win at the Harrogate Festival was Durham's first of the year against first-class opposition. In May, Stewart Hutton, his place under threat now Sherwin Campbell had arrived from the West Indies versus New Zealand series, was suspended for three games for 'disciplinary reasons' after a dressing-room argument at Lord's. Campbell had been the first visiting batsman to score a Riverside century, for West Indies in June 1995, and was recommended by tour manager Wes Hall (Jones suggested Stuart Law, Darren Lehmann or Jamie Siddons). Campbell scored 1,019 Championship runs and averaged 38 but made just one century, against Nottinghamshire at Trent Bridge.

Durham became only the fourth team since 1946 to go an entire season without a Championship victory and only won once in the Sunday League. 'We had some characters who showed their emotions,' says Collingwood. 'When you're not winning, it's a nightmare. It was really tough; there was lots of soul-searching. I remember being at Sussex [where Durham lost by an innings and 67 runs] and just getting an absolute rollicking from Rosey [Roseberry]. Giff's [coach Norman Gifford's] pipe used to start shaking a little bit more when things were going badly. It almost shapes you.

'I was still trying to find my own game and it took a long time for me to put performances in which warranted my position. That was the thing about Geoff and everyone, they really stuck by me when I wasn't performing that well.' Robson once told me: 'If you can see in somebody that they're really committed and able to achieve, you've got to give them the benefit of the doubt.'

Roseberry's form continued to suffer. After finding his feet at Middlesex in his first three years, his seasonal first-class average had not dipped below 30. In two years as Durham captain he averaged 19.08 in the Championship, with a top score of just 60. Three weeks before the end of the 1996 season he resigned as captain and his father left the board. When I asked Cook about Mike's captaincy, a very long pause followed. 'There were a lot of internal politics within the club,' he says. 'There was always a little bit of friction between a couple of the directors but you try to detach those things from any decisions.

'Mike was an experienced player and John Morris was a fine player but we had a callow team. We suffered a lot of broken fingers and people didn't really want to bat here in the end. One of the many mistakes I made in terms of trying to get the club moving was always trying to get overseas batters in but, probably because it was such a bowler-friendly wicket, bringing in a top-class overseas bowler might have been a better way of winning matches. We were just trying to get enough runs on the board to help us survive, really!'

With vice-captain Morris also struggling for form – he made three Championship fifties and no hundreds in 1996 – Simon Brown was asked to add captaincy to carrying the attack for the final three matches, all lost. Fortunately, a solution was in hand. Cook was in Tasmania, speaking to another overseas batsman. David Boon was being persuaded to change Durham for the better.

5.

The Production Line

IT is a cold early Wednesday evening in February and the Riverside's indoor cricket school is packed. Inside the main door, the floor and seating are littered with bags and equipment, the balcony fills with parents and siblings as training nears its end. Like me, they are watching four lanes of cricketers.

In the first, boys pit their wits against a bowling machine. To their right, first-team bowling coach Alan Walker chats away, occasionally illustrating points with a swirl of the arm. In the far net, Gareth Breese works with the spinners. Geoff Cook stands in the lane between them, largely passive. Academy director John Windows buzzes around, feeding balls into the bowling machine, talking to those waiting to bat and bowl, but most of all to Cook. As the session finishes, the next group warms up.

One of those in Durham-branded kit will probably play for England, possibly more. It seems inevitable given how prolific this production line has become. When Mark Stoneman made his Test debut in August 2017, replacing his former Durham opening partner Keaton Jennings, he became the academy's ninth full England international, following Stephen Harmison, Liam Plunkett, Phil Mustard, Graham Onions, Scott Borthwick, Ben Stokes and Mark Wood. In 2017 Kyle Coetzer became captain of Scotland, for whom

Gavin Main and Dylan Budge have also played, while Barry McCarthy and Peter Chase have represented Ireland. Paul Collingwood made his Durham debut before it opened. The academy has even produced an international umpire after ex-England Under-19 captain and two-time England A tourist Michael Gough fell out of love with opening for his home county and retired aged 24. Gough was the Professional Cricketers' Association's umpire of the year every summer from 2011 to 2018, and has officiated Test matches since 2016.

Giving north-east youngsters the chance to play professional cricket was a big reason why Durham turned first-class. Nova's 1990 promotional video featured a dream sequence with 16-year-old Brendan McCreesh striding across the farmer's field that became the Riverside, while on the voiceover Tom Graveney imagined a Durham player one day making that walk to face the West Indies. McCreesh never lived the dream, scoring 26 and not bowling in his solitary Second XI Championship appearance for Hampshire in 1994, but others did.

On 18 June 2007, Shotley Bridge-born Collingwood walked across that land, raising his bat to the crowd after making 128 in the fourth Test against the West Indies. At the non-striker's end was Harmison, three years earlier ranked the world's number one bowler, and part of the academy's original intake. It was one of 300 England appearances Collingwood made in all formats, 55 as limited-overs captain. The winter of 2018/19 was Collingwood's sixth as a part-time England coach and it would be a surprise if he did not become head coach one day. He was, after all, the first – and to date last – man to captain them to a major global trophy, the 2010 World Twenty20 Championship.

Given how harnessing local talent came to define Durham, it is surprising an academy was not part of their original plans. 'It was important to me right from the very start, and that's no exaggeration,' insists Cook. 'But it took a lot of persuasion to convince the board. Just when Durham got first-class status, a Durham Senior League club called North Durham folded. I was being a bit greedy and I thought it was a fantastic chance to take their place as Durham Academy – but that was poo-pooed by the board. A lot of them were league men – [Don] Robson, [Bob] Jackson, [Tom] Moffat – and didn't want to upset the applecart. That was understandable but gradually people realised first-class cricket was quite a hard game, and giving the youngsters a bit of a cushioned education could possibly be a good thing. The committee's idea right from the start was for young players to get an opportunity, but not as an official group. The forming of that official group was the thing I thought was going to sway the issues.'

Jackson confirms: 'It wasn't unanimous. Some people thought we should bring in established players from other counties, but Geoff Cook was absolutely right. He saw in young cricketers something that could be developed. Even when Clive [Leach] was chairman and the board went to the limit with wages, there was a real commitment to protect the academy.'

Having run Durham's under-19s, Robson was passionate about developing cricketers. 'Don was always talking about the success of the academy right up until he died,' says Jackson. In 1993 Robson revealed: 'When we became a first-class club, other chairmen told me we'd be lucky if we produced one home-grown player in the first five years. We are certainly keen to have home-bred players in the side. That's the main reason why we pushed for first-class status.'

Nevertheless, it was not until the end of Durham's fourth first-class season that the academy opened. 'I didn't really spend that much time in it,' says Harmison, one of nine initial recruits, along with Hartlepool's Gough. 'It was basically four months in the winter and, by the time the [1997] season started, I was in the first team. But there were some good players who went on to bigger and better things, and some good players fighting hard to get into the second team. You could see Durham were going to progress.' Gough, Marc Symington and Ian Hunter, who later joined Derbyshire, also played for Durham. Chris Hewison represented Nottinghamshire, Ian Jones Somerset and Middlesex; Simon Birtwisle and Paul Lindsay played for Northumberland. When Phil Carlin represented his country it was on military service, having not played above second-team level for Durham.

David Boon, who became Durham's captain in 1997, saw the academy as a no-brainer. 'Any academy is going to have good results if it's run well and financed well,' he argues. 'Kids are the strength and the soul of your future, the heart and lifeline of the cricket club. When you had a board like ours, and especially a very charismatic chairman in Don Robson – a wonderful man who just had a vision and wouldn't let anything get in the way – the academy was always going to be good.

'When Durham were initially admitted to first-class cricket it appeared to me it was a little bit of an end of the line for players. It's quite logical, and we did it in Tasmania [when they turned first-class]. A lot of those blokes are good friends of mine like [Graeme] "Foxy" Fowler, "Beefy" [Ian Botham], [Wayne] "Ned" Larkins, Paul Parker, Jonesey [Dean Jones]; but it probably didn't do the young kids of the north east a great service because they were only there for a year or two. When they all retired it was, "Shit, there's a ski field and we're slowing down!" Things had to be rebuilt and the academy was a very important part of that. Over the years it's proven to be really good, with the production of quality players. Thankfully it's still doing fantastically well.'

In 1989 Yorkshire opened an academy – one of the best decisions made in English cricket because not only did it brilliantly supply their team and England's, it also inspired Durham. 'Yorkshire have a massive amount of young cricketers but I'd admired the way they'd directed them and given them a structure,' says Middlesbrough-born Cook. 'I always thought in terms of youth cricket Durham was a bit of a mini-Yorkshire. We have the numbers. Community cricket at places like Eppleton, Hetton Lyons and Shotley Bridge has a history that stands young cricketers in good stead.'

Durham's presence inspired would-be local cricketers, and still does. Neil Killeen was 16 when they joined first-class cricket, Collingwood a month away. 'Doug Ferguson used to send a lot of north-east youngsters to play for Northamptonshire but now we had our own county to play for,' says Killeen. Collingwood admits: 'Until Durham were a first-class county I didn't really understand what it was all about. I knew if I wanted to become a professional cricketer there was a good chance I would have to go to the MCC, or some people had gone to Northants. But when you're 12, 13, you don't really think about all that. It came around at the perfect time.'

In 1996, the Test and County Cricket Board became the England and Wales Cricket Board (ECB), with Robson one of its most influential figures, and county boards were created to develop recreational cricket. Robson chaired Durham's until handing over to Jackson in 2012. Windows, Breese and Alistair Maiden – now England women's assistant coach – began their coaching careers there before moving into Durham's academy.

The academy shrewdly exploits its geography. Thanks to Harmison and Wood, many cricket-lovers think Ashington is in County Durham, not Northumberland. Stokes, Graham Clark and Jamie Harrison grew up in Cumbria, Coetzer in Aberdeen, and Teesside was raided for the likes of Plunkett and James Weighell. 'It's the region's club,' says Jackson. 'The three recreational boards [Durham, Northumberland and Cumbria] meet often to discuss items of mutual interest and Durham's academy is held up in very high esteem by them.'

From December 2003 to January 2011, a Durham player appeared in all but three England Test XIs. 'I still get excited when Durham players get in the England team,' says Jeff Brown. 'Yet for all the call-ups there's still a slight suspicion that if we weren't so far away... It's absolutely ludicrous Graham Onions only won nine caps – and Mark Stoneman goes to Surrey and he's suddenly in the England team.'

Norman Gifford's 1996 appointment as first-team coach allowed Cook to focus on the academy until 2007, and after a spell as first-team coach it became his main focus again in his final five seasons as director of cricket. 'You don't get many people comfortable coaching a school's year-two class, then stepping up to coaching international-standard players,' says Windows, Cook's academy assistant from 2002–07. 'He's happy and outstanding at every level, and that comes from massive knowledge about cricket. He can gauge situations and he's a great reader of people. He's got a knowledge for personalities and the character people will turn into; it's prophetic really.'

Cook's eye for a cricketer is legendary. 'Liam Plunkett was a batter who bowled a little bit,' recalls Mustard, who played 516 times for Durham and won 12 England caps. 'One day we were in the nets and Geoff said, "This player is going to play for England. As a bowler." Geoff recognised he was a strong boy with a lovely action, so he changed him into a bowling all-rounder. Graeme Bridge was a left-arm fast bowler getting wickets for fun at Ryhope, but Geoff recognised he wasn't going to be tall enough because his mum and dad weren't, so changed him to a pretty good left-arm spinner. He just sees something others can't and he can look one, two, three years down the line. He works everybody out individually. It wasn't just one rule for all, which is how it tends to be in county cricket because not many people have the skills to treat everyone differently.' That people believe they took contradictory things from the academy proves Mustard's point.

Cook's 2013 heart attack lowered his profile in his final five years at Durham, but not his commitment. 'Geoff's enthusiasm for grassroots cricket in particular isn't readily known by many members,' says Jackson. 'Last year a game at Lintz [Jackson's club] was off so I walked up the road to the new [Burnopfield] ground and there was Geoff, just sitting by himself. I went in for a pint and some of the people in the bar didn't even know he was at the match. I had a word with him, then off he went. He rang somebody up and found there was another league match going to last until about eight o'clock.'

Talent-spotting is only part of Cook's recipe. 'There's no compromise on cricket standards – you could be the best player in your age group, but if you haven't got the characteristics that mean you'll be successful, you're overlooked,' Windows stresses. 'It gives you much more chance to put the nuts and bolts on in the cricketing environment.' When I recorded the *Bunny's First XI* podcasts with him in 2015, Onions said: 'You often get asked why Durham keep producing so many outstanding young cricketers and I just believe Geoff gives you responsibility. There's been times when I doubted if I could play second- or first-team cricket for Durham, but he gave me that belief.'

Ten years younger than Onions and born in Johannesburg, Keaton Jennings has a different perspective. Cook knew Ray Jennings through their time playing in South African domestic cricket – Cook for Eastern Province, Jennings for Transvaal – and invited his son, then national under-19 captain, for a season-long trial in 2011. Ray, who coached South Africa in 2004/05, knew former Durham Twenty20 import Albie Morkel and then-player Dale Benkenstein, and his wife Alison was from Sunderland. 'As a family we've always been aware that the UK system was probably one of the best in the world, and there was no better place for Keaton to go and play,' he told me. 'I don't think [South African] players get the rewards they should do, but the whole system in the UK is really professional.' Bizarrely, the son of Ray's successor as South Africa wicketkeeper – former ICC chief executive Dave Richardson – also came through Durham's academy, as would Michael and Keaton's compatriot Brydon Carse.

When Jennings joined, Cook was Durham's first-team coach, so he believes '"Steamy" is probably the main reason why the academy's a success.' Jackson is also a fan of 'Steamy' – aka Windows. 'He was a magnificent support to Geoff, not in just saying, "Yes Geoff," because he's got his own mind and he's a deep thinker about the game,' Jackson says. 'He was very, very helpful in the discussions about merging the cricket board and the club. I've always used John as the litmus test for all the age-group teams [run by the cricket board]. Whilst he's been a club employee I've given him real licence to establish that set-up, working with [cricket board development manager] Graeme Weeks.'

Windows began coaching in his early 20s. 'Collingwood and Killeen were my vintage,' he explains. 'I played for Northumberland against them at junior level, then I went to university with a view to trying to become a cricketer, but I was never any good. I tried at Glamorgan, at Worcestershire and with Durham. I went to Australia to forward my playing career and Mike Hirsch [a coach based in Perth in the winters, Durham in the summers] gave me a coaching job in a private school over there. I quite enjoyed that.

'When I came back, cricket development was just taking off and I was fortunate to team up with Nick Brown as [Durham Cricket Board's] second development officer. It was a bit of a luxury position because it was mainly coaching, and I did secondary schools and county age-group squads for three years from '99. Then the ECB started to fund the academies and I was taken on by Durham's to be assistant to Geoff and help support the coaching at county age-group level. I had five brilliant years as Geoff's understudy and, when he became first-team coach in 2007, I was lucky enough to take over the academy. When Geoff recovered from his heart attack he oversaw the junior programme and provided day-to-day guidance and support.'

Like Onions, Jennings now plays for Lancashire, but recognises his debt to Durham. 'When you're in the academy you almost hate Steamy because he challenges you, he nails you,' he says. 'You feel it's unjust at times, but suddenly when you move out of that academy environment it makes sense. He loves the game and is careful about the way he goes about his coaching. A lot of the guys, as soon as they have any trouble, they go straight back to Steamy, even though when they were in the academy they were whinging, "Steamy's done this", or "Steamy's done that."'

It is noticeable how ingrained so many around the club are. Alan Walker joined as a player in 1994. Between 1997 and 2018 Jon Lewis worked up from opener to captain, second-team coach, then head coach. There from the start, Killeen is also on the coaching staff as well as working on various England development programmes. 'The loyalty is unbelievable,' says Boon, who captained all three. Windows's assistant James Lowe made nine first-class appearances for Durham between 2003 and 2006. 'These guys have the right values and all the usual corny words,' says Cook. 'Whilst they want to progress as coaches because it's another way of earning a living, I think they want to repay the opportunity Durham gave them.'

Andy Fothergill's complaint that Durham's 1992 team lacked identity no longer stands. 'You're always asked what are the values of the club, and if you tried to crystallise it you could spend hours talking a load of rubbish, but Whack [Walker] and Killer [Killeen] know what it is to represent Durham and know the values of the area, and Jon Lewis was our leading batsman,' Windows argues. 'Even through the language they use and the stories they tell, you can't fail to get the point. I don't think it's an explicit thing, it's just evolved. There's always a counter to it that you've got to stay fresh and up to date, so I'm always conscious of getting stale, but Yorkshire are so similar – they keep a lot of their ex-players involved.' I ask Cook to define Durham's values. 'It's always to do justice to the north east,' he answers. 'You can talk about core values but it's beyond that.'

The academy's importance is reflected in how the club is run. 'Only Yorkshire would have their academy at the centre of the club too,' argues Windows. 'Alan Walker and Jon Lewis were at 80 per cent of the junior sessions, and myself and James Lowe are probably at 90 per cent of senior practices, so it's an across-the-board integration. A lot of academies operate in isolation but I don't think our players ever really leave the academy environment.'

Lewis began his career at Essex. '[The youngsters] changed in the away dressing room and it was a rite of passage when you crossed the border for your first pre-season with a peg,' he recalls. 'It was a bit of "them and us". The second-team guys were treated like dirt in some respects – they bowled for hours in the nets and never got a bat, except the first bat of the season as the net-tester. Geoff was always inclusive. It is a cultural thing and I don't think it's particularly common.'

Yet Jennings argues: 'Steamy was very good at that separation – you're not a professional so you don't put your bags over with the professionals. You are bottom of the food chain essentially. He was good at hammering home the point that that's where you want to get to, but you can't have all the privileges of it yet.' Windows explains:

'You want the same values, same ethos, same attitudes, so fellas feel comfortable going all the way through. But you've also got to realise you're stepping up, so more's required. If [Matty] Potts has played one day for the academy and the next day he's playing for the first team, on the day he's playing for the academy he's not welcome in the first-team dressing room; but when he's a first-team player he feels comfortable because he deserves to be in that room.'

Windows thinks one reason northern academies are successful is hard to copy. 'We have really strong club cricket and not the dominance of big private schools,' he points out. 'To have success in that [league] environment you've got to have something about you. Haseeb [Hameed] was asked how he found playing Test cricket, and he said, "I've played in the Bolton League." Rocky [Mark Stoneman] said something similar. When you're selecting fellas out of club cricket, to have reached a level they've got to have a bit of fight and independent spirit. I think that would be unique to the north. I don't think there's such strong league cricket elsewhere in the country, where the best players are in independent schools.

'Our fellas are playing against really good recreational cricketers who are teachers, plumbers or whatever, choosing to play a really high level of cricket on a Saturday. You've got to be blummin' good to battle against them. Nottingham has some good club cricket but they've also got some big independent schools, and I don't want to do down independent schools, but when you've got three or four confident young lads coming in halfway through the season it kind of erodes that.'

Luton-born Will Smith came through a private school and university background and joined Durham first from Nottinghamshire, then again from Hampshire. 'When I was at Hampshire, the guys in their mid-to-late 20s who had come through their academy – guys like James Vince and Liam Dawson – were unbelievably mentally strong in some situations, but maybe they'd had too many opportunities and too many one-on-one sessions,' he says. 'The mindset here seems to be that if a guy's talented, great, but he needs to find his own way. Durham's academy still produces players with the mentality but also the attributes to cope with the rigours of professional cricket day in, day out. I'm sure that must come from the way they're selected and prepared.'

South Northumberland have won the 45-over National Club Cricket Championship three times since 2006, Chester-le-Street triumphed in 2009, and 2018 winners Richmond play in the North Yorkshire and South Durham League (NYSD); while South North have also twice claimed the Twenty20 version, which began in 2008. Since Collingwood's 2011 retirement, Stoneman's 11 England Test caps are the most for a state-school-educated specialist batsman or wicketkeeper, a major concern. Of the nine Durham academy graduates to play for England, only the one born outside the north east – Jennings – went to a fee-paying school.

'I think it's the biggest factor,' Collingwood replies when I ask what part league cricket plays in the academy's success. 'When you play against adults at 11, 12, 13, you quickly experience failure and you've got to find a way to overcome that. It makes you grow up very quickly. My life was at Shotley Bridge Cricket Club, literally seven days a week. I'd come home from school, put down my bags and walk to Shotley, whether to help my dad on the roller, or to get into the nets. I played in midweek, you were travelling around and there was the banter. Other people would finish work at five o'clock and have a mad rush to get to Thornaby or somewhere like that for six o'clock to play a cup tie.

'I used to call Alan Smith, the groundsman at the Racecourse, "Uncle Alan" and push the covers on at a young age. I remember watching quite a few [Durham] games there when Anderson Cummins was playing, but Shotley Cricket Club was the ultimate to me, and my brother [Peter] was my hero. He was four years older than me and the competition we had meant it was him I looked up to. A lot of my early learning was done at club level and playing against my brother in the back yard. I only played a handful of second-team games [11 in the Championship before graduating to the first-team version] and there wasn't an academy, just age-group cricket at Durham and the England Schools Cricket Association.'

One suspects Collingwood might have found his way to Northamptonshire or elsewhere, but Stephen Harmison insists: 'There's not a cat in hell's chance I'd have played professional cricket if it hadn't been for Durham.' Onions was a county badminton player and Mustard a footballer – neither considered cricket as a career before Cook spotted them. 'I wanted to play football but I just followed my brothers around to Boldon CA Cricket Club,' says Mustard. 'Once you start getting older you begin picking up a bat. Hylton had never been renowned for bringing through youngsters but my dad set up the under-13s. My mum and dad split up, so every Saturday I would get the bus to Boldon, my dad would pick us up and we'd go from there. My dad played at Hylton and his cousins were Alan and Joe Rushworth [father of Chris], so you had eight or nine family members playing cricket. We went to the cricket ground every other day. You wouldn't have enough kids to make up the numbers in all the age groups, so when I was 11 I'd be playing in the under-13s as a leg-spinner.

'I never thought of being a wicketkeeper. My brother Kevin was a wicketkeeper but when I was 15 he had problems with his knee. It left them short one night and I was a bit of a goalkeeper/striker as a footballer and I loved diving around. I was 15 playing under-18s, and within two or three weeks I was getting picked for the second team, and once you get into the first team your name gets out there. One day, aged about 16, I got a phone call from Geoff saying would I like to play a second-team game for Durham?

'Just before I played that game Geoff got myself and my mum in. We sat in one of the boxes [at the Riverside] and Geoff said they'd like to give me a contract. I was at Middlesbrough and football was still my number-one sport – cricket wasn't even on the radar, I just played because I enjoyed it. I didn't even think it was a job but I knew football was – that's where my head and my heart were taking me. But I was going to get paid, which I hadn't been before – £50 a week in the winter's not too bad when you're 16. Middlesbrough rang to say they weren't going to keep me on but they were happy to put my name out to different football clubs for trials. I went to Hartlepool for a bit and I wasn't enjoying it, so when I had to choose I went for cricket because they gave me my first contract and told me what was happening.'

Nicknamed 'The Colonel' after the Cluedo character who shared his surname, the charismatic Mustard became a key part of the Durham story and, having lost his father to a heart attack, the academy played an important role in his personal, as well as cricketing, upbringing. 'A lot of it was communication and structure,' he explains. 'You knew what was happening two or three weeks in advance, you were asked to get time off school to play. At that age you don't really learn cricket, you just learn life skills. They left it up to you to decide what you wanted to do and they'd support you to deliver your best cricket, which was amazing.

'Geoff was very calm, you never felt under pressure, but he knew what he was talking about. In that phase of my life Geoff was the father figure to me. I respected what he said and he respected my mum was a mother of four working full-time to keep us afloat. He realised every time we had training I'd be catching the bus. If we were in at eight o'clock I'd get the bus two hours early because it arrived at five past the hour or something like that. He respected that. One day he said that on top of my £50, the club were going to buy my bus ticket, a £32 ticket to get me to the ground every day.'

Durham Academy initially played in the Durham Senior League, but when the Northumberland and Durham Cricket Boards created the North East Premier League (NEPL) in 2000 they joined with a guarantee they would never be relegated. Now the Durham Cricket League and Northumberland and Tyneside Cricket League feed into the NEPL, and the NYSD also has premier league status. 'When the cricket boards were formed there was a suggestion the NEPL should come under the board,' Jackson explains. 'Don was chairman of the cricket board and I was secretary. We were adamant the league should have autonomy.'

Durham Academy withdrew from the NEPL for 2019. 'We haven't got a very big playing staff so I think we need these guys around and I want them to experience and see it [first-team cricket], to be involved in it,' explains chairman Sir Ian Botham. 'One of the problems the club had previously was that they spread themselves too thin. We're not going to go down that route. It could be re-assessed in a year or two's time. Nothing is set in stone. We'll go with the flow.'

The result will be a smaller academy staff, but more support for county age-group players from under-11 to under-19 level. 'Many of next season's recruits are already playing important roles for their clubs' first teams,' argues Windows. 'With clubs now finding it harder to turn out sides and there not being the volume of players to support a playing side in the league for a full season, I feel this is the right time to move the emphasis of the academy into a training environment supplemented by midweek playing opportunities, and ensure the players perform for their home clubs with distinction on the weekend.'

Durham chief executive Tim Bostock, a former minor counties cricketer, believes the switch 'will give them a better education because they can be too cosseted playing in their own world of 18-year-olds, and they can start to get ahead of themselves. If they're in a changing room of talented amateur cricketers, some of them bloody good players, they will grow up a lot quicker and learn some alternative skills. Plus, those clubs did develop them in the first place and it should strengthen them.'

Durham's production line quickly became self-perpetuating, its successes inspiring, advising and pushing others. Onions, Mustard, Gordon Muchall and Nicky Peng were born in 1982, Gary Pratt 1981, Graeme Bridge and Mark Davies 1980. 'We had a really good team ethos,' says Onions. 'You need good coaches – and Geoff is the best I've worked with, but we also had Jonny Windows. They were people you actually wanted to play for. It was a little bit unstructured. If there'd been loads of structure at that stage I don't think I'd have been into it. I quite liked just playing, enjoying it and learning. We were all good mates, all local lads, and literally everybody wanted to play for Durham.

'I remember looking at these guys thinking, "Wow, they're unbelievable players," but, whereas they'd been at the academy four or five years, I was just starting. Nicky Peng was driving a brilliant car and I thought he must be earning a fortune. I wanted to reach their level and catch them up.'

Not that the academy worked for everyone. When Sunderland-born leg-spinner Ben Whitehead made his Durham debut at Worcestershire in an August 2018 Twenty20 game, he was one of four visiting players released by the academy, only to return after spells in league cricket. 'I think he'd openly admit he didn't take it seriously enough,' says Killeen. 'He's gone into league cricket, performed well, and we've brought him back and he's done really well.'

Chris Rushworth was released in 2005. 'I joined when I was 15 and I was 19 when I was released,' he recalls. 'I probably got ahead of myself because your instincts are to think, "I'm a professional cricketer, I've made it." Getting released was a bit of a shock and a massive disappointment. My first thought was probably that it was not meant to be and I was not too fussed, but when I had that first winter away from it, missing things like indoor training, it made me realise I did want to get back.'

Like Whitehead, Rushworth was fortunate to have NEPL cricket to drop into during four years working in call centres and selling satellites door to door. 'Before I joined the academy I played for Sunderland and I went back there,' he says. 'Simon Brown was a coach and he was quite close to [then-second-team coach] Jon Lewis so when I was doing well he would be saying, "I think you should get Rushy in for a look." One winter I went back, did OK, did pre-season nets and was asked to play a few games at the start of the [2010] season.' With Mitchell Claydon nursing an abdominal strain, Harmison, Onions and Callum Thorp suffering back injuries and Luke Evans on loan at Northamptonshire, 23-year-old Rushworth made his Championship debut at Headingley in April, and 419 first-class wickets later he was awarded a testimonial for 2019. 'Usually people end up playing elsewhere, so to come back to my home club and grasp this chance, I'm massively proud and honoured,' he says.

Graham Clark was released in 2012 but rejoined after a year with MCC Young Cricketers, while the injury-prone James Weighell responded to being cut by spending his winter playing club cricket in Australia for Tallangatta, Killeen's old side, then averaged 70 with the bat and 19 with the ball for Stokesley in the 2015 NYSD League. 'I got in the mindset of thinking it [being released] couldn't happen,' he admits. 'Cricket was my life and my job, it was all I'd done since leaving school so the mindset was, "What are you going to do now?" Realising I was fit again to bowl was massive for me.'

Windows concedes: 'Quite often I end up arguing against the academy because one, it provides everything so there's not that sense of having to go out and get it yourself, and two, you're predisposing there's a chronological order to development. You can't keep fellas going at 21 and 22, it can be counter-productive. Teenagers have a predisposition to be a spoilt teenager when the nets aren't right or the pitch isn't good, so being independent, resourceful and taking responsibility for your own game can often be bred out in academies. It's about trying to keep a system that rewards them but, to be a frontline bowler especially, you have to do tons of fitness work behind the scenes. You could do that if you didn't have access to the strength and conditioning support we have but it would take a specific type of person, a certain motivation and a bit of luck.'

Killeen argues: 'Sometimes you've just got to ask where the opportunity is for them first-team-wise. If it's not there, maybe it is time to send them out. If that's a way of them taking more responsibility for themselves and their own actions, and if they're prepared to look after themselves outside of our environment, that ticks a lot of boxes. We've got to look at the players individually and ask, "Is that the best place for him?" That might be the case in terms of their NEPL clubs. We'll never tell anybody they have to play for someone but we'll give advice.'

Most importantly, Durham are prepared to grant patience and opportunities not available everywhere. 'I don't know how people do my job in some other clubs because it must be soul-destroying,' comments Windows. David Harker was Durham's chief executive through some hard times financially, but one thing was always non-negotiable. 'We had an academy before you got money for having academies,' he says proudly. 'We'd get a hundred grand from the ECB for it and spend about £250,000 on it. It's probably the only bit of the business that's been ring-fenced. By their own admission other counties receive £100,000 and spend £50,000 with no consequence. Once the academy goes, our whole reason for being here goes. In 2017 we opened a women's academy too. Someone coming in new would bin the academy, recruit Kolpak players principally for Twenty20 and run it from there if all you were worried about was sustaining Durham as a business without any interest in its contribution to the wider community. If Mike Ashley owned Durham [rather than Newcastle United], that's what he'd do.'

Pulling out of the NEPL might seem to contradict this, but Botham insists not. 'We've got a lot of young players coming through and that's why we want to develop our facilities for the club sides,' he says. 'Some of the clubs felt we were taking but not giving anything back. I had a long chat with Bob [Jackson] about that and that's something we'll definitely put right. We're going to have finals on this ground – under-15s, under-13s, area and district finals, league finals, whatever. They'll bring their parents and their families. I want everyone to feel part of it. We're not an elitist club – and never will be.'

As the 21st century approached, Durham had developed the structure to convert raw talent into top cricketers. To really work, though, the youngsters needed someone to change the club's mindset.

6.

Boon Then Bust?

JUST looking at the league tables over the following five seasons, you might think Durham squandered David Boon's work the minute he left. The Australian signed off in 1999 by booking his team's place in the new County Championship Division One, arguably their first significant achievement in professional cricket. They returned to the wrong end of the table as soon as he left, but the mutual affection between Boon and Durham remains strong.

'I think he left his mark on Paul [Collingwood] and he definitely left it on me,' reflects Stephen Harmison, who was given his debut by Boon. 'Jon Lewis learnt a lot from him because he travelled everywhere with him. There was no team bus then so we travelled in twos and threes. There's still a little bit of David Boon lingering around the club.' Boon was only at Durham for three seasons, but between them Harmison, Collingwood and Lewis served more than 60 years, passing his legacy on. As we talk on Skype about cricket from another millennium, Boon could scarcely be more removed from it. But, speaking from Tasmania on a summer's evening while snow falls on a bitterly cold north-east morning, he keeps instinctively referring to Durham as 'we'.

After some uninspiring post-Dean Jones overseas signings, Durham needed a heavyweight for 1997, so Geoff Cook went back to Australia for one. 'We were just starting to get a few green shoots coming through in Melvyn Betts and Paul Collingwood,' Cook explains, 'but because they'd lost so many games as a group, getting someone to harness their potential and show them the way forward on the pitch was pretty much essential.

'We'd been looking for someone like Boon for a while, someone who'd be available for most of the games. We'd looked at people like Steve Waugh and [Hansie] Cronje to help the young players realise it was a tough game. In cricket when the fire's quite hot and you show a little bit of weakness, people are going to walk through you. We needed someone to stand up to that and show the others how to stand up.' Director of cricket Cook did not deal with budgets, he just identified players. 'If we wanted a player, a way was found,' he says. 'Somebody of David Boon's stature was obviously going to help the club, so money was jiggled around.'

Cook's sounding board John Hampshire and Lancashire's Jack Simmons were Tasmania's overseas players when, in December 1978, they handed a debut to 17-year-old Boon in the Gillette Cup semi-final. Batting at nine, his 18 not out from ten deliveries included the winning runs as Queensland were beaten by one wicket off the penultimate ball. Five days later Boon made his first-class debut against the same opposition, before playing in January's cup-final victory. He went on to score 7,422 runs in 107 Tests and was man of the match in the 1987 World Cup Final, before retiring from international cricket in January 1996.

As England's 1996 season neared its end, Cook touched down in Hobart. 'When Geoff and I spoke it was purely cricket stuff,' says Boon. 'He was mainly sussing me out. He obviously had goals and he wanted to see if I fitted in with those goals. I dare say they'd had a recommendation from Jack Simmons at Old Trafford.' Boon's debut season was only Tasmania's second in first-class cricket. 'Playing county cricket was something I hadn't done so it really interested me, and I think what probably attracted me most was that Jack said there were a lot of similarities between Durham and Tasmania in our formative years,' he explains. 'That, in a funny way, made me feel this might be the best place to go. I'd at least have the experience of those formative years in Tazzie.'

With Cook concentrating on the academy, Boon was handed a two-year contract and control of the first team. 'I wouldn't have minded if I wasn't captain but the club and the board wanted me to do that,' he says. 'I was very grateful for Don Robson and the board's support in saying they would back anything I wanted to do. It wasn't really specified but I think Blind Tommy the Miner could have seen what they wanted – a combination of winning some games, or initially being competitive, and starting to produce players.'

Since retiring, aged 48, from a playing career that included 15 Test caps and captaining Worcestershire to the 1974 Championship, slow left-armer Norman Gifford had been an England selector, assistant manager and A-team coach. Sacked as Sussex manager in August 1995, he became Durham's coach in 1996. 'Boon and Gifford was a really good combination,' says Lewis. 'Giff deliberately took the role of number two. It was never stated but it was very clear that they worked together to make sure what Boon wanted happened. Giff had an extraordinary depth of knowledge and a really nice manner, particularly with young players who weren't as robust.'

Toughness was one of Boon's best qualities, but Collingwood insists it was not Durham's problem. 'Rosey [Mike Roseberry] was flipping tough, Jesus!' he says. 'It was all about going out there with your heart on your sleeve, showing a lot of pride and fighting like hell but, if you haven't got the personnel, it doesn't matter what kind of leader you are.' Boon also dismisses the idea he inherited a feeble-minded squad. 'It was just a lack of awareness,' he reflects. 'It was a little bit, "Oh, we're playing first-class cricket – wonderful, we've got a contract, let's go and play." It was just a little bit cruisey.' Lewis faced Durham six times as an Essex player. 'They were a good side who didn't know how to win,' he says. 'I couldn't tell you why but they certainly had enough individuals capable of putting in performances.'

Boon immediately imposed an Australian mindset. 'I'd always want to bat first unless it was really green, and then the bowlers would ask if I had confidence in them to take 20 wickets, and I said I had. That sort of changes the mentality,' he explains. 'When I signed up I basically asked for a few lines on each player. I just wanted a semblance of character, and not enough to give me a preconceived idea. What I found was that there were a lot of guys in their early to mid-20s who had been at the club for a number of years but had played very little cricket – were they not being given an opportunity, or were they not good enough? A prime example was Jimmy Daley – he'd been there for five years and hardly played. What I found out over those first few months was that he could actually play!

'There wasn't a selection committee [a dying breed on the county circuit but still Australia's favoured approach] so I floated the idea at the end of my first year. When I first arrived I said I was going to ask them to do something they'd probably find very difficult, and that was to select the best-balanced team we could put on the park regardless of where we were playing or what the pitch was reputedly like. Whoever they picked would play the first six games without even being questioned. The only thing that would intervene was injury, and if we made a change it would be after that sixth game and the players would know that. They were a bit, "Oh dear, oh wow!" but I really thought that would give the players the opportunity to play their natural way, learn how to play first-class cricket – or at least start to.' The top seven and lead spinner James Boiling played all six matches, although ten bowlers shared the remaining spots.

'As we started to progress we introduced a little bit more stuff about honesty and reading the game,' Boon continues. 'I did ask at one session, "When do you win a cricket match?" They said, "When you take the last wicket on the last day." I said, "Can't you win it in the first session? What if you get four or five wickets? Do you think that's the time to realise, shit, we can win this game if we do the next step?" I said I didn't care if we lost trying to win, what I wouldn't like is if we just folded.'

Neil Killeen says: 'I first got involved as a 16-year-old in an era where we'd bought some big players in and it was almost a survival mentality. David Boon stopped us thinking, "How do we not lose?" and got us thinking about how we would win games. He always said county cricket's 80 per cent mental, 20 per cent ability. Test cricket was 90-10. Once we got our head around that we developed as players.' For Collingwood, 'It was a breath of fresh air. It showed ambition. We had a quality player but also a quality man in the dressing room leading us. He didn't come in with any Churchillian speeches, he didn't actually say that much, it was just his presence.'

Boon recalls: 'One of my targets was to produce players capable of playing for England and who wanted to play for England. Simon Brown had played one Test; I remember asking an open dressing room and, from about 20 blokes, there were two, maybe three [who said they wanted to]. I thought, "Shit, we've got some work to do here! What are we playing for?" If we could produce some players who could play for England or England A, then on the way we would start to win cricket matches. We were really lucky that we had some young blokes like Jimmy Daley, Paul Collingwood and in the second year a 19-year-old Harmison, Melvyn Betts, Nicky Phillips, Michael Gough, Neil Killeen, big Johnny Wood, and some young blokes in the academy pushing the door a bit. Then we had experience with Simon Brown, Johnny Morris, Nick Speak, Martin Speight and JJ Lewis. We had a lot of real good triers who gave me faith very quickly that they wouldn't give in. It was just a matter of slowly introducing the nuts and bolts of how to play. It wasn't my job at that stage of my career to take over at the top [of the batting order where Boon made his name]. I had to be more of a stabilising figure in the middle. I thought, "Jeez, this is fantastic, batting at number four and five – blimey, sitting down, having a breather." It was wonderful stuff!'

Lewis also joined for 1997. 'I was at Essex and it was going along OK but I was a squad player – I'd get a game when Goochie [Graham Gooch] or Nasser [Hussain] were at the Test match,' he says. 'I was 25 and I thought this was more or less the time when my career needed to be happening. Geoff Arnold was Durham's bowling coach and I'd known him quite a long time so I asked him if he'd speak to Geoff [Cook]. I'd looked at a couple of others but only had a conversation with Durham. They weren't the strongest and I was looking at somewhere where I'd get the chance to forge a career. In typical Geoff style, it went very quiet for three months. I was in South Africa for the winter and I had a contract offer from Essex I didn't really want to sign, but I was kind of getting to the point where I was thinking I needed to so I could get my head straight, when I got a call from Geoff offering me a deal at Durham for a couple of years.

'What Boony asked of the players was always very simple, which was important for what, with the exception of Simon, was a fairly young bowling group. He was clear and consistent, a proper leader, a guy players would follow. Captaincy's not a tactical position. Anyone on the field can be the tactical genius, the captain needs the personality to be the leader.'

Boon's mentality was made for Collingwood, a born cricketer. 'It sounds arrogant but I remember the careers officer came into my school and asked what I wanted to go in to,' he recalls. 'I said I was going to be a professional cricketer and play for England. That was as a 12-year-old. She thought I was in cuckoo land, so when she asked what I was actually going to be I said I wouldn't mind being a PE teacher. I was going to go to university and go down that route but I got a [Durham] contract in 1996.'

A back injury delayed Collingwood's unremarkable competitive debut until Somerset's Sunday League victory at the Riverside in August 1995. The 19-year-old's next appearance came against Kent at Scarborough. 'Graham Cowdrey panned me everywhere, I was absolutely devastated,' he says of his 7-0-66-0. 'It used to really upset me when I got hit around the park.' It was, though, only a festival game – 'At lunch they were drinking pints' – and he top-scored with 74 in Durham's 54-run defeat. 'I was really proud of playing those one-day games,' he says. 'I was in the squad at Hartlepool and they gave me a shirt. I wore it everywhere for three days.'

Collingwood's only previous overseas trip had been skiing in Slovakia until a winter in Melbourne where he helped Bulleen to their first league title. His Championship debut followed at home to Northamptonshire in Durham's opening game of 1996. Collingwood had already taken and dropped a catch before David Capel drove at his first delivery and lost his middle stump. 'The youngster was so astounded he instinctively turned to umpire Kevin Lyons, as if to assure himself there was no need to appeal,' Jeff Brown wrote in *The Journal*. Collingwood says: 'I remember getting the ball in my hand, being nervous as anything. It came out like a powder-puff. It pretty much went under his bat and did him for lack of pace.'

Durham were 44/3 replying to 320 when Collingwood came in. His first boundary was a six hooked off England left-armer Paul Taylor, and he added 107 with Mike Roseberry. 'I just enjoyed getting runs and the excitement of getting close to a hundred,' he recalls. Collingwood's 91 was instrumental in Durham's first draw in two seasons, in the year points were introduced for them. He had warmed up for it by top-scoring in the Sunday League game, making 54 not out when Durham's next best score was Stewart Hutton's 17. But he says: 'I had an excellent start but I struggled that season and it quickly gets on top of you. My first four or five years were really mediocre.' He did have one huge advantage. 'You wouldn't put him up there technically but he's arguably one of the top two or three in the world mentally,' says Harmison. At top-level sport it counts for so much, as Killeen can testify after 607 wickets in all formats for Durham. 'I wasn't the most talented person but I got out of myself every bit I possibly could through a strong mental capacity,' he comments.

'Boony identified Colly [Collingwood] quite early; I would never say I identified him as an international cricketer straight away,' comments Lewis, who made a 290-run opening partnership with the 20-year-old on his own Durham debut, at Oxford University in 1997. When a hand injury ended Collingwood's season in July his Championship average was just 21, but he had impressed the new captain. 'I got to know him really, really well because we used to stand at first and second slip and chat a lot,' says Boon. 'At times I would ask him to captain – not visibly, but to tell me what to do. He wanted to learn, he was a sponge. You could tell in the nets by the way he spoke that he was taking things on board. You could see he was going to be a huge captain.' As usual, Collingwood makes light of it. 'It was probably because Boony was so bloody lazy!' he laughs. 'I just learned from how he went about things in the middle.'

Boon acknowledges: 'Colly probably was a little bit of a kindred spirit. He had that little bit of aggression and he loved a fight. He really wanted to win. You had to harness his aggression but he learnt how to do that quite quickly. They were all a bit aggressive – "Put a brick wall in front of me, I'm not going to stop."' If ever there was a case of the pot calling the kettle black... 'David Boon had Chris Balderstone by the throat in the showers at Cheltenham,' Harmison recalls gleefully. Boon made a first-innings duck in Durham's 86 all out, then saw Gloucestershire declare on 471/6. Not out 66, he had the smell of a second-innings century in his nostrils. 'Boon was given out lbw rocking forward on the front foot and it hit him on the knee roll. In Australia, that's just given not out. I went into the shower and he had the umpire by the throat saying, "It's the flattest wicket I've ever played on in this fucking country and you've given me out lbw after what I have to bat on!"

'We played South Africa in '98 and Nantie Hayward, Allan Donald and Brian McMillan were playing. We were three or four down for not very many and Donald and Hayward bowled rapid. Boony was finished – 37, two years retired from playing for Australia. They were gunning for him. Donald hit him in the helmet from around the wicket and bust his grille. I remember thinking afterwards, he could have thought, "I'm not facing this," and chipped one up in the air, but that just summed up David Boon and what Durham meant to him.'

In June 1997 Boon's occasional off-spin took the final wicket as Durham beat leaders Kent by 135 runs for their first Championship win in 24 games. It hardly burst the floodgates. Victory over

Derbyshire six weeks later, with Lewis passing 1,000 first-class runs for the summer as he made 160 not out, was Durham's only other Championship victory of 1997. 'We noticed a couple of times that our membership weren't exactly supporting us in the way I felt your own membership should,' says Boon. 'I went to the chairman and the CEO and said, "I would like to introduce a members' night say once every month and a half and I will always be there, but after the first one I will bring in one of the kids." I wanted them to get to know us, where we were heading and that they could expect some hiccups, but I hoped they would support us if they understood. I floated it towards the end of the first season, but we started it at the beginning of my second season. We had almost immediate results. Here was this bloke who had played Test cricket for Australia and he'd come over here, taken over our club, and I hope they thought, "Shit, he's human!" We became mates, the members and I. I can remember some of those faces when we started winning games. The biggest thing for me was that if someone didn't succeed on the day, or we lost a game trying to win it, they would still clap. That was a massive psychological turning point for our players.'

Batting at seven, Collingwood started the 1998 season with his maiden Championship century at Edgbaston. The following week Harmison took his first five-wicket haul and his 12 runs prevented Durham following on at home to Gloucestershire. Harmison had made his Championship debut aged 17 in 1996's final match after dismissing Martyn Moxon and Richard Blakey at the Scarborough Cricket Festival days earlier, but the competitive stuff was harder, Leicestershire hitting 77 off his nine overs. The champions won by an innings and 251 runs inside two days, and a back injury restricted Harmison to playing as a batsman for Ashington seconds in 1997. 'I was asking, "Do I really want to play cricket?"' he admits. 'I wasn't really brought up in it, it was always football.' A miserable 1996/97 tour of Pakistan had not helped.

'I'd heard snippets about this young, gangly thing from Ashington that could bowl a bit,' says Boon. 'I'd heard he'd gone on an [England]

Under-19 tour and hated it. You should want to play. I got an email halfway through the winter [of 1997/98] saying they'd been having a chat to him and he was softening about maybe having a bowl. When I got back to Durham they told me he was coming down for a bowl so could I come and have a look? They asked me to sit in the grandstand because he might get a bit nervous if he saw me wandering around. I was hiding in the dressing room and I reckon I saw three balls, then I thought, "I'm not sitting here any longer." I walked straight out and said, "Morning Stephen, my name's David Boon, lovely to meet you. Do you think you will be fit to bowl in three weeks?" He just looked at me with a funny expression and asked why. I told him I wanted him to play.

'We formed a great relationship. It was like having a fourth child. Collingwood could bowl, he could bat, he could field, he had a good cricket brain, he was eager to learn, but Harmy [Harmison] was one of those out of a bag – he had something special if it was harnessed. To try and control him mentally when he's travelling and he hates it – even going to the south of England – had to be managed. He was still maturing; a young man who hadn't yet found out he actually had talent.'

Harmison agrees. 'I didn't understand the game – some of the rules and the fielding positions, I didn't have a clue,' he admits. 'I don't think people realised how raw I was. I used to think an away trip was a little jaunt that cricket got in the way of, but as it got more serious and recognition started coming I did things differently. I learnt a lot about my body early on – how to abuse it and then get it back!

'I couldn't speak to Boony for about three months, I was so in awe of him, but he always says he couldn't speak to me for six months because he couldn't understand a word I was saying! I'd grown up watching cricket and this little man with great stature and aura, and all of a sudden I was a teenager sharing a dressing room with him. He's one of the best people I've played with as an all-round guy. He was very tough on the group, there were standards you adhered to. He didn't say much but when he spoke, he spoke with authority and a hell of a lot of sense. He didn't lose his temper many times but when he did he let you know what was happening.'

Harmison's talent was obvious. 'If you can have a bloke like Justin Langer say to me in Harmy's first year, "That's the quickest thing I've faced all year in any form of cricket," that tells you something,' says Boon. 'Harmy hammered him [although Middlesex's Australian opener escaped being one of his seven victims at Lord's] so we knew we had something special. It took two or three months but we had a good group around him and he started to feel more at home. He cared deep down, but on the surface he didn't care about anything – he was just as happy playing drafts, darts and having a beer with his brother and his dad at their local. Mind you, we did play against Hampshire at the Riverside and I remember asking Colly if he could translate for me because Harmy had got very excited about wanting to get somebody out – or hurt them. I got the message back – "Do not take me off until I have got this bloke." That showed me there was a little bit of something there.'

Having previously won comfortably at Trent Bridge, beating Langer's Middlesex by one wicket at Lord's in early June put Durham second in the Championship. Harmison took 49 wickets in 1998, John Wood 61, as Durham claimed all but three of 68 available bowling points.

The problem was no one made 1,000 runs. Not that the old excuses about the Riverside pitch washed now. 'I felt from my tours of England with the Australia cricket team that some of the English pitches were actually some of the best to bat on in the world, but you were always going to get the odd one that does a bit,' Boon says. 'We had to learn to play it and we worked hard at it in the nets and became very honest and open with each other.'

Bizarrely, Lewis passed 1,000 first-class runs in each odd-numbered Durham year until injuries caught up with him in 2005. 'I realise now I was a much better bad-wicket player than good-wicket player,' he explains. 'Coming here brought me to a place where I could be better than average. I had an appalling conversion rate from fifties to hundreds [66-16], but on a pitch where 220 is not the worst team score, a bloke who can get 60s and 70s is quite valuable.'

Durham were 14th in the 1998 Championship, their highest finish, and reached the Benson and Hedges Cup quarter-finals. In the winter Harmison and Betts toured Zimbabwe and South Africa with England A, while Michael Gough, Marc Symington, Ian Hunter and Graeme Bridge were called up by England Under-19s. The biggest indication things were moving in the right direction was Boon's one-year contract extension. 'I was really enjoying myself, the kids were enjoying school, and my wife was enjoying it,' he explains. 'But there was still some work to do and I thought I had one more year left in me.

'Some of the things I talked to them about, I think they thought I was a lunatic. I told them to spend ten seconds looking in the mirror on their own at the end of the day answering a little question. About 12 years later when Colly was captain of England he rang me and said, "I think I understand what you were talking about now!" Harmison had moved forward and we had some hard nuts. Browny's ability in a relaxed manner to help our young quicks was a massive advantage and we had some experience in the middle order with [John] Morris and Nicky Speak scattering Collingwood, [Jimmy] Daley and Gough. You can put every single name down who played over those three years as a contributor to where the club went. Then we got presented with what was probably the gold at the end of the rainbow – a split County Championship to be decided in my third year.' English cricket would enter the 21st century with its flagship competition divided into two divisions for the first time, just as the 50-over National League was a year earlier. The top nine would go into Division One.

The season did not start well, and in June the Netherlands knocked Durham out of the NatWest Trophy by five wickets. 'We were sat on a concrete floor in a changing room in Amstelveen and we said, "This can't get any lower. How can we get this higher?"' Neil Killeen recalls. 'The answer was to believe in ourselves.' Durham were bottom of the Championship when they hosted Nottinghamshire the following month, but after a first maximum-points victory for four years Boon declared: 'This gives us a realistic chance of pushing for a place in next season's first division.' Derbyshire and Gloucestershire were beaten in the next two games.

Durham went into the season's finale needing ten points at Leicestershire to achieve their goal. Player-of-the-year Killeen's 7-85 helped secure four bowling points once the match belatedly got going on day two. When two batting points followed, thanks partly to Boon's 53, a draw would suffice, and rain secured it. Durham's final wicket of 1999 was a diving slip catch by the captain. 'Boon strutted because he was so proud of the young players but it was his ability to bring them to where was necessary,' comments Bob Jackson.

'I had an absolute ball for three years, made some great friends, and I still follow the club sincerely and closely, and still talk to JJ regularly,' says Boon. 'I felt so much pride when they won their first County Championship, when any of them got picked for England – even if I didn't know them, because they were still part of Durham and part of what hopefully was a legacy I left.'

The unenviable job of replacing Boon fell to his vice-captain, Speak. Lewis 'didn't realise at the time how big the task was – we'd have to finish sixth [to avoid being one of three relegated sides], which from ninth being your best finish was a bit of a stretch. There were some difficulties with Nick. Tactically he was a really good captain, but his relationships with a couple of players didn't work very well and they were important players, so it probably wasn't the greatest environment. Important guys in the dressing room were starting to get dragged away by England too [Harmison was named in three Test squads without making his debut].'

Harmison and Collingwood found 2000 tough. 'I've got nothing against Speaky, I got on really well with him, but the captaincy was possibly just a bit too much for him and it was the closest I got to leaving Durham,' admits Harmison. 'It wasn't financial because the offer I'd have chosen, Lancashire's, was about 30 per cent less than Hampshire's. I must admit I wasn't very good that year as a person or as a cricketer. I was young and still very, very naïve. One of the biggest shames was that Norman Gifford left; he was such an unbelievable human being. We had a young overseas, Simon Katich, who batted brilliantly for him but not many others stood out.'

Katich and Collingwood scored more than 1,200 National League runs between them, yet Durham finished seventh in Division Two. Betts and Wood, with 110 Championship wickets between them in 2000, left for Warwickshire and Lancashire respectively, while Katich earned an Ashes call-up and Morris's contract was cut short. Nicky Peng had left school at Christmas and was not on a full contract when Gough's back injury brought his Championship debut aged 17 years and 227 days against a Surrey side en route to retaining the title in 2000. Opposition captain Adam Hollioake described the Newcastle-born batsman as 'the best young player I've ever seen' when his 98 helped Durham win by 231 runs. Sadly it all seemed to come a bit too easily to Peng, who left for Glamorgan in 2005/06, retiring two years later aged 24.

The season's lowlights included a 217-run defeat at Grace Road, a 232-run reverse at Derby, and being bowled out for 91 in the NatWest Trophy. 'I tried to erase that time from my memory,' says Collingwood. 'You had a guy who would openly say he was a tactical genius but he just lost the dressing room. With me being an artist, he got me in at eight o'clock one day and made me draw in big letters on the dressing room wall, "There are no rules". People were coming in asking what I was doing. There was a blame game going on and it made for a tough environment. It upset Giff a hell of a lot.'

Speak was replaced by Lewis with two games remaining. 'I was in charge when we got relegated here against Hampshire,' Lewis recalls. 'We had to win and I remember setting the declaration. We had a bit of rain so we set them 291. I remember staying at the ground after the game and drinking quite a lot with Simon Brown. Although we knew we were probably going to get relegated anyway – there was another game to go – it was a bit of a low point. When the captaincy was offered permanently I asked to think about it and, as I walked out the door, I thought, "I don't know what the hell I've got to think about because I know full well I'm not going to say no.'" Durham avoided bottom place because Derbyshire were docked eight points for their pitch.

The Riversiders finished one from bottom in Division Two in 2001 but won one-day promotion. Injuries were catching up with Brown, who retired in 2002, and when Daley did likewise in August, the last of the 1992 squad had gone, replaced by a largely young, home-grown and injury-prone group. They lost 11 Championship matches in 2002, were 47.75 points adrift at the bottom of Division Two and relegated in the 50-over league. Five Championship wins in 2003 was only good enough for sixth.

Herschelle Gibbs was meant to join for 2004 but South Africa's new Twenty20 competition, then his national team's concerns over fatigue, delayed his debut eight years. Gateshead professional Marcus North replaced Gibbs, but the second overseas slot was a mishmash of the returning Shoaib Akhtar, Reon King, Tahir Mughal, Pallav Kumar, Andy Blignaut and Shaun Tait, who shared 11 Championship games and 25 wickets at 42.92. Shoaib arrived with a stress fracture of the rib but recovered in time to play at the Asia Cup and ICC Trophy. King conceded 0-21 from 20 balls on his debut in Hampshire's successful run-chase. Zimbabwean Blignaut bowled 11 no-balls in as many overs in his Championship bow against Derbyshire – yet Tait outdid him with 26 in two games, including four in his first over. Combined figures of 18-0-176-0 meant Tait could not be risked for a third match. For the second time in three years, Durham finished bottom of the Championship.

'The club has two objectives: we want to be successful on the field, but we want to allow talent from the north east to not have to go anywhere else to fulfil their potential, their dreams, their ambitions,' Lewis stresses. 'Andrew Pratt, Gary Pratt, Gordon Muchall, Mark Davies, Liam Plunkett – we had a lot of youngsters who might not have had first-class careers, so we were fulfilling that part of the remit. Muchy [Muchall] went on an England A tour, Plunkett played for England, Mark Davies's first-class stats rank with anyone in the world, Andrew Pratt for a while was considered the best gloveman in the country; so we were still having an influence on cricket in England even when we weren't winning many games.'

Of Durham's eight English-born players in Lewis's final game as captain, at home to Leicestershire in 2004, he was the only one not from the academy. 'We had to go backwards to come forwards,' Harmison argues, 'but I think Geoff, [Gifford's successor] Martyn Moxon and Jon Lewis knew it would come good eventually, and when it did it didn't really stop until 2016.'

7.

Outside Influences

DURHAM'S 2005 season was one match old and already Jon Lewis could feel the difference. 'As I was taking my boots off at the end of the game, I was reflecting that this is different. This club is now not the same as it was six months ago,' he says. 'I felt we could really achieve things now.'

It was not just on the pitch where Durham had changed. Although new captain Mike Hussey led from the front with 253 in an innings-and-215-run win at Leicestershire, he was just one of those who altered the club's mentality.

'Hussey sat us down [after the match] and said, "If you want to win things in this game, you've got to get even better,"' recalls Graham Onions, Durham's 12th man at Grace Road. 'We'd had four years of losing and he was giving us a rollicking, and I was thinking, "That's amazing." He was that good you had to take notice and practice became more structured, better, with more intensity. I remember Mick Lewis bowling in the indoor nets and Hussey said to him, "Come on, I want you to bowl properly." He started sending down short balls and people were playing it properly and you thought, "This is elite level."' Stephen Harmison, who had been playing international cricket for two years, reflects: 'There are parts of your career when you think the outlook of the game's changed, and that was one.'

Although Durham won promotion in first-class and one-day cricket in 2005, the shift began in the miserable 2004 season, which they finished in their customary bottom place in the Championship. Durham and Warwickshire had been the only counties to oppose increasing the number of overseas players allowed per county to two for 2003, but soon they were packing their team with players born outside Britain alongside home-grown talent.

The first signing under the policy shift was Gareth Breese, a 28-year-old Jamaican with one Test cap. Because his father was Welsh, he was not part of the cast of thousands who represented Durham as their 2004 overseas players. 'At first I didn't want to come back to the north east because my first professional club job was at Etherley, just outside Bishop Auckland,' admits the off-spin-bowling all-rounder. 'I'd just turned 20 and I guess I didn't know what league cricket was all about.

'There wasn't much practice, I was in a really quiet village way out in the country, there wasn't much to do – two pubs and a village shop – and I had no car. I found it really hard, although I made some good friends. I thought, "If this is what Durham is, I don't want to come back!" But the next time I came was to watch a friend, who was doing a master's degree at Durham, play for the university. I spent a week with him staying in Durham City, we went out in Newcastle a couple of times and went to the Riverside, and it made me realise there was a lot more to offer.

'Just after my first-class debut I played against Lancashire on their [1996] pre-season tour and somebody mentioned to me, "Why don't you try and play county cricket?" I didn't think I was good enough [even though he scored 124]. I'd only just turned 20. I'd never thought of it because my dream was always to play for the West Indies. It came up again quite a few years later after my solitary Test match – I got dropped and it was a bit of a tough time for me. I was playing in the Liverpool leagues [for Newton-le-Willows] and my agent said, "Have you ever thought of playing county cricket?" I said I couldn't because I'd played Test cricket now, but he said that was a year ago and, having a British passport with my dad being Welsh, I'd only have to wait a year to qualify.

'I had a trial with Worcestershire, then a couple of trial games for Durham, at South North and Seaton Carew. The trials kind of stopped and I thought I probably wasn't good enough, but then I was offered a contract to start in 2004 and I never really looked back. If it had been league cricket I wouldn't have wanted to come back but I was very grateful for the opportunity to play county cricket; and it wouldn't have mattered who I was playing for, it was about trying to prove yourself and fit into a team. The only dilemma I had is I was captain of Jamaica. Omari Banks also had dual nationality and the West Indies brought in a rule that we could play as overseas [players] within the regional competitions. From 2004–07, I played basically 12 months a year.'

Breese scored 165 in his third Championship game as Durham made 453/9 to beat Somerset, but their only other victory came nearly three months later against Yorkshire when he became the eighth player to take ten wickets in a first-class match for them. 'Not only was there an inferiority complex but everybody who played against us seemed more experienced,' he says. 'We would turn up for games as the beating sticks. We went through quite a few overseas players [in 2004] and it made for quite an unsettled environment, but I felt I gelled quite well into it.'

Three days after Breese's Taunton century – his second in first-class cricket, eight years after his first – Clive Leach became Durham's chairman.

Bob Jackson had stood in for ten months when Bill Midgley resigned following the unpopular decision to allow a gym to be built at the Riverside – providing £400,000, on top of funding the 2,000-seat County Durham Stand. 'I asked the board would any of them like to be chairman and I asked myself as well – and I said no, and they said no,' Jackson explains. 'Therefore [chief executive] David Harker and I were charged with bringing a number of candidates to the table. Clive was streets above, he was impressive in his interview.

The Callers came off the board and it was obvious there would be a fundamental change.'

Leach, then 69, was born in Bombay (now Mumbai) and lived in India until his British parents moved to Suffolk when he was five. He played 39 times for Warwickshire between 1955 and 1958, and made 66 appearances for Durham during six years as Bishop Auckland's professional. He opened with Colin Milburn when the 17-year-old scored 101 against India in his only appearance before turning professional, and Bob Taylor was one of Leach's victims when his left-arm spin took 12-49 against Staffordshire in 1959. He had been chairman and chief executive of Tyne Tees Television, who sponsored Durham's early overseas players. Midgley opposed the Championship splitting into two divisions, wary money and talent would drain towards the elite. Leach wanted to be part of that elite.

'He encouraged ambition on and off the field, and that was to be admired,' says Gordon Hollins, then Durham's commercial manager. 'He encouraged the organisation to look up the way, rather than down the way. Clive's belief was that if you competed on the field, you would attract investment off the field for the broader project.'

August's extraordinary general meeting voted overwhelmingly to turn Durham into a limited company. Jackson remained cricket club chairman but Durham Holdings was formed to take on its assets and liabilities – including £1.8m of debt – and drive development of the ground and team. Sir John Stevens, head of the Metropolitan Police but once Northumbria's chief constable, was brought in as president, more for his contacts than cricket knowledge.

'We'd sort of half begun to build an international stadium without international cricket, then we get international cricket and the ECB begin to impose requirements on international venues like covered seating, media centres, etc., so the club is in the position of either pulling right back, not further developing the ground and doing without international cricket and the financial consequences of that, or we commit to try to further develop the ground to ensure a better share of international cricket in the hope that will bring the revenues to go forward,' Harker explains. 'The club chose to do the latter. The question then is: how and where do you raise the money? We couldn't borrow any more and, as a company limited by guarantee, we couldn't raise any equity, so Durham CCC Holdings created a vehicle to attract outside investment.'

On-field recruitment was therefore crucial in 2004/05. Durham have never done it better. 'I remember sitting down with [coach] Martyn Moxon and [director of cricket] Geoff Cook and saying that if we were going to improve the team's fortunes and they could have anyone in world cricket, who would they have?' Harker recalls. 'They both very quickly, and at the same time, answered, "Mike Hussey".'

At Northamptonshire – as captain – and Gloucestershire, Hussey proved himself the best county cricketer not to own a Test cap, albeit he was an Australian one-day international. His Gloucestershire opening partner Phil Weston advised against joining his dad Mike's old club, but Hussey was struck by Durham's ambition. 'The club said, "Whatever you need, we'll get. No expense spared. We really want to go places",' he recalled in his autobiography. Durham had propelled Simon Katich and Martin Love into Australia's Test team (Brad Hodge would follow), one of two ambitions Hussey outlined in Durham's yearbook, along with winning promotion in both forms of cricket. With Jon Lewis making way as captain, Hussey signed a two-year contract to lead the team as an overseas player from 2005.

'He threw himself into what Durham were trying to achieve,' says Cook. 'He flew into Dubai to be with the team [in pre-season] and took people's breath away with his dedication, professionalism and ability. We knew what we were getting – you just needed to look at his record and his longevity. He wasn't an established international but he kept performing and striving to reach that level.' Breese says: 'When people put themselves out for you, it's hard not to try and give your best back. It showed he cared, he really wanted to do a good job for the team.'

Before his first game, Hussey showed the same Australian mindset predecessor David Boon had. 'It was a damp day and the wicket was the greenest I'd ever seen, it was like six stumps on the outfield,' Stephen Harmison recalls. 'He got us into a huddle and said if we won the toss we'd bat first. I just looked at him and said, "Excuse me?" He said that's the way he wanted to do it.'

After calling correctly, Hussey batted nine hours, 50 minutes, for 253 in Durham's 523/8 declared. '[The ball] was literally going sideways, the wicket was green and tacky,' says Onions. 'I don't think he gave a chance. It was unbelievable.' Lewis opened alongside Hussey. 'I was the first player to score 50 in that game!' he points out. 'Ottis [Gibson] was extraordinary for Leicester, I think he bowled the whole of a session. When Hussey was on about 180 he took the second new ball and bowled a really good spell at Hussey – a great player with a massive hundred already, and a great warrior determined to do something for a side that was not the best at times. Then I think the first two balls Colonel [Phil Mustard] faced he put straight over the sightscreen for six.'

Mustard only made his debut in 2003, but Hussey quickly identified him as a future England player and he became such a key figure that at the end of the 2005 season Andrew Pratt was released – the first in a long line of wicketkeepers seen off by the man from Washington. 'When I was growing up I was always pestered by Alan Walker and Geoff to say, "You're the core of the team,"' Mustard recalls. 'They wanted me to be intense, the worker of the team. I had a free rein to chat shit because people couldn't understand me anyway! I think it made a big difference. I was still dropping a few catches and letting a few byes past until the last ten years of my career, but they wanted me to be the core of the team.' He was by no means the only player to raise his game. 'I went from being on the periphery to feeling like a leader myself,' says Neil Killeen.

'The injection of energy and quality that Huss brought into the dressing room, he just led from the front,' marvels Paul Collingwood. 'Everything in practice, he did it at 100 per cent intensity, so it was a bit of an eye-opener to see how he went about his business and how he spoke to people. When he got a double hundred in his first game it was, "Wow, this boy can play!" So the confidence we gained from that was incredible.

'There was a bit of ribbing about the Ashes [in England that summer] and we did a Q&A when he first arrived. I thought we were going to win the Ashes and he was a typical Aussie, saying they'd win 5-0. It was almost a little bit of a competition between us that year and I honestly think he dragged me to one of my best seasons. In an environment like that, the quality of everything you do goes to a new level. Everybody knew their roles, we had clarity about how people were going to go about it, so when you watched people bat you knew what shot they were going to play. It was really enjoyable, a really fun dressing room.'

Collingwood made six Championship centuries in 2005. Already a key member of England's one-day side, he played two Tests in Sri Lanka in December 2003, but it was on the back of his 2005 season that he cemented himself as a Test player. So did Hussey. One-day international and Australia A call-ups limited him to ten Championship games, yet he still made 1,074 runs at an average of 76.71. Australia's Ashes defeat allowed the 30-year-old to take his form into the Test arena that winter, scoring 897 Test runs at 74.75. He never looked back.

'He hated his reputation as Mr Cricket, but it couldn't be denied that he had a real love for it and was capable of infecting people around him,' says Lewis. 'It could be really cricket-orientated but it wasn't dull or dry, it was that cricket was fun and we really enjoy it. Christ, he worked hard and set that example – a bit like [Graham] Gooch in my youth. Hussey really positively influenced those around him and they really enjoyed playing cricket under him.'

Incredibly, Hussey was not even Durham's best signing that winter. The 2000 Cotonou Agreement was designed to allow countries free trade with the European Union, but had a transformative effect on cricket thanks to Slovak handball player Maros Kolpak. When Germany's TSV Ostringen tried to release Kolpak because they were only allowed two non-EU players, he took them to the European Court of Justice. In 2003 it decided citizens of any country with EU

Association Agreements must be granted equal rights to live and work in the Union. As South Africa, Zimbabwe and many West Indian nations had agreements, it became far harder for county cricket to restrict non-English players.

Durham's first 'Kolpak signing' was their best. Dale Benkenstein quickly delivered on the ambition outlined alongside his out-of-focus headshot in their 2005 yearbook: 'To make a difference to cricket at Durham.' In 2004, Benkenstein's agent circulated his name around the counties, and the Riversiders offered him a trial second-team game against Yorkshire at Stamford Bridge in July. 'I was rooming with him,' Mustard recalls. 'I didn't know him from Adam – in those days you didn't really use Google. I said we were all going down to the bar but he said he'd just chill – typical South African mentality, ring the wife and kids and have an early night. He didn't know anybody and I was young and wild then. We went down for breakfast the next morning and he was still in bed. I said to the others, "This guy is a right boring old git!" When we got to the ground Geoff asked me how my room-mate was and I said we didn't speak to each other. He said Benki [Benkenstein] had told him I was farting, swearing and snoring and I denied it – so I had a go at him for that, then all of a sudden he goes out and gets a hundred. Wow! He played like God!'

Onions was also playing. 'People were thinking, "Why on earth have we signed a Kolpak when we've got amazing youngsters coming through?"' he recalls. 'I bowled quickly and I thought I bowled really well and so did the others. Benki said, "I think we should have bowled a yard fuller." He didn't say anything during the game. He basically just said if you want to get better you have to learn to adapt to different wickets. I walked away thinking about it, which I'd never done before.'

Benkenstein's 123 not out earned him a three-year contract starting in 2005. 'It was fascinating to see a different way of playing cricket, even just the way he pulled the ball,' says Mustard. 'You realised he was a proper cricketer.' If Benkenstein was an unknown quantity to the youngsters, his pedigree was understood by their more-travelled team-mates. Benkenstein captained Natal for eight seasons and, in his first, aged 22, they won the domestic four- and one-day competitions. Born in Rhodesia (modern-day Zimbabwe), he moved to South Africa aged six, won 23 one-day caps and led the A team.

'I'd heard a lot about what a good character he was but the one thing people always said was what a good player he was,' says Harmison. 'I knew Neil McKenzie very well and he told me when Graeme Smith got the South Africa job it was either him, Smith or Benkenstein for the captaincy. They went with Smith and the rumour was he wanted them nowhere near, which is probably why Benki decided to go down the Kolpak route. He captained Natal with Malcolm Marshall, then Shaun Pollock and Lance Klusener. We knew we were getting a good player but he was one of the best characters I ever played with – nothing was ever a problem. If a fielder told him the ball had carried, he walked off. "This is how we're going to play, and if it doesn't work it's our fault." He had a loose side as well, he liked a laugh and a drink.'

Onions believes: 'Benki, Hussey and Michael Di Venuto were the best blokes and the best players Durham ever signed. Comfortably. I'm talking about volume of runs, the way they practised, playing all forms. They were absolutely brilliant and their captaincy was fantastic as well. Benki would stand at mid-off and he liked to tell you what to do. He'd say, "Bowl a short ball," and I'd be, "Really? He's quite good on the short ball." I'd do it and he'd say, "Go again." I'd say, "Really?" Then, "Now pitch it up," and I'd get a wicket and I'd think, "You can have that wicket!"'

Cook has no doubt Benkenstein was the best player he brought into Durham. 'Sport is about making the right decisions when luck shines on you,' he says. 'Dale was available to play a second-team game, and a few days later he was a Durham player. It was just his perspective, really, his priorities. His view of young cricketers was absolutely brilliant and that never changed. He was selfless.'

Benkenstein made 9,055 first-class runs in 137 appearances at an average of 45.96, and was the first to score more than 1,000 in a season five times for Durham. 'Benki struggled for the first couple of weeks of that [2005] season and I remember having a conversation with him where he was grasping a touch,' comments Lewis. 'I don't think I ever saw it again. It was a month at most. He was struggling to come to terms with the Duke ball in April and he wouldn't be the first. He was asking a few questions but he pretty much worked things out himself throughout his career. He was quite self-reliant. He was quiet, not out in your face, a calming influence, but he had a fire in him and we saw it once or twice.'

Future team-mate Will Smith says: 'Some guys are calm and you're lulled into thinking they don't really care. With him you could tell there was this edge, he wanted to win and everyone to play their best. It was genuine joy when other people affected games in a match-winning way, that gave him more pleasure than when it was him. Some people say that and you can tell they don't really mean it, but you could tell he was overjoyed. That fostered a really good spirit. He's just a very good man, someone you respect and trust and could always talk to knowing he had your best interests at heart. And he was a bloody good batsman and an unbelievable fielder, even when he was getting on.'

Of the three 30-year-olds signed in the winter of 2004/05, Callum Thorp was easily the least heralded, which is probably how he preferred it. The seamer made his name taking 4-58 for Western Australia against England on the 2002/03 Ashes tour when combining cricket with window-cleaning. A late developer, he only appeared in six Sheffield Shield games but he and Hussey grew up 20 minutes apart and had come through the state system together since they were 11. Like Breese, Thorp had British parents.

'One of the best things that happened in that era was Huss brought in a bowler who we'd never heard of, Callum Thorp,' says Mustard. 'That was probably the start of the new way Durham wanted to play – not crash, bang, wallop, more of a structured, cautious approach. If you bring in a bowler who just bowls line and length and doesn't go for runs, it changes the whole dynamic – bowlers can bowl around him. Thorp did that job unbelievably well and people don't realise how influential he was – not so much off the field because he was very quiet, very humble. His bowling was very, very simple but he brought a new dimension with Hussey. That is when Durham changed and they're probably like that to this day, with one, maybe two characters playing that role and the whole system based around it.' Breese says: 'He had so much time for everybody around him. The players we signed then brought younger players on and would have had a massive impact on them moving on to international honours.'

Durham's second official overseas player, Australian Ashley Noffke, missed the first six weeks of the 2005 Championship with back trouble but Harmison, who had not featured in 2004 because of England commitments, took 27 wickets in the opening four games, all won. It was 30 May before Durham lost a match of any type. Their progress slowed mid-season, winning two of eight Twenty20 games and beaten by an innings and 228 on the resumption of the Championship, with Lewis breaking his collarbone. In early August, a stress fracture of the back put Mark Davies out for nearly 18 months.

Benkenstein skippered when Hussey and vice-captain Paul Collingwood were on international duty, and at times even when the latter was not. Noffke's replacement, compatriot Mick Lewis, had to leave early to give evidence in the trial arising from former Australia batsman David Hookes's death, having taken 26 four-day wickets at 23.61. When Australia A called Hussey up to tour Pakistan, stand-in Jimmy Maher scored 18 runs in four Championship innings – but produced some match-winning one-day performances. Durham limped across the line, claiming the third promotion spot in the final season before two-up, two-down and – thanks in no small part to Breese's seven half-centuries – won 40-over promotion too.

Recruiting good characters, not just good cricketers, tipped the balance. 'Geoff has an eye for a player which in my observations is unrivalled, certainly in terms of players we've recruited for the longer term. In any sport once you get to this level the innate talent and skillset is almost a given, it's the character that makes all the difference,' says David Harker. Cook explains: 'A lot of it is experience – knowing the make-up of a team, what makes a cricketer tick, what makes him fit into a group, where he's performed, his skills, what levels he's performed at, and what pressures he's performed under. You get a sixth sense that this could be the right man.'

Harmison argues: 'It was either great luck or great research. It's probably a bit of both. I'm sorry, you couldn't do all that research, get all those players in and still do what he did day to day, although it wasn't just Geoff. Martyn Moxon signed Michael Di Venuto and Ottis Gibson, and Hussey recommended Thorp. There were not many selfish characters there.'

Keaton Jennings did not make his Durham debut until 2012, yet still had the benefit of Breese, Thorp, Benkenstein and Di Venuto's wisdom. 'For the younger guys to still be calling Gareth Breese now for advice shows the calibre of person,' he comments. 'That's probably more important than someone who's guaranteed 1,000 runs [a season]. Durham created a good environment and a good nucleus of players. I know I've left but I think that's why guys want to play for Durham and win games of cricket for Durham.'

Maher and Mick Lewis returned as overseas players for 2006. Former West Indies bowler Gibson, English-qualified through residency, joined from Leicestershire, and off-spinner Paul Wiseman signed a two-year contract late in the campaign. Wiseman had 25 New Zealand Test caps, 15 one-day international appearances and a British passport. Australians Di Venuto and Mitchell Claydon arrived for 2007, along with Englishmen Will Smith and Will Gidman. Di Venuto was an overseas player for his first season but, once he retired from Australian first-class cricket, he played under his Italian passport, Claydon a British one. West Indian Shivnarine Chanderpaul joined mid-season as an overseas player.

Like Hussey, Tasmania opener Di Venuto was a proven Championship performer, having joined Sussex in 1999 then spent seven years at Derbyshire. He missed 2004 through injury when he was due to captain, and was frustrated when he returned as vice-captain. 'I couldn't get the team to play the way I wanted,' he told me on joining Durham. 'They played in a negative fashion which goes against my upbringing.' When Derbyshire released Di Venuto to get 'the right overseas player to complement our young players', Moxon was quick to sign a batsman he had long admired. 'He would run Benkenstein close as one of the top recruits,' comments Cook.

Three weeks after a Hussey-style debut – 155 not out from Durham's 313 as Worcestershire were beaten by 241 runs – Di Venuto made an unbeaten double hundred at home to Kent. Again, though, it was his impact on others, particularly a talented left-handed opener from Sunniside, Gateshead. 'Mark Stoneman's career didn't really get going until he got to stand side-by-side with Michael Di Venuto,' says Harmison. 'He learnt how to prepare, how to be a first-class, then a Test, batsman – he turned into him at one point! Put two Mark Stonemans together then and you're not going to go anywhere.'

Stoneman says: 'Diva [Di Venuto] brought a real sense of purpose and was far from someone who was happy to pick up an overseas gig and see how it went. His attitude was one of demanding excellence from himself, which resulted in some unbelievable performances with the bat in his hands and also his slip catching, but he dragged other players along with him and fully bought into trying to take the club forward, so it was no longer just about competing, but winning.'

It is uncanny how many of that Durham team became coaches. Di Venuto was Australia's batting coach before taking over at Surrey. Gibson had two spells as England's bowling coach, as well as being in charge of the West Indies, then South Africa, with former Hampshire coach Benkenstein as his batting expert. Jon Lewis, Neil Killeen and Breese joined Durham's staff, Wiseman and Mick Lewis also coached domestically, and Onions and Kyle Coetzer qualified while still playing.

Others just set an example. 'Kyle Coetzer in 2007 was one of the best young one-day players in the country and that had a hell of a lot to do with Shiv Chanderpaul,' Harmison stresses. 'Mike Hussey rubbed off on Muchy [Gordon Muchall] especially.' It was, says Breese, 'a good environment for young players to see how to be professional'. Harmison believes: 'If you've always got somebody to look up to in a dressing room, you've got a great chance – especially if that person has got good work ethics, as well as being very, very good at leading from the front.'

Jon Lewis can 'vividly remember Shaun Pollock being here [in 2008] and saying a couple of things to the bowlers with me looking at them thinking, "We've been saying that to you for months!" but they were looking at him like he was God. That stature can be used extremely well by those individuals. I sometimes think they don't necessarily understand how fortunate they are to have that instant gravitas. They've earned it but it puts them in a great position to have influence.

'After Boon, Hussey would be the next example of that; Benki and Di Venuto had a big influence. Shivy, it was more by example. You could engage him in conversation about batting but you probably had to work harder. Kumar [Sangakkara, who played two matches in 2014] was unbelievable in such a short period of time. Some of the guys in the dressing room fell in love, I think.'

Players of that calibre did not come cheap and Leach looked overseas for investment too, mainly from Asia. 'Foreign investment worries me because the question was often asked if they were really interested in the cricket, or were they after something else?' says Bob Jackson. In 2008 brothers Gautam and Hiren Radia, Indian radio station owners, quietly invested around £2.4m. Singapore-based businessman Jhaveri Darsan put in around £6m. 'I only met Gautam Radia once and never saw the others,' says Jackson. 'It used to get my back up. I'm not a sophisticated financial man, I'm a cricket man, and although I'd ask the odd question to challenge it, people were very strong for it. Radia sounded OK. I asked was he interested in the cricket and he said yes. He came across as very pleasant.

'My problem with spending the money was that if the north-east public and particularly the business world didn't support it, that was a risk. They were very, very good in the initial years, buying boxes and helping us to build the ground, but the attendance at matches in terms of hospitality has never been strong. T20 changed it a little bit but there are still empty boxes. But after the Holdings board was formed, the club's audit committee had some very big hitters. The chairman was Richard Bottomley and you had Bryan Sanderson, former chairman of BUPA and senior man in BP, and Frank Curry, a local businessman. Their recommendations were supportive [of greater investment], particularly when outside individuals were discussed.'

Harker says: 'Gautam Radia was a business associate and friend of Clive's and, as is common with a lot of Indians, he had a love for cricket. He liked what we were trying to achieve and had the means to get involved. It was unfortunate he was unable to honour his original commitment of £5m because in 2008 the world [economy] fell off a cliff. It wasn't that his involvement was secretive, it was more that he was, and is, a private sort of guy. Like Clive, he wasn't driven by ego, they weren't doing this as some sort of trophy asset, and he just preferred not to draw attention to himself. It was all publicly documented so it wasn't something we were trying to keep secret. I didn't have an awful lot of contact with him. He came over from time to time and took an interest. He'd send me occasional emails about who we were facing in the next match and who to watch out for. He was a fan who had the best interests of the club at heart. He felt that he was able to help, then couldn't to the extent we needed.'

Jackson's suspicions were aroused by the fact that around this time there were discussions about a franchise Twenty20 tournament to ape the Indian Premier League. There was talk of 49 per cent stakes in franchises being sold for £50m, and of £85m in sponsorship, broadcasting and matchday receipts. The ECB have decided to go down a similar path from 2020, but this was led from the Test-match venues.

'A couple of the chief execs had a few meetings but we weren't party to that,' Harker insists. 'You have one eye on how the world of cricket might change but there wasn't a masterplan for people to put their money in and we'd convert it into an IPL or whatever. I think when [ECB chairman] Giles Clarke got wind of the conversations some of the fellas were having, he soon stamped on that. I think they were curious more than anything, looking to understand how it worked. [An "English IPL"] was so far off that I don't think it would have been a big factor in the investment. You could see it was an interesting time, and who knows what might have developed, but they weren't sold it on that basis.'

In 2012 there was even a link-up with Shanghai Cricket Association to share playing and coaching resources and spread Durham's name. What Leach called 'a pretty epic sort of thing' soon petered out.

'I think the success would suggest we got the balance about right,' says Harker. '[From 2005] players who had talent were growing into a successful organisation which set the right standards. I think our success in developing players would have been hampered had there not been that balance between the experience we had to recruit, and the younger local guys who were now coming into a different sort of dressing room.'

Other are not so sure. 'I like to think if I'd still been treasurer we'd have done things differently,' says Tom Moffat, Durham's president from 2006–08. 'Let's say Clive and I didn't always get on. My problem with Don [Robson] was that I wasn't a yes man – I'm very arrogant – and it was the same with Clive. The minute I finished as president I was jettisoned.'

Leach's ambition held sway over Jackson and Moffat's caution. 'That was the start of the really exciting times for Durham,' says Killeen. 'It snowballed.'

8.

Full Steam Ahead

SUNDAY lunchtime, 19 August 2007, and a train is rattling up the East Coast Main Line. A group of Durham supporters huddle around a radio nursing hangovers and listening to their team closing out victory at Lord's for the county's first major silverware in their 16th first-class season. When Liam Plunkett bowled Shane Warne to secure it, 'the carriage went up', recalls Chris Rushworth.

In the previous 12 months alone Durham faced three sliding doors moments which could easily have derailed them. Instead, Ottis Gibson stared down Championship relegation and any personal demons, and the 11th-hour departure of the coach who signed him was turned into a catalyst for Durham's golden era.

Like David Boon's before him, Mike Hussey's on-field legacy was threatened as soon as he left. When Hussey's burgeoning Test career prevented him returning for a second year, the captaincy passed to Dale Benkenstein. Hussey was not the only Durham player on the Test scene in the winter of 2005/06. With Plunkett making his debut, Stephen Harmison established and Paul Collingwood cementing his place, Durham had three players in England's Test XI for the first time.

Injury restricted Mark Davies to eight Championship overs in 2006, Harmison only bowled 32, and Plunkett none. Having taken just three Championship wickets in 2005, Callum Thorp topped Durham's 2006 bowling averages, Gibson claimed 49 scalps in his debut campaign, and Graham Onions 50. Benkenstein scored 1,427 Championship runs and the returning Jimmy Maher fell just short of four figures.

Durham finished second in their 50-over Friends Provident Trophy group but in 2006 only the winners progressed. They finished bottom of the Twenty20 Cup's northern group, and even a final-day win over champions Essex could not prevent Pro40 Division One relegation. Three days later they were at Headingley, facing the very real prospect of following 2005's double promotion with double demotion.

Fortunately for Durham, 2006 was the first season where only two sides were relegated from the top flight and Middlesex had all-but booked one spot. It left a three-way fight with Yorkshire, half a point behind, and Nottinghamshire, 9.5 in front. With five batting bonus points available, three bowling, four for a draw and 14 for victory, a loser in Leeds seemed certain to return to the division they had just come from. At the end of day one, it already looked like Durham.

In his final appearance for them, Darren Lehmann made Yorkshire's second-biggest individual score – 339 of their 677/7 declared. The first chance the Australian offered came on 202, and Benkenstein – close in at point – dropped it. 'Lehmann was taking the piss,' says Onions. 'He was almost getting to the stage where you were bowling bouncers at him and he was watching it and glancing it off his helmet. He'd walk across and knock it into the off side, so you'd move everyone over there and he'd walk across and knock it into the leg side. It was like indoor cricket, I've never seen anything like it. I thought, "I've got no idea." We were dead and buried.'

A glimmer of hope came from Trent Bridge, where Nottinghamshire were hurtling towards a one-point defeat against champions-elect Sussex. A draw with maximum batting points would keep Durham up but, when Phil Mustard, Ben Harmison and Gareth Breese were dismissed in the space of four deliveries to send Gibson striding out to join Benkenstein on 176/6, 400 looked virtually impossible.

'I remember sitting in the old changing rooms in the freezing cold with pad rash and it was quite surreal,' Onions recalls. 'Ottis and Benki just kept on batting. Ottis got a bit giddy at one point where he started hitting sixes and you thought, "Just bat!" But Gibbo in that period was just incredible. What he added to the team was remarkable. To come in when you don't really know anybody and just fit in so well, he was great – a real legend.'

The pair added a Durham-record 315 for the seventh wicket. A Gibson six secured the fifth batting point, but Benkenstein was out for 151 with 22 needed to avoid the follow-on, and when Gibson went in the next over for a career-best 155, it was the second of four wickets for 12 runs. Asked to bat again 159 behind, Durham had 48 overs to survive. They lost openers Maher and Gary Scott with just 16 chalked off, bringing Benkenstein back to the crease after 62 minutes away. The captain scored only 26 this time – but 100 not out from Garry Park, a South African wicketkeeper who made his Championship debut at Lancashire the previous week, kept Durham up by half a point. It appeared Park might solve Durham's long-standing problem at number three but he only made two Championship appearances in 2007 and one in 2008 before leaving for Derbyshire averaging 50.42.

'That was a crucial part of Durham's history,' Mustard reflects. 'It just gave people the fighting qualities they needed, and knowing we had that gave confidence to the board to put us on the map properly.' Relegated in 2000, the injured Stephen Harmison appreciated the significance. 'We needed to stay in that top division,' he remarks. 'Once Gibbo got started, Yorkshire weren't that bothered about creating a result. It typified the people involved that 36 months later the players who kept Durham up had two Championship medals and a Friends Provident Trophy.'

Breese admits: 'You never know how things would have panned out [had Durham been relegated]. Maybe we wouldn't have been able to sign [Michael] Di Venuto, and probably it could have knocked some of the confidence that was starting to build. Maybe some of the young players might have gone back a bit. The way we stayed up showed our character. That's what professional sport's about – fighting to the bitter end. It felt like a win and we'd started to understand what it was like to win.'

Six weeks before the 2007 season began, coach Martyn Moxon resigned. The former opener joined from Yorkshire in the winter of 2000/01 amid recriminations over who should pay his wages while with England, but he had laid the platform for their first Championship title for 33 years. A reunion always seemed likely, but when his successor Wayne Clark was sacked in 2003 Moxon signed a contract extension. 'The fact Durham were wanting to extend my contract, particularly given the season we had last year, shows a lot of faith in me,' he said. 'I think that deserves some loyalty on my part. I feel there are exciting times ahead.' He was, however, still commuting from Wetherby, and when Yorkshire came back in 2007 the lure was too great. 'I sensed something was in the air,' says Geoff Cook. 'He was finding the travel very difficult so it wasn't a total surprise.'

It was a big loss. 'Moxon was amazing,' says Breese. 'You knew where you stood and I liked his way. He really got the guys to understand what professionalism was about and he was quite structured, which is probably what our younger players needed. When he decided to leave he was probably gutted because that was the year we put our mark on county cricket, but he had laid the foundations and Geoff Cook and John Windows had done the work of getting the young players really ready.'

Offering Cook the job 'seemed the obvious thing', comments then-chief executive David Harker, who spoke at the time of creating an 'Anfield Boot Room-style' culture. Cook says: 'It came at a good time for me. The academy had been going pretty well, and I was more than happy to take on a fresh challenge and try to bring in my experience of a lot of first-class cricket, and a lot of knowledge of the young guys in the squad. I had a brilliant experience doing different roles at Durham, meeting different people and having to react to different age groups and take on different responsibilities. I'd had ten years at the academy and you think, "Is that long enough?"'

Not everyone was convinced. 'I was in charge of the pre-season trip to South Africa because Benki was still captaining Natal, Colly [Collingwood] was away, and I remember Geoff getting us all in a room and saying he was going to take over,' Harmison recalls. 'I said to Geoff I didn't think it was a good idea because what he had done up until then was produce cricketers for England and I didn't think it would be a good idea for the club to jeopardise that, even though I knew John Windows had grown into the role of seeing cricketers through Geoff's eyes.

'I believe some of the best coaches, best managers, shouldn't be at the top, they should be at the next rung down. The list of players he produced was endless, for Durham and England, but Geoff was adamant he wanted to do it. It was not in any way, shape or form about his coaching ability – which was second to none – or his leadership skills, it was just I thought he would be more important finding the next generation but he kept doing that as well.'

Moxon and Cook brought different approaches ideal for their times. Moxon inherited a talented but raw group which needed to be taught cricket's disciplines. 'Martyn provided clarity,' opener Jon Lewis explains. 'The message was definitely consistent, which is a good thing for young players. He was very good at structure and process. Giff [predecessor Norman Gifford] had a softer touch around younger players, whereas Martyn was probably a bit more direct.'

Few youngsters were rawer or more talented than Mustard. 'You had to be clean shaven – do you really need that?' he asks. 'That was one rule for everybody. Did it suit me? I was still raw so yes, it taught me a few harsher things. Frog [Moxon] took over a team that was getting beaten very comfortably every game and realised we needed to be more structured, more solid, have a system. That's his management style. People bought into it and we started moving forward. One of the things Frog would say to everyone was, "I don't care what you get up to tonight, don't get arrested and be there at ten o'clock tomorrow." Then you realised you were in a professional environment. It was what Durham needed.'

By 2007 it was a different club. 'You'd got people who knew how to do their jobs and understood how to play the game and what it takes to survive and be successful,' argues Harmison. 'There was less hand-holding and it was basically, "Get on with your job." You didn't have to teach Ottis Gibson or Callum Thorp how to play. Michael Di Venuto just wanted his bag in the right place, he'd put his kit on and go out and play.'

Lewis began coaching the second XI in 2006, before succeeding Cook in 2013. 'You could argue myself and Martyn have the same skills and strengths – structure, process, directness are more comfortable for me,' he reflects. 'I'm not always the most sensitive but you learn these things. Geoff's very good at the softer skills and he had a side that knew their games pretty well so it allowed Geoff to trust them. I probably learnt from working with Geoff that even young players need a degree of freedom.'

Onions blossomed into an England A bowler under Moxon, touring Bangladesh in 2006/07. 'Geoff had that feel of "it doesn't matter", but actually he was a really good man-manager and I think that was lacking by the time I left [in 2017],' he argues. 'There might not have been much actual coaching but the man-management when I wasn't convinced I could do it was massive. Geoff just gave you little bits of help along the way. Martyn Moxon gave it a bit of structure and Geoff let things flow. I do like structure, but when you get on the field you don't want to feel like the shackles are on. You want to cross the white line and think, "I'm just going to be me." As long as you've structured your practice right you can think, "I've had a bad day but I've done everything right." I always felt I could have done better, which was a good thing because it made me want to work harder. People say I was grumpy but if I wasn't happy it was because I wanted to get better.'

Mustard was also ready to be unshackled. 'When Geoff took over you'd think he wasn't watching, but he took every little bit of the action in,' he says. 'I didn't realise until he brought them out one day but he took notes of everything in this brown book. He'd just say, "Colonel, can I have a word?" And you're thinking, "Oh no!" People were scared of him because they respected him, and what he said was probably right. He'd not do it in front of everybody, just casually ask how you think you're playing or how things are at home. If you did good things he'd tell you, but when things weren't good he wouldn't shout at you. You know if you've done something right or wrong so he'd just ask questions he already knew the answer to rather than just say, "Do this, do that."

'I went from four years of Moxon – strict, structured – then Geoff came in and relaxed all that. It was a bit of a free-for-all really, from one extreme to the other. I don't know if Froggy would have changed his coaching style but everything started falling into place because you had young guys surrounded by serious experienced characters like Gibson, Di Venuto, Benkenstein, then outside of that Harmy, Plunkett, [Mitchell] Claydon, Onions.'

Cook explains: 'You don't want to inhibit people of immense ability with too many structures but, equally, there was a little bit of research about what players from other counties thought about Durham, and the big message that came back was a feeling that there was a real inferiority complex and Durham didn't have the belief that they could win the games. Those were the simple messages that Dale and I tried to get across to the group, that every one of them could be match-winning cricketers, such was the high level of talent.' Personally, it felt like the inferiority complex went under Hussey – Harmison and Collingwood agree – but Durham undoubtedly stepped up under Cook.

They started 2007 with eight players born outside the country, but only Di Venuto as an official overseas player until signing New Zealander Scott Styris, one of the world's best limited-overs all-rounders, in June. Arriving with a knee injury, which restricted his bowling, then picking up a calf strain, which limited him to three Twenty20 appearances, his end-of-season statistics were underwhelming, but Cook remembers a crucial Friends Provident Trophy contribution. 'We were playing at Yorkshire in the qualifying stages and he ended up getting 98,' he says. 'I remember one shot when [Darren] Gough, who was a master of the inswinging yorker, was bowling. Styris played a shot you see pretty regularly now to lift this yorker off the middle of the bat over backward point for four into the Western Terrace. It was one of the best shots I'd ever seen because I hadn't seen it before. He went on to play a match-winning innings. Things like that reflect that things might be going in your favour.'

Durham won by 53 runs at Headingley and would top the northern group on net run-rate, securing home advantage for their semi-final against Essex. Harmison was nursing a hernia problem, having the previous day played in a seven-wicket Test win at the Riverside. 'I wasn't supposed to play but I said, "Fuck it, I'm playing!" because it was a good chance for us,' he smiles. 'I didn't have an injection but I was overdosing on painkillers. I was desperate to play because I'd played at Lord's for England and I wanted everybody else to have that chance. [England coach] Duncan Fletcher went ballistic when he found out!'

The bad weather which blighted the Test delayed the start until 12.10pm. Benkenstein won the toss. 'Teams from the south come up here and don't know what a good score is, so it's best to put them in,' he explained. Dropped from the Test, Plunkett took 4-15 as Essex were 71 all out on the slow pitch. Gibson took 3-21 off six overs, his new-ball partner Neil Killeen 3-9 off seven. The visitors managed more ducks than boundaries. 'With 72 runs needed you think, "We'll just knock this off,"' Benkenstein reflected. 'The next minute it's looking like a bloody mountain!'

Durham had scored just six by the time Di Venuto, Mustard and Collingwood were finished for the day, and 39/7 off 11 overs when Danish Kaneria dropped Gibson at mid-on. When Graham Napier no-balled the next delivery, Plunkett toe-ended the free hit for six. He scored 30 of the 34 runs he and Gibson needed to take Durham over the line, from 35 deliveries. The game lasted 41.1 incredible overs.

Durham suffered three consecutive Championship defeats either side of the semi-final and, instead of proving his fitness for the upcoming India Test series, Harmison aggravated his groin fielding in the last of them, at Sussex. Six days after surgery, he captained Durham against Sri Lanka A to demonstrate his readiness for Lord's. Harmison bowled ten overs across two innings, taking a wicket in each. Two days later he bowled seven overs in a Pro40 defeat at Canterbury, then nine against Surrey the next day before a back injury with internal bleeding likened to a car-crash victim's ended his season. 'I bowled about 25mph at Kent but I just wanted to prove I was fit enough to play,' he says. 'I felt a little bit like a spare part [at Lord's] but it was the bigger picture, what it stood for.'

When New Zealand ordered the injured Styris home, Durham turned to Shivnarine Chanderpaul. The left-hander had just averaged 148.6 – including a Chester-le-Street century – in the England–West Indies Test series, and 202 in the one-dayers. Although he would have to leave at the end of August for the World Twenty20 Championships in South Africa, Cook called the signing 'a statement of intent'.

Durham had nothing to fear against 2005 winners Hampshire. 'It never occurred to me that anyone thought they were going to do anything other than win,' says Jon Lewis, invited along for the ride. 'That side hadn't really been together very long but it was pretty vibrant. At no stage did people seem intimidated by Shane Warne, Kevin Pietersen, [Michael] Carberry or [Dimitri] Mascarenhas. It wasn't that we had a right to win it, but we expected to.' After Essex, Breese says: 'We almost felt like we'd played our bad game.' Their opponents were confident too. 'Having spoken to guys at Hampshire who were involved, they had a real belief because they were the one-day kings,' says Will Smith, who later played for them. 'They thought, "Great, we've got Durham in the final – they'll be overawed."'

Smith had lost his spot after an unconvincing first ten Championship matches for Durham. 'I'd played all the group games [bar one], and the quarter and the semi, but the final was after the T20, and I wasn't in the T20 team,' he explains. 'I'd scored 103 against Worcester and played a part, but Kyle [Coetzer] had been going well and the rest of the batting line-up picked itself. While I was disappointed, I had no qualms.'

Onions was sweating on his place. 'We arrived on the Friday and it might have been raining so there was talk we might put another batsman in,' he recalls. 'I was lying in bed praying I was going to play, rooming with Gordon Muchall, who was praying he would. When they told me I was going to play I felt nervous but fantastic. I was excited.'

Mustard dealt with excitement his own way. 'When we got on the bus Benki said, "I don't want us to get nervous,"' he recalls. 'We stopped off at a services and some guy stopped Benki with a white racing pigeon that had got lost. Benki told him we were off to London and the guy said would we mind taking the bird with us and letting it out there? Benki being Benki, he took this pigeon in a box. We're thinking, "What are you doing? This is not right!" When we had practice he let it off.

'That night everyone had a beer together and enjoyed talking around the bar. Gibson, Di Venuto, Benkenstein, Colly weren't modern professionals – they did it right but they enjoyed a Guinness. All the girls had come down and they arranged to go to a show. Colly took us to a pub called the Landsdowne and we decided to spend the night together. It was perfect, just three or four Guinnesses, a pizza and a good laugh. We got back about half-ten, 11, and the girls had come back so we had a drink in the bar with them. All the TV commentators were in there and the fans. We had another beer and I was talking to Nasser [Hussain], Knighty [Nick Knight] and the girls, so I had another beer, then I got talking to the supporters and some of them had known my dad, and all of a sudden you're another four beers deep. I had eight to ten pints and I was feeling a bit ropey so Louise [now his wife] said to me, probably about half-oneish, I should go to bed. I was happy, not "drunk drunk". In them days I could drink, get up and not bat an eyelid. I didn't do it because I was nervous, I did it because I'm happy having a beer with people, happy to make friends. I'd had a few beers before some of the games earlier in the season and I'd still been able to perform. If you go to bed you're twiddling your thumbs thinking about tomorrow.'

It had been a big season for Mustard, scoring his maiden one-day century in the four-wicket group-stage win at Northampton. He jointly held the record for Durham's fastest first-class fifty for all of six days before deputy Lee Goddard outdid him against Sri Lanka A in his only first-class appearance for the county. As well as claiming more dismissals than any Championship wicketkeeper (62 catches and three stumpings), Mustard was the country's top-scorer in both 50- and 40-over cricket.

Opening the batting happened by chance in 2006's final 40-over game. 'I still played football then on a Sunday,' he says. 'I was a bit naïve thinking I'd never get injured. I was a striker and one day I walloped into a goalkeeper, full force. I had a bruise from my knee to my elbow, I couldn't move, I couldn't drive, I was in agony. I really could not run but I said I'd be all right. I went for physio and said I'd been in the gym and dropped a dumbbell, then I got hit by a golf buggy. The stories didn't add up. Benki and Frog said if I couldn't run, why not go at the top of the order and slog it? I never looked back.'

Mustard made 84 from 86 deliveries and was given the job in all limited-overs cricket from 2007. 'I had an amazing year,' he reflects. 'Frog was big on execution and all of a sudden I had to convert that into match-winning performances. He kept saying, "Execution, execution!" And that meant nothing to me. If Moxon hadn't left, where would I be? Who knows? I was scared to hit a few shots, but the change [of coach] was quite good for me. Geoff knew me like the back of his hand and he knew how to coach me. The first year I opened was 2007 and I got more than 1,000 runs in limited-overs cricket. That's when cricket started being a proper job.'

His fearlessness set the tone after Hampshire put Durham in and removed Di Venuto in the ninth over. 'I just said, "Right, I'm going to take them down!"' Mustard says. 'I might have still been under the influence, but I started playing as I'd been playing all season.' Onions argues: 'Phil Mustard's at his best when he doesn't think about it. He can play pretty much every shot and, on his day, he can take attacks apart. That was his day.'

On 49, Mustard was lbw to James Bruce. For the first time in a domestic final, players could refer decisions to the third umpire. 'It didn't even cross my mind,' Mustard admits. 'I thought, "That's out!" Then when I looked back on it I was trying to hit it to the leg side so maybe it pitched outside the line. If the umpire gives you out, you walk off. People on the balcony were saying, "Turn around! Review!" By then it was a couple of minutes and [umpire] Ian Gould told me to get off the pitch. People keep bringing it up now but it didn't cross my mind.' His 38-ball innings did its job.

Durham's least experienced player, 23-year-old Coetzer, batted at three. Coetzer made his debut at Cardiff in 2004 but had not played a competitive game for Durham in 2005 or 2006, and his contract was up at the end of the season. When he made an unbeaten 153 against Durham University in May, he kept his place and, having missed out to Smith for the semi-final, he scored 142 at home to Warwickshire with the final a fortnight away. 'I got told [I was playing] a few days before,' he told me in 2014. 'I was very grateful because it gave me a little bit of time to get my head around it. I was still a young guy trying to push my way into that team so any game I was selected for I thought, "Oh brilliant, I'm playing!" Things were going really well and I was as confident probably as I ever have been. Cricket has its ups and downs but at the time I was backed.'

Coetzer added 111 in 119 balls with Chanderpaul. 'Kyle Coetzer played the innings of the day really,' Onions recalled. 'You expect it from Chanderpaul, Collingwood, Di Venuto or Benkenstein, but Kyle hit one ball right into the top of the stand for a massive six and, when we got to 35 overs, we had the chance of a big score. It was nice as a tail-ender not having to put the pads on and it meant we could put them under pressure when we bowled.' Coetzer's 61 came from 74 deliveries, and Chanderpaul was on course to mark his competition debut with a century until being run out for 78 off 79. The heavy artillery kept coming. 'They were pretty much all international-class or just under,' says Collingwood, making his sixth limited-overs appearance for Durham in two years. 'I hit it like a dog but everybody else was smacking it everywhere.'

Benkenstein smashed 61 not out off 43 deliveries. 'He hit a boundary to get his fifty and he was that much in the zone he didn't even realise,' chuckles Smith. 'The whole crowd was clapping and he didn't raise his bat, he was that focussed – or he'd lost count!' Lewis recalls: 'He kept depositing [Daren] Powell, their West Indian bowler, over the short boundary – that was bullying.'

Even walking out with only 13 deliveries remaining, Gibson made an impact. 'Chris Tremlett bowled a beamer and Ottis almost threw his bat at him,' says Onions. 'I know Chris Tremlett really well and it was a genuine mistake, but the next ball was in the slot and he hit it for six. What would have been a good score on that wicket after being put in? We probably would have taken 250. With 180 we could have potentially won the final with nerves around.' Benkenstein hit the final three balls for six, four and four to take Durham to 312/5. 'By the end of it you think, "Surely we can't get beaten?" and "I can't wait for Gibbo to get the new ball in his hand,"' says Mustard. 'He could bowl some fast balls and he was telling us he was going to get KP [Kevin Pietersen] and all this malarkey.'

It was Gibson's year. He was 37 when he joined Durham in 2006, 15 years after his first-class debut with Barbados. Spells with Border, Glamorgan, Griqualand West, Gauteng and Leicestershire followed, plus two Test and 15 one-day caps for the West Indies. He also played league cricket for Enfield, Rawtenstall and Haslingden. When Gibson moved to England in 2001 it was to coach, and after spending the summer playing minor counties cricket for Staffordshire, he sat out 2002. He had worked with England's under-15s and under-17s, and his two-year Durham contract would be a last hurrah before coaching full-time.

Despite Gibson's end-of-season heroics at Headingley in 2006, Smith thought he detected doubts the following pre-season. 'We played in Cape Town, I think,' he says. 'Maybe he'd come into it not having done much over the winter, but he got smashed all over the place by a young South African lad. He was sat in the dressing room after the game and looked a broken man. I didn't know much about him then and thought, "This isn't good!" It obviously flicked a switch in his mind and he said to himself, "Sort yourself out." I don't know how he did it but he was phenomenal that year. It was just his experience, his desire and his incredible pride in what he did. It was a joy to play with him.'

After five wickets in 2007's first three Championship matches, Gibson was dropped for the 157-run defeat at Kent. With Harmison, Collingwood and Plunkett at Lord's for the first Test, he made a low-key return at Edgbaston, then exploded into life against Yorkshire. Gibson was one of five Durham half-centurions and claimed a career-best 7-81, followed by 3-63, in the six-wicket home win. 'He half made light of it and was half trying to set an example,' explains Smith. 'When Liam Plunkett or Mark Davies or one of the younger lads was left out and kicked up a bit of a fuss or didn't act as you should, he kept coming out with this line: "Don't get bitter, get better."'

Gibson took 80 Championship wickets in 2007, including all ten in Hampshire's first innings at the Riverside about a month before the final. He was only the third bowler in 50 years to do so in the Championship. Gibson had 5-31 at lunch. '[Benkenstein] said at my age I wasn't going to get many more opportunities to take all ten,' he revealed. He had a career-best eight when rain gave him an hour-and-a-half's break after 17 overs, then took wickets with his second and third balls after it. 'I remember him just running off like a 16-year-old schoolkid,' Smith says of the football-style celebration. Gibson took the first two wickets of the second innings but, with rain and bad light taking so much play out of the game, an unbeaten century from Michael Brown – the only player Gibson was unable to dismiss – meant Hampshire batted out a draw.

Gibson's hold over Hampshire continued at Lord's. 'I was having lunch with Nigel Kent, the physio, and a few other lads in the lunch room at Lord's, which is out the back,' Smith recalls. 'The TV was on but there's a delay of a couple of seconds. I didn't realise they'd started [Hampshire's innings] but suddenly you hear this massive roar and think, "What's happened there?" You watch the TV and Gibbo's running in and gets Michael Lumb. I thought, "What a start!" Things settle down, you keep eating, and it happens again. You think, "It can't be. Surely." This time it was Sean Ervine, then Pietersen. I thought, "Oh my God, this is unbelievable!" After that, they were never getting into the game.' The left-handers fell to the first two balls of the innings, brilliantly caught by second slip Di Venuto. Pietersen was lbw to a delivery which kept low in Gibson's fifth over.

John Crawley led the resistance with 68 until being bowled by Collingwood. With Hampshire 158/5, the result was beyond doubt when rain stopped play at 5.20pm. Rather than use the Duckworth-Lewis Method, the final had a reserve day. 'It was a real travesty which has been rectified now,' argues Lewis. 'From a player's point of view, it probably wasn't too much of a downer because you've still got your win, but for the members it didn't culminate in the day they should have had.'

Released by Durham two years earlier, Chris Rushworth was one of 6,000 Durham fans at Lord's on the Saturday. 'I had a lot of friends who I played with in the academy playing, so to watch them was an amazing experience,' he recalls. 'Seeing them win a trophy only grew my hunger to be part of that.' Not that Rushworth saw Benkenstein lift the cup, he only listened on the radio from the train.

'You thought the job was done on Saturday night,' Mustard admits, 'but you were still a bit cautious. That night was quieter than the night before. This time it was, "It's not over yet." The chief execs were in and you could see them watching you so it was probably an early night's sleep. On the Saturday when you walked to the ground they were queuing up outside, on Sunday it was one man and his dog. It took the oomph out of Durham's first trophy.' Neil Killeen recalls: 'My parents were staying in the same hotel as

Hampshire. They'd organised a winners' party at the hotel for the Saturday night. It was pretty clear by Saturday evening Durham were going to win so I think a few of the Durham fans staying there gatecrashed the party!'

The second day started at 12.30pm and lasted just nine overs, Collingwood and Plunkett taking the last five wickets for 13 runs. 'To win that first trophy was something I never thought would happen back in 1992,' says Killeen, the only player remaining from Durham's pre-season tour of Zimbabwe. 'I've got a picture on my wall of myself, Paul Collingwood and Stephen Harmison with the trophy. It was one of those moments you live for in sport.'

There was the possibility of more silverware in 2007. 'With a quarter of the season left in the Championship and five one-day games remaining, we owe it to ourselves as a team to keep going,' Benkenstein said. The Riversiders lost at Taunton on the Thursday but it was their last 40-over defeat en route to winning Division Two. The season finished at Canterbury, where Durham were outsiders in a three-horse Championship race with nine points to make up on Lancashire, three on Sussex.

A two-day defeat at Blackpool a fortnight earlier appeared to end Durham's chances, but later that week Mark Stoneman's maiden century secured a nine-wicket victory over Sussex. The West Indies' surprisingly early World Twenty20 Championships exit allowed Chanderpaul to play in Kent. Lancashire were at Surrey, Sussex at bottom-placed Worcestershire. Benkenstein made 117 at Canterbury, where the next-highest score was 54, and when Durham clinched their eight-wicket win at 12.19pm on day three, they went top of the Championship. Surrey beat Lancashire, but Sussex won at Hove to claim their third title in five seasons.

Canterbury was Gibson's farewell before becoming England's bowling coach and, compared to the legendary Adam Gilchrist by Warne at Lord's, Mustard joined him in Sri Lanka as back-up Test wicketkeeper and limited-overs first-choice. He kept his white-ball place in New Zealand, but it would be a short-lived international career. The following winter Mustard was working as a landscape gardener. What Durham achieved was more enduring.

'You could tell it was the start of something, we were ready to take the whole country by storm,' says Harmison. 'The southern teams were beaten by the time they got to Nottingham because they'd have to have two stops on the bus and, by the time they got to Leeds, they were still two-and-a-half hours away thinking it was going to be freezing and they didn't fancy facing Harmy, Plunkett and Onions, or getting Diva and Benki out. For us, 2007 was the turning point.' The last words of Cricinfo's match report from Lord's read: 'It may be their first trophy; it won't be their last.'

9.

Playing the Numbers Game

ONE would have thought England's newest first-class county and its 21st-century format ought to have been a good mix, but Durham have been slower than most to get to grips with Twenty20 cricket – on and off the field. International 20-over matches have always been well-attended at the Riverside, but it has never come close to selling out for a domestic game, despite heavy investment at times in some of the best players to grace the format.

Incredibly, in its first 16 seasons the Twenty20 Cup has been shared around 12 counties – but not Durham. Only Derbyshire and former champions Middlesex have won fewer matches in the competition. Durham's stirring performances in 2016 and 2018 improved crowds, and the consistent form of the second XI has raised hopes the tide could turn but, for now, their 20-over record is patchy at best. Nothing highlighted the county's muddled thinking more than their first appearance at Finals Day, at Hampshire's Rose Bowl in 2008.

Durham won their maiden Twenty20 match, beating Nottinghamshire by six wickets at the Riverside in 2003, but in the first five seasons of the new competition they recorded just eight victories from 34 games, finishing bottom of the northern group twice, and one-from-bottom in the other three summers. It was 2008 before they reached the knockout stages, and when they got there it was shambolic.

Eight minutes before the quarter-final between Durham and Yorkshire was due to start, spectators in the Riverside were informed it had been abandoned. Those who stayed at home to watch on television found out first. 'We've looked like amateurs,' said an angry David Harker. It had come to light that Yorkshire had fielded an ineligible player in the group stage, where they were one of two best third-placed teams.

Off-spinner Azeem Rafiq had not taken a wicket or batted in Yorkshire's nine-wicket win over Nottinghamshire ten days earlier – his biggest contribution was messing up a run-out by knocking the bails off with his hand – and was not in the squad to play Durham. The 17-year-old was born in Pakistan and, although he had lived in Barnsley for seven years, did not have a British passport or a permit to live and work permanently in the country. Yorkshire had quietly been fined £500 for not filling out the necessary paperwork. They were not the only team Rafiq had played for, either – he also captained England Under-15s and Under-16s, and played for the Under-17s. The ECB called off the quarter-final while they worked out what to do next.

It was an important decision. That winter the Champions League was born, bringing together eight teams from the Indian, Australian, South African and English Twenty20 leagues. The Twenty20 Cup finalists would compete for the £2.5m prize fund, £1m of which went to the winners. The English champions would also be invited to play an exhibition game in Antigua as part of the ill-fated Stanford Super Series, which was reckoned to be worth between £100,000 and £190,000. Having won their group losing only once (they also had a tie and two no-results), Durham fancied their chances.

Nottinghamshire would have qualified for the quarter-finals had they beaten Rafiq and Yorkshire, a tie would have seen Glamorgan through. Durham's right to be there was indisputable, but a bye into

Finals Day would deny them a bumper pay-day, with 6,000 tickets sold for the derby. Durham might also be without both their South African internationals for a rescheduled game. Albie Morkel's contract was due to run out after the original date, and Shaun Pollock was supposed to be commentating on the second England versus South Africa Test, which could clash with a fresh match.

When the game Rafiq played in was awarded to Nottinghamshire, Glamorgan appealed and instead neither side was awarded points from the game, putting the Welshmen into the knockout stages as the next-highest-placed team. Durham's quarter-final was played 15 days late, only four days before Finals Day. The ECB offered to fly them back after their Sunday game at Uxbridge to play on Monday night, but Durham preferred an extra day's preparation, even if that meant paying for a bus back. They also had to install the temporary floodlights needed for Wednesday's Pro40 game against Somerset a day early, and donated the receipts from the new quarter-final to charity. They did at least have Pollock available after Sky Sports and *Test Match Special* released him without having to be asked – although, as it turned out, the Test did not run into Tuesday anyway.

Shivnarine Chanderpaul made his Durham Twenty20 debut as Morkel's replacement, but when the West Indian was out in the seventh over Durham were 49/4, having been put in. As with Phil Mustard and Paul Collingwood, a poor shot was to blame. Batting at five to accommodate Collingwood and Chanderpaul, Will Smith was dropped on 36 and lucky to escape an lbw shout on 45, but rode it out to make 51 from 38 deliveries. Liam Plunkett scored 12 off the final three deliveries to see Durham to 163/8, then took a wicket with the opening ball of Glamorgan's innings – removing their top three in a decisive spell of 3-0-16-3. Mike Powell's wicket owed much to a brilliant low catch from man-of-the-match Smith, who also ran out Alex Wharf. 'They were never really in the hunt,' says Smith.

Durham were through to Finals Day at the Rose Bowl but, with the Boat Show also on in Southampton that weekend, there were no rooms in the city's inns for supporters to stay at such short notice. I was fortunate my brother Ross lived there. Maybe the last-minute preparations were a factor in a semi-final performance against Middlesex which Geoff Cook called, 'a bit surreal… brains did not kick into gear', but Gareth Breese is not buying it. 'No excuses,' he says. 'When you turn up on a big day and don't play well, you're going to lose.' Durham's most experienced player let them down.

Later that day Chanderpaul went top of the world Test batting rankings but, although he had 241 limited-overs caps for West Indies, this was only his 13th Twenty20 game, and his last for Durham. 'All I remember was Shiv's batting,' says Collingwood. 'I remember the game for the wrong reasons because we turned up all excited and it was a bit of a damp squib for us; we performed really poorly. We were kind of blown away before we'd known it and we were very conservative, whereas in 2007 [in the Friends Provident Trophy Final] we were all guns blazing.'

The wickets of Mustard and Michael Di Venuto brought Chanderpaul to the crease at 34/2. His 48 from 47 deliveries might have been useful in different circumstances, but saw Durham to just 138/6. 'We were almost playing risk-free cricket,' Dale Benkenstein reflected afterwards. 'I asked Shiv if he realised it was 20 overs, not 40, because he was batting well for a 40-over game.'

Smith, who made 21, 'was trying as hard as I could to push it on but every time I went for a big shot I'd mistime it and it would skew out to the sweeper or whatever. Shiv was just knocking things around and we kept chatting in the middle and I kept saying, "I think we've got to go." I was trying! I remember looking at all the guys to come and there was this real conflict thinking, "I'm trying as hard as I can to score as fast as I can," but, bar trying to get out, what else could I do? Time ran out for the people coming in. We got nowhere near enough. Even 150, 160 gives you a little bit more – it's funny the difference between that and 130 in T20 because it just takes one or two good overs and 160 gets tricky.'

Fast bowler Stephen Harmison was bemused. 'It was bizarre,' he says. 'I don't think we read the conditions on a slow pitch and we

got nowhere near enough runs. You look at the side we had – Jesus!
– ten internationals and Will Smith, so to lose in the manner we did
against a decent side… To this day I just can't put my finger on what
happened, we just got bogged down and it was a long way to go to be
rabbits in the headlights.'

Promoting hitters up the order once Chanderpaul and Smith were
out, Benkenstein did not bat or risk bowling his or Collingwood's
medium-pacers with so few runs to defend. Middlesex's Tyron
Henderson smashed seven sixes in his unbeaten 57 from 22 deliveries.
Durham only managed two. Named in the England squad that day for
the first time since the tour of New Zealand, Harmison's 3.4 overs cost
47 runs. The Crusaders won by eight wickets with 26 balls remaining
– a Twenty20 hammering. Durham had to watch Middlesex win the
final on television because they were rushed out of their dressing
room to make way for second semi-finalists Kent.

Although Pollock was a Kolpak signing, and although he and
Morkel played in the Friends Provident Trophy semi-final and Morkel
filled in for a Championship match, they were essentially the first
overseas players Durham signed specifically for Twenty20. 'Shaun
Pollock was a significant investment for us at the time – it doesn't
seem so now – but that was when Clive [Leach, the chairman] was
wanting to try and be competitive on all fronts,' recalls then-chief
executive David Harker. 'He was a bit like Hussey in so far as he had
a particular reputation, not only for his playing ability, but the type
of individual he is.'

Durham's joint-leading wicket-taker with Plunkett lived up
to his billing. 'I loved having Shaun Pollock around because of his
enthusiasm for the game,' comments Smith. 'He had such a love of
being active. Every practice session we had suddenly took on a new
meaning because he would be charging around setting scenarios in
the nets and giving everything a spark, which I'm sure had a huge
effect in getting to the final.' Breese says Pollock 'had a huge impact in
a short period of time and had similar characteristics to Benkenstein
– it's no surprise they went to school together.'

Twenty20 cricket was fast becoming vital to county balance sheets. A shorter form of the game was first suggested by the ECB in 1998 but shelved after opposition from the counties. When it was revived, Durham were expected to vote against, but chairman Bill Midgley's late change of mind meant they were one of 11 counties to vote for it, with the MCC abstaining. It really took off in late 2007 when Zee Telefilms missed out on the broadcast rights for India's internationals and, taking a leaf out of the Kerry Packer manual, Subhash Chandra set up his own competition, the Indian Cricket League (ICL). Like Packer's World Series Cricket, it controversially sat outside of the established order. Benkenstein was prevented from playing for Natal that winter because he joined the ICL, and Durham were initially unsure if he would be available to them in Twenty20. More significantly, the Board of Control for Cricket in India launched the Indian Premier League (IPL) in April 2008, and it quickly became the world's most lucrative and successful domestic competition.

It was therefore important to Leach and his Indian investors to take Twenty20 seriously and, even as they started to rein in their overseas signings in other formats, they continued to press ahead with trying to sign 20-over stars of the present and the future. 'I think our policy to try and encourage our own players in the longer forms of the game is the right one, but in Twenty20, which is more about entertainment, excitement and individual performances, we think it's right to sign overseas players,' Cook argued. Harker believes: 'Some people are coming for a cricket match and they want to see top players and an exciting game, and then there's the people coming for an evening out and the cricket's kind of the backdrop. I don't think the game generally has ever fully got its head around what it [Twenty20] is meant to be. That will be really interesting for the new competition [The Hundred], which is being promoted as a competition for non-cricket people, to see whether they can make that work.'

In 2009 Durham were stargazing. Australian opener David Warner had only made one first-class appearance but was already a Twenty20 international. The Riversiders signed one of 20-over cricket's most exciting talents – even though once he had played for Delhi Daredevils in the IPL semi-finals, then for Australia at the World Twenty20 Championships, then for Australia A in Pakistan, they got only three group games but 113 runs out of him. When Durham finished second in the northern group, the plan was to fly Warner from Australia for the quarter-final in Canterbury and he would either head straight home or hang around for Finals Day, depending on whether Kent were beaten. In the end, Warner travelled halfway around the world for four balls. He didn't even take a catch. Di Venuto made way for his compatriot and, with Mustard already out for a golden duck when Wayne Parnell dismissed Warner too, the visitors were 5/2 chasing 150. Ian Blackwell was run out without facing a ball in the 56-run defeat.

Albie Morkel returned for 2010 but he, like fellow overseas player Ross Taylor, was delayed by the IPL. Durham decided against signing stand-ins. Morkel and Taylor's experience was worth waiting for. The South African had played in two IPL finals for Chennai Super Kings, winning the 2010 game, while Taylor was a runner-up with Royal Challengers Bangalore in 2009 and had played in a Champions Trophy Final and World Cup 50- and 20-over semi-finals with New Zealand. The pair finished first and second in Durham's batting averages, but the Riversiders were eighth in their nine-team group, winning four of 16 games. For the next seven seasons, the county never filled both available overseas slots.

In 2011 they went for another rising star in David Miller, who averaged 41 playing Twenty20 for South Africa, but only 27 for Durham. They reached the quarter-finals, but were bowled out for 99, their lowest score since their last-eight appearance in 2009. Collingwood missed the game with back spasms, while Hampshire's top-scorer was Neil McKenzie, who had not played Twenty20 when at Durham in 2008. The Riversiders went into the game top of the Championship and joint-top of their 40-over group, but after the 55-run defeat Benkenstein said: 'We have to learn to perform on the big occasions.'

In 2012 Durham were inspired by Perth's run to the Big Bash Final, signing Mitchell Johnson and Herschelle Gibbs, Collingwood's team-mates with the Australian side the previous winter. Johnson's IPL deal with Mumbai was cancelled because of a foot injury, but Durham signed him because the indications were that, despite having recovered, he would not make Australia's one-day tour of England. When that was proved wrong, another contract had to be ripped up. Collingwood missed the entire competition with a broken right hand, but at least 38-year-old Gibbs topped Durham's batting averages. That year the format went back to three groups of six, and Durham missed out on the knockout stages with the worst record of the third-placed sides.

'The club's ambition was obvious,' Cook reflects. 'If you look at the players we signed at no small expense – Pollock, Morkel, Ross Taylor, Gibbs, Warner – they've all been top-class Twenty20 players. I suppose the hope was that they could provide the magic formula because we had our own players too like Mustard, and Dale was a top-class player, but we never clicked.'

There was a sense too that Durham were sometimes lukewarm towards the format. 'I don't think it was intentional, I just think once we'd got a one-day trophy, we'd got a squad together, the next thing was to push for a Championship, then it was to back it up,' says Breese, regarded as a limited-overs specialist during the glory years. 'It just kind of took its course so when [Graham] Onions and people were doing well you would manage their workloads and give other people opportunities in limited-overs cricket.'

Jon Lewis, who was the county's first-team coach from 2013–18, believes: 'We'd always been a very strong red-ball [first-class] county; we always put quite a lot of stock in that. The traditions of the game are important to Durham and of all the punishments we got hit with in 2016, losing first-division [Championship] cricket was, from an ego point of view for the club, quite a hard one to take because we probably measured ourselves almost exclusively by it, even though our first trophy was in the 50-over comp in '07. We came second in the Championship that year and we probably saw that as being as important in some respects.'

Cook insists Twenty20 was never taken lightly. 'I've always found it a mystery,' he replies when I ask him to explain the disparity between Durham's Championship consistency and their comparative 20-over struggles. 'In four-day cricket the planning was always on a softly-softly basis, whereas, at that time, T20 would hit you in the middle of the season and everything would be suspended so you think, "We've got to do some really specific planning for T20." The volume of chat and tactics and individual practice far outweighed anything that ever went on in four-day cricket, but unfortunately it wasn't reflected in performances.

'Maybe we were putting too much pressure on the players because it meant a lot to the clubs. The winners went into the Champions League so there were substantial rewards. I think the board were living in silent hope rather than putting on pressure, saying, "We have to win the T20," but when it came around I sensed if we didn't win a game there was a little bit of a "Here we go again" attitude. Possibly our inferiority complex lingered a bit longer in T20. Until you actually achieve something, there's always that sense of "Can we?"'

Few English cricketers have more Twenty20 expertise than World Championship-winning captain Collingwood. 'I think confidence and momentum are the key things and we've probably lost games that have dented our confidence,' he says. 'It can happen in that form of the game. If you're going to win things you've got to err on the more aggressive side of the line and I guess we've probably been on the more conservative side. But it comes down to people in form at the right time and all that kind of stuff.'

In 2013 Durham had one of the country's leading wicket-takers when Usman Arshad claimed 22 in 13 games, and only the fifth player to make 100 Twenty20 Cup appearances in Mustard. They were missing Collingwood for the final four group games, but an in-form Ben Stokes more than made up for it as he smashed 72 not out,

46, 41 not out, and ten not out as Durham reached the quarter-finals with four straight wins. Again, though, they fluffed their lines, an 89-run opening stand between Northamptonshire's David Willey (46) and Kyle Coetzer (44), who left Durham in 2011, quickly putting the game out of reach.

It was not just on the field where Durham were struggling to crack Twenty20. 'You would think it would be a natural sell,' argues David Harker. 'You wouldn't have to convert many of our [region's] natural football fans to have a good crowd. Whether that's because we simply haven't been good enough at marketing it, selling it and getting the understanding out there, or whether this is such a football area that Twenty20 is still perceived to be cricket for cricket fans, rather than a form of cricket for sports fans, I don't know. One of the consequences of not having any money is that you're not in the position to make the investment you might always like to in the marketing team, the website, ticket systems, etc. We kind of had to do it on a bit of a shoestring.'

Perhaps the biggest problem is the Riverside's location. In the early 1990s, building sports stadia was all about out-of-town locations with lots of land and car-parking space, which is why the Rose Bowl was constructed on the outskirts of Southampton in 2001, and why a 57-hectare site just off the A1(M) felt ideal to Durham's pioneers. Twenty20 cricket changed the landscape – it is a city game. Durham prefer to host Sunday afternoon games as family affairs, and the long queues when the home players sign autographs at the end of Riverside games shows why, but when the competition was spread across the whole season in 2014 – and rebranded as The Blast – the ECB tried to concentrate on Friday nights as an after-work (alcohol-fuelled) spectacle. The Riverside is poorly served by public transport on Friday evenings – most trains on the East Coast Main Line zoom through it, only stopping to pick up passengers to and from Newcastle and Sunderland every couple of hours – and from early Friday afternoon A1(M) traffic reduces to a crawl, usually more than doubling journey times.

Harker smirks when I ask where, if given another chance to build Durham's ground, he would like it to be. 'St John's Wood,' he says, flippantly. 'There was talk at the time this was built about the Racecourse at Durham and also around Gateshead Stadium. The way the game is going, being on an effective public-transport network would be interesting, but it's pointless even thinking about it. Pre-Twenty20, good county crowds were in a few thousand. If the event's big enough it doesn't matter where the ground is, people will come, so for international cricket it hasn't mattered so much. It's domestic cricket where if we were on the [Tyne and Wear] Metro or something like it, it would make a big difference – or you would think so, but who knows?' Steve Coverdale, part of the TCCB's working party when Durham turned first class, thinks north-east rivalries had to be considered too. 'You've got to be very neutral in terms of Newcastle, Sunderland, Durham and Middlesbrough,' he argues.

Like his fellow director Tom Moffat, Bob Jackson is adamant Durham made the right decision. 'I think the Riverside is a good location,' he argues. 'It's perhaps just a tad far away from the cities – Sunderland and Newcastle – but I think it's good; the parking's first class, the only thing it lacks is a hotel. I've never had any doubts about my support for that location.'

Nevertheless, the numbers do not add up. In 2010 only four counties recorded smaller Twenty20 gate receipts than Durham, whose combined 31,253 attendance was less than half London-based Middlesex and Surrey's. In 2016 Durham's average 3,606 crowds were, as a percentage of capacity, the lowest of any county; only Leicestershire, Derbyshire and Northamptonshire's aggregate gates were smaller. In 2017 Durham's new board introduced a bus service for fans and targeted a 25 per cent increase but, not helped when their derby with Yorkshire clashed with Sunderland's first football match of the season or by their miserable form, had to settle for 15 per cent. The seven per cent increase in the 2018 group stage was well ahead of the national average, but even a 5,887 crowd for the quarter-final, where juniors were allowed in for free, paled into insignificance alongside the grounds chosen instead to host the new 100-ball franchise competition from 2020.

Even the increased crowds have been a mixed blessing, but the good outweighs the bad. 'We've had so many more kids in during 2018, which is fantastic,' says Harker's successor as chief executive, Tim Bostock. 'The downside is they don't drink beer so whilst our attendances are up the revenues are down slightly, but there are long-term benefits.' The youngsters on the field offer hope too. Durham reached Finals Day in the Second XI Twenty20 four times between 2013 and 2018, and although they lost all those semi-finals, the 332-mile bus journey from Chester-le-Street to Arundel, where the games are played, was probably a big factor.

Where once Durham's academy churned out orthodox cricketers who learnt the fancier short-form skills later, the process is being reversed nationwide. 'You see 12- and 13-year-olds playing paddles and "Dilscoops" but that's the nature of beast, it's what they see,' shrugs Neil Killeen, Durham's coach at all four second XI semi-finals. 'I've got a 13-year-old son who is captain of the county under-13s and doing very, very well, but I come in and he's watching the Caribbean Premier League or the IPL. Although he does watch Test matches at times, he's more into them. Now they're more likely to be thrown into a T20 or a one-day game [for their debut] so they have to have those skills and you then have to teach them consistency for the four-day game. North-east club cricket stood me in good stead because we played 20-over cricket, and they still do that, but the cup competitions are not as strong. Youngsters don't actually learn the clever stuff, they just do it.'

Despite that, academy manager John Windows insists: 'The long-format stuff still floats the boats of the really exceptional players. The red-ball stuff is still what they spend most of their time on. Having said that, you're more likely now to make your debut in white-ball [limited-overs] cricket than you are in red-ball, so the preparations required to get them ready for that initial experience at a young age is much greater and there's more to do to get them up to speed, from a tactical point of view as much as anything. No players have come on to the radar that you would develop purely as a Twenty20 player, it's always been a multi-format approach. I think it's down to strength and power because that's the name of Twenty20, and you're not going to get that until past [the age of] 20 anyway.

'England are nearly the world's best side at Twenty20; [Ben] Stokes and [Mark] Wood didn't play Twenty20 at academy level and they're some of the best. They've learnt all these Twenty20 skills without having that at a younger age. They haven't played it that much at county level, either. The best players in the world adapt. Power-hitting comes into it, but if you can bat, you can bat — and with the bats nowadays you don't have to be that powerful to belt the ball.'

Former coach Lewis believes attitudes have changed at the Riverside since Breese retired in 2014. 'I'd say the emphasis has shifted a little bit,' he comments. 'Without detracting from the way we viewed red-ball cricket, we had to drag our attention on white-ball cricket up a little bit. Some sides who are traditionally not as strong in red-ball cricket have been [focussing on Twenty20] for quite some time. Without diminishing red-ball cricket, we tried to give white-ball cricket equal status, which I'm afraid in the modern game traditionalists might not like it, but you have to do that. Two-thirds of our season [in terms of the number of games] was white-ball cricket so it had to at least be an equal, but I don't think it will get to the point where it becomes the priority [for Durham].'

Killeen believes Durham are now well equipped for Twenty20. 'We've got a good group of genuine all-round cricketers who are all the right sort of age,' he argues. 'It's quite an exciting group who are young and stick together, and there are exciting lads underneath. You have to target those competitions because it provides excitement from outside and the crowds we got in 2018 were brilliant. To keep pushing for those comps is great. Personally, I'd like to see the second XI competition run before the first XI competition so they can see the players that stand out. You might just pick up a couple of gems.'

The cruel irony could be that Durham are belatedly getting to grips with Twenty20 just as, domestically at least, it is about to be put into the shade by a glitzier, more glamorous and shorter little brother in The Hundred, a new competition for 2020 which will be played by franchises, not counties. Understandably given its attendances, Chester-le-Street will not be a host venue, but the first-class counties will continue to play the existing 20-over competition. 'There's a part of me that thinks if The Blast suffers, that means the 100-ball's been successful and, with the money going into it, it has to be successful or we could be in trouble,' comments Lewis. 'It's hard to see how we can have a really vibrant and successful T20 full of quality overseas players if we're also going to have a vibrant, exciting and noticeably better – it has to be noticeably better – 100-ball tournament. If it's just about the same standard, there's no point. 2018 was probably the most successful Blast and there's a lot to be positive about. We'll do it as well as we can regardless, but if it doesn't get the exposure or the attendances that might be because The Hundred is going well and usurping us.'

Tim Bostock is more confident the competitions can live together. 'You couldn't do The Hundred with 18 teams but I think the two can exist alongside one another,' he argues. 'Because The Blast is played over two and a half, three months, and because the 18 counties have got a soul, their own identities and even accents and dialects – England's a unique place like that for a fairly small island – I think it can survive. It could definitely co-exist as a feeder into this five- or six-week really glitzy event.'

Quite where Twenty20 cricket will sit in the future of English cricket, and where Durham establish themselves within it, remains to be seen but, on the bus back from the Rose Bowl in 2008, it probably felt like a rather painful distraction. The good news for the Riversiders as they made the long journey home was that they still had the incentive of another Championship title race to focus on in the final two months of what would be another historic season.

10.

'We Didn't Want That Journey to End'

'**M**Y best day in cricket was walking off the field at Canterbury in 2008, and it will always be,' insists Stephen Harmison. The fast bowler won the Ashes twice – the first time ending England's 18-year drought, the second in his final Test appearance – but it could not compete with helping Durham claim their first County Championship alongside his brother Ben. Although the Harmisons are rooted in Ashington in Northumberland, in cricketing terms Durham is their county.

The 2007 Friends Provident Trophy winners badly fluffed their lines in the semi-finals of the 2008 competition and the Twenty20 Cup. To lose as poorly as they did against Middlesex weeks after their trophy defence went up in smoke at home to Kent could have disrupted Durham's confidence as much as the different styles of cricket could disrupt their flow, but this team was having none of it.

'We'd always try to say, "Make sure we've got something to play for in the last quarter of the season,"' Gareth Breese stresses. 'You want to be involved in everything as deep as you can to keep that interest, that desire going. If you're out of everything it can be a long last six weeks or so!'

Harmison says: 'If you look at the characters in that team, that tells you why it didn't disrupt us.' Will Smith believes the separation of limited-overs and first-class teams was important, arguing: 'Having the likes of Shaun Pollock and Albie Morkel who didn't feature a huge amount in the Championship probably helped but equally the Championship team was pretty experienced. They'd seen everything.' In the winter of 2006/07 Michael Di Venuto was integral to Tasmania's first Sheffield Shield title, Dale Benkenstein captained Natal to two Currie Cups, Shivnarine Chanderpaul won the West Indies' domestic first-class competition once outright and once shared in the 1990s, and Smith the 2006 Championship with Nottinghamshire.

Durham were fortunate to only play in one of 2008's weather-hit opening three Championship rounds, drawing at home to Surrey, before a big defeat at Old Trafford. England released their centrally contracted players, but Durham were without Benkenstein, who was attending the birth of his third child in South Africa, overseas batsman Neil McKenzie, who was best man at a wedding, Graham Onions, who was on England Lions duty, and the injured Liam Plunkett. Di Venuto led the side rather than vice-captain Paul Collingwood because of his greater familiarity. Collingwood scored just four runs and took two wickets; Lancashire's Andrew Flintoff bagged a pair but made up for it with seven wickets; Harmison's match figures of 1-100 contrasted with James Anderson's 9-77. Although Mark Davies took 7-33, bowler Mitchell Claydon's first-innings 40 was the only Durham score above 25 as they were hammered by 232 runs.

A week later, Durham defeated Yorkshire by an even greater margin – 295 – with Di Venuto and the returning Onions starring. The opener cracked his left index finger after his first-innings 184, not that it stopped him helping Benkenstein set up a second-innings declaration, making 45 not out from number eight. Then Onions followed his 5-75 by removing three of the top four, only to suffer a heel injury.

Di Venuto soldiered on but the run-scoring burden on him and Benkenstein was about to ease. Smith's debut season had not gone as planned in 2007, dropped after 397 runs in 19 Championship innings. Born in Luton, Smith captained Durham University and began his professional career at Nottinghamshire. 'My first Championship hundred was against Middlesex at Lord's and fairly soon after they announced they'd signed Will Jefferson [another Durham University graduate] from Essex as an opening batter, so that made me think I was at an age where I had to see if I was good enough and go and play,' he explains. 'It wasn't going to be at Notts. I got the sense it was a club that always wanted a slightly bigger name. I floated my name around a little bit and there was a bit of interest from elsewhere, but it was Durham pushing the most and it just felt right having spent three years at university here and played against them quite regularly. I liked the people and Martyn Moxon seemed like a nice guy.

'I spent that winter in Sydney playing grade cricket and I got a call from him on a night out. He sounded quite emotional, saying he was really sorry having signed me but he'd got the opportunity to go back to Yorkshire and he felt it was right for himself and his family. There was me stood in the middle of Sydney with skyscrapers everywhere thinking, "That makes things slightly interesting," because I had no idea who might take over. It was decided fairly quickly that Geoff [Cook] would. I had a few conversations with him and met him properly around early March. I presume he'd had a large part to play in signing me because he had a say in most things that went on, so I was always fairly confident it would be fine.'

Despite a century in the Friends Provident Trophy group stage, 2007 was a season of struggle. 'I made a few battling 30s and 40s while Diva was peeling off chanceless 150s,' Smith comments. 'The first [Championship] game was at Worcestershire and I remember walking out to bat with him thinking, "This is brilliant." I really wanted as much of that as I possibly could and maybe I just searched a bit too hard in that first year. I wanted it too much, maybe, instead of relaxing and letting things happen.'

Smith was recalled for Durham's fourth Championship game of 2008. Having previously opened with Di Venuto, he returned in the position he had relinquished in the 50-over side, at the fall of the first wicket. Ask him what the most significant change was, and he replies: 'I think it must have been a more relaxed mindset. That winter I was living in Hitchin and I did some work with *All Out Cricket* magazine. I did a sports journalism course in Stoke but I ended up pulling out halfway through because it was very football-centred and I got the hump with it!

'I'd drive to Stoke on a Thursday and come up here Thursday night, do a bit of training Friday and Saturday and stay with Kyle Coetzer before driving back on Monday to go to *All Out Cricket* for three days. I was enjoying everything. I was doing enough practice but not too much, so every time I did come to practise it was really focussed and still fresh. The previous winter I'd met Kat, who is now my wife, and she was best friends with Kyle Coetzer's fiancée. That had a huge effect too. I was pretty happy with everything.

'I had a shocking pre-season – I didn't score a competitive run in April and there were a few washouts. At Campbell Park, Milton Keynes [in May], I got 99 and 146 and played really well. It coincided with Kyle not scoring many in the first four Championship games [54 in total] and they saw fit to make the change. I scored 100 in my first game at Sussex and put on quite a few [205] with Benki from 11/4. [Pakistan leg-spinner] Mushtaq Ahmed had got me out a few times previously so I had a think before the game. Previously I was just sat in my crease waiting for something to happen so I decided to take the game to him by trying to sweep every ball, basically, and it worked. I got my pad outside the line of off stump and swept everything and I managed to survive and score a few off the other guys.

'By the end they had a short leg, a short fine leg, deep backward square, a man just in front of square on the boundary and a man just in front of the [square-leg] umpire saving one because it was the only shot I was playing. I thought if I tried something else I'd probably get out. I ended up nailing a sweep hard to the man at square leg [Chris Nash], who took a one-handed catch. I thought afterwards there was no shame in it because it was what I'd been doing all innings, and we ended up winning by seven wickets.' It was champions Sussex's first home defeat since 2004. Some good 50-over performances kept Smith ticking over until his next significant four-day score, only the third Championship double hundred by an Englishman for Durham, as Surrey lost by ten wickets at Guildford.

With Smith, Benkenstein and Di Venuto scoring runs, Durham were fortunate to see plenty of one of the world's best fast bowlers. Harmison won his 50th Test cap in May 2007, but between England's final Test that year, in Sri Lanka, and their last against South Africa in the summer of 2008, he made just one international appearance. England's 189-run defeat to New Zealand in March 2008 was the last time Matthew Hoggard wore the Three Lions and it seemed the same might be true of Harmison, who took 1-121.

Having retired from one-day internationals in autumn 2006, Harmison made 12 Championship, 14 one-day and seven Twenty20 appearances for Durham in 2008, playing like a man with a point to prove. He insists not. 'I was past caring,' he says. 'I wasn't enjoying playing for England because I didn't enjoy the set-up. I was more old-school and it was starting to become a little bit more cut-throat. But 2008 and 2009 were two of my happiest years playing cricket because I was enjoying playing with the likes of Benki and Diva more than with an England side which had lost its edge, with Simon Jones, Hoggard, Michael Vaughan, Geraint Jones and Ashley Giles gone, and Flintoff playing on one leg.

'At that time if you gave me a ball in a feel-good environment, I couldn't give a flying fuck who was 22 yards away, I always believed I was better than them. When I got on a roll I felt as though I was hard to stop and in '08 and '09 Durham couldn't have got me at a better time in first-class cricket. People will say I was trying to prove a point to the ECB, but honestly I wasn't – I was trying my best to win matches for Durham and the ECB benefitted, but I wasn't putting two fingers up at them or the selectors, I didn't care what they were thinking. I was quite happy moving on to the next venue and turning the next team over.'

Despite only two five-wicket hauls – he also took a hat-trick at Hove – Harmison claimed 60 Championship victims in 2008. Only James Tomlinson, Tim Murtagh and Adil Rashid had more, all at a higher average. Top of the national averages was Mark Davies, although 30 of his 39 wickets came in three games, and Durham lost two. Callum Thorp took 50 Championship wickets but it was Harmison who put fear into the opposition and confidence into his team-mates. 'When you've got one of the world's best bowlers and you bring Liam Plunkett through and you've got Callum Thorp, Graham Onions, Diva, Benki... Durham built a prolific team,' says Phil Mustard.

Harmison argues: 'If you've got somebody to aspire to, your younger players will perform at their absolute maximum, like I did under David Boon. Plunkett and Davies weren't there to get the five and six wickets, that was my job. I felt more pressure playing for Durham than England because I felt I had to perform, but it inspired me because I loved playing for Durham and I wanted my mates to be successful.'

Their first chance of 2008 glory came in the Friends Provident Trophy, with Harmison's 16 wickets a big factor in escaping a tight group. At the Riverside, Yorkshire were beaten by five runs and Lancashire six, but away from home Derbyshire won by one run, while Steven Croft hit the six Lancashire needed off the final ball at Old Trafford. Level on points with Yorkshire, group winners Durham progressed to the quarter-finals where Gareth Breese's 34 not out saw them through another thriller, beating Nottinghamshire by one wicket.

Durham rolled out the big guns at home to Kent but lost a disappointingly one-sided semi-final as Shaun Pollock and Albie Morkel failed to fire. Harmison took all four Kent wickets, Smith made 56 and Benkenstein 80 not out, but the South Africa all-rounders had combined bowling figures of 17-0-126-0. Morkel made nine runs, Pollock 18.

Kent's Joe Denly and Robert Key added 96 for the first wicket and after Harmison removed his good friend, Denly and Martin van Jaarsveld made centuries. If 301/4 looked imposing at the start of Durham's innings, it was even more so nine balls in on 2/2. They were bowled out 83 runs short. Losing their Twenty20 semi-final heavily too could have broken Durham's season. They were ten points off the Championship pace in third with a game in hand, having won four of eight matches. Durham cleared their Twenty20 hangover with an equal share of the spoils in a rain-hit game at leaders Nottinghamshire, then took revenge over Kent in a controversial match at the Riverside.

Although rain wiped out all but the first 16 minutes before lunch, there were 15 wickets on day one and 23 on a second day curtailed by bad light. Durham were 146 all out after being put in, but it looked an awful lot better once Kent were dismissed for 78. After the hosts made 108 second time around, Key promoted number-ten Amjad Khan and number-nine Ryan McLaren to three and four respectively to swing the bat at their target. At an equally seamer-friendly Stockton two years earlier van Jaarsveld led the way with the season's fastest century – this time his 65-ball 53 was the game's only fifty, but still Durham wrapped up a 43-run victory on day three. Without Harmison, recalled by new England captain Kevin Pietersen, Davies claimed match figures of 10-45.

The pitch panel convened on day two decided no action was needed, perhaps considering the pre-match rain's disruptive effect on groundsman Dave Measor's preparations. Having seen the same reaction at Stockton in Grangefield Road's final Championship match, Key was furious. Normally the media ask to speak to players after the match, so when it happens in reverse, you can usually expect something good. 'The pitch liaison committee were down and we had an interview,' Key revealed. 'It was a bit of a Muppet show in hindsight because by all accounts there was no excessive seam movement, which is absolutely ridiculous. I just worry about the integrity of the rest of the tournament. What has to happen for a pitch to get docked points?' Umpire John Holder reported no extravagant movement or variable bounce, but Key felt the pitch was two-paced and the seam movement extravagant. He accepted the track was not dangerous, but argued: 'If you're not going to do anything about a pitch like that why are you wasting your money paying these blokes a salary to go around the country looking at these wickets?' Getting it off his chest cost Key £1,000.

For only the second time in Riverside history, there was not a ball bowled when Nottinghamshire visited in the wettest part of a damp season. Durham went to Basingstoke in sight of the Championship summit only to lose a game they controlled for two of the three days needed to produce another low-scoring thriller. Hampshire were 48/0 in response to Durham's 156, yet somehow surrendered a 60-run advantage, Davies taking 8-24. Set 240 to win, Hampshire were 77/5 until Sean Ervine found the support to see them home with 94 not out.

Smith, though, continued to churn out scores, making 144 against Lancashire. 'I ended up getting 925 runs from 12 games, and I thought, "If I'd just started the [16-game] season I'd have got 1,200, 1,300!"' he says. 'Three or four games out I had 600 and I set 1,000 as my aim. Previously I'd never set a target.'

In 2008 the number of permitted overseas players was cut from two to one, and in his eight Durham innings, South African Neil McKenzie failed to make a half-century. Morkel played as a specialist batsman at Headingley before Shivnarine Chanderpaul returned to make two fifties and a hundred in 12 knocks. 'I'd been playing against Shiv since I was 17 and I played with him for West Indies,' says Breese. 'It was good for him to have someone from a similar background to bounce off because it's a long way from the culture you're used to. He fitted in really nicely because he also knew Benki.'

Chanderpaul contributed 183 runs to Durham's final two games – at home to Sussex and at Kent – to Breese's 184. Until then the latter had not featured in a Championship game since acting as an emergency opener in early July 2007. 'It came out of the blue because that year we had Gordon Muchall score five second-team hundreds, Garry Park got two,' Breese admits. 'I don't particularly know why it was me, I didn't ask. I'd put in some fairly consistent performances for the last couple of seasons in one-day cricket, doing well in pressure situations; it helped me relax.'

While Breese only contributed one century to the second XI's Championship-winning 2008, he played just three games to Park and captain Muchall's 19 combined. Only Smith averaged more than Breese's 67, and the Jamaican topped the bowling averages. 'It was a bit of a masterstroke to get his experience and calmness in,' Smith comments. 'All credit to Breesey too, the ultimate team man. He had two games to make a difference. A lot of people would have thought it was a bit annoying, but throughout his Durham career he just wanted the team to win and if he could help out in any way he would, whether it be as a 12th man, off-spinner or batter.' Breese warmed up for the Sussex game with 3-8 and 20 not out as Durham beat Gloucestershire by five wickets to secure their highest 40-over league finish of third.

Having been inserted, Durham were 143/4 in the Championship match when Breese joined Chanderpaul at the crease. Breese made 63, Chanderpaul 138, as the Riversiders claimed four of the five available bonus points, then bowled Sussex out 78 behind to take three more. With the game not starting until half an hour into day two and bad light interfering on every day, bonuses were important in the inevitable draw.

'You can say you contribute by creating a strong second team but if you don't actually play in the first team when they win, part of you is always thinking, "I didn't really get on the field,"' Breese reflects. 'That was the big part for me – trying to be a part of something. I think that's why I never thought about leaving – I enjoyed what we were building and from a limited-overs perspective I felt an integral part of moving the club forward so I thought if I wanted to play four-day cricket I just had to work hard and put performances in.'

Paul Collingwood was less anxious to contribute. Having only made two four-day appearances in 2008, he was notable by his absence at Canterbury. Harmison, Ravi Bopara, Samit Patel, Matt Prior, Owais Shah, Luke Wright, James Anderson, Ian Bell, Stuart

Broad, Andrew Flintoff, captain Pietersen and Collingwood were members of both the Test and one-day international squads that finished the summer against South Africa and started the winter in India. The first six played in the final round of Championship matches while the latter six rested. When Durham opened their Friends Provident defence with a narrow home win over Yorkshire in April, Collingwood was watching his football team, Sunderland, at Newcastle United. England were using central contracts aggressively to protect their players and because they were paying the wages, the counties could not argue.

'I wasn't a Durham player then, and to be honest with you, I didn't want to be either,' Collingwood admits. 'I wasn't the most talented person so I had to work extremely hard to stay in the England team. I always felt I was the one people wanted out of the team so it was a constant mental battle. So, when I had the opportunity to have a week off, the last thing I wanted to do was play for Durham. It was almost like the start of a new career and being part of a totally isolated team, putting all my efforts into it. When I had a week off I would want to recharge my batteries.

'I don't remember too much of the early [Durham] games because I was so focussed on playing for England, but if you ask me about any England game I played I can go "Bangladesh!" and I remember it. The Durham stuff, the early years were all personal development and making sure I was performing and when I got in the England squad it was only England, I had to give myself the best opportunity to do it for as long as possible. From the point where I got the captaincy [of Durham in 2012], I can remember everything.'

Collingwood was first named in an England one-day squad the day before his 25th birthday in 2001, and although he made his Test debut at Galle in late 2003 when Nasser Hussain had flu, it was only in late 2005 that he became an all-formats regular, remaining so until 2011. In that period Collingwood played 245 games, including warm-up matches on England tours. Only four were in the Championship, making a high score of 58 and taking six wickets. He played just 13 limited-overs matches for Durham and did not make his domestic Twenty20 debut until 2008, playing six matches where he excelled as a bowler and disappointed as a batsman. Between returning from the Caribbean in early April 2009 and the mid-May Riverside Test, Collingwood only faced 20 deliveries, having not featured for Delhi Daredevils at the Indian Premier League. Despite that, he turned down the opportunity to play for Durham in the Friends Provident Trophy at Bristol and Hove. At Chester-le-Street for the pre-Test press conference I noted 'Collingwood has the look of a stranger in his own supposed home' as he surveyed the new scoreboard and second tier added to the County Durham Stand.

His international performances justified it, and Durham benefitted once his England days were over. 'In many ways that was why I came back [to play county cricket] because I knew fine well that I didn't give anything during that period,' Collingwood says. 'You want to give something back once you've finished putting all your efforts into international cricket. You've got to make strong decisions and be really focussed and understanding on what you need as a player. I found international cricket mentally really tough so I never worried about what people thought. I was in the bubble, completely seeing England as my number-one interest. Harmy would have felt a lot closer to Durham. I kind of just wanted them to get on with it.'

There was, says Harmison, no hard feelings from him. 'I didn't think I was a Durham player either,' he admits. 'You've got other priorities and Durham had other priorities too. Paul was playing all formats [for England]; I'd retired from one-day cricket in 2006 so I'd have five or six games back at Durham no matter how much Test cricket I played. I dipped in and out and it gave me a bit of energy. Colly didn't have that, he had total detachment.' Collingwood more than compensated for five lukewarm seasons with eight more of total commitment, including six and a half as captain, after his international days.

With Harmison back after facing South Africa, Onions and Plunkett were left out of the final three games of the 2008 title run-in. The heel injury the former suffered against Yorkshire kept him out for six weeks and, although he played three more games, he only took three wickets. Durham at least gave both votes of confidence with two-year contracts, Onions ignoring interest from Warwickshire to sign his. It meant Durham ended their Championship season with more players born outside England – Di Venuto, Benkenstein, Chanderpaul, Breese, Paul Wiseman and Callum Thorp – than in it.

For the second year running, Durham arrived in Canterbury as title outsiders. They were third, two points behind Somerset, who hosted Lancashire. On the back of crushing Surrey, Nottinghamshire were a further eight points in front and the television cameras and the trophy followed Hampshire to Trent Bridge for a coronation. Durham had other ideas. 'There was a real drive having finished second the previous year,' says Smith.

Nottinghamshire started with six wickets before lunch, and despite resistance from Nic Pothas and Dimitri Mascarenhas, ended day one needing one more first-innings wicket, soon taken the next morning. Despite rain delaying the start and bad light hastening the finish, it was similar at Canterbury, where Benkenstein put Kent in and Stephen Harmison took four wickets. Unsurprisingly in late September, the ball was even on top at Taunton, where Lancashire closed on 56/4 in reply to Somerset's 202 all out.

'We didn't actually hit the top of the table until the last game but I had this feeling,' Smith recalls. 'I'm stupidly positive at the best of times but all along I was thinking and saying we would win it. I had no doubt. Maybe I conned myself a bit.' Durham more than doubled Kent's 225, Smith making 81, Phil Mustard 83, Di Venuto 90 and Breese 121 not out. It was the first time since Headingley in 2006 that Durham had scored 500, and that was not the only parallel. Again, Nottinghamshire were self-destructing live on television. Eight behind after the first innings, Hampshire declared on 449/5 in the second.

'The third morning at Canterbury was the first time that season I thought we could win the league,' Harmison admits. 'We thought we'd finish second, Notts couldn't make a mess of it. The third day was extraordinary because all of a sudden they had a bit of a wobble and it was, "Christ almighty, we can win the league here," then, "We're going to win the league here!"

'Notts lost that league. It was in their hands. To this day I still don't know how England lost the 2004 ICC Trophy Final and Notts probably think the same about the 2008 Championship. They were out in front going into the last game. It probably took the pressure off. It was our last game of the season, playing away with a bus journey back and you'd have a few beers. You just wanted to finish on a high and then all of a sudden Notts were wobbling.'

As Hampshire piled on the runs at Trent Bridge, Somerset were heading for defeat, with Lancashire 122/0 chasing 182. Durham had five more wickets to take but Davies was struggling with injury and Harmison cracked a bone in his left wrist when Geraint Jones hit the ball at him in the gully. No matter, Thorp had taken the first five himself.

'I remember waking up on the fourth morning and it was foggy, and bizarrely that was the only point I'd ever felt nervous about it throughout the whole season,' Smith claims. 'I suddenly thought, "This is going to happen? Surely nothing can go wrong?" In the morning we had a little huddle as usual and Benki was just so calm, so measured. He said every day we'd gone about our business in a really confident and assured fashion, just do the same today – or words to that effect. A lot of captains would get ahead of themselves and become emotional or frantic but he kind of calmed my nerves a little bit.'

Harmison had already shown his determination not to miss Durham's big day. 'I'd broken my wrist and been to hospital,' he recalls. 'I came back with a cast on and the management were twitchy as anything. It was the first time I'd seen them like that. There was a misfield, someone kicked the dirt and the dressing room was getting heated up. It wasn't enjoyable. I thought, "I can't sit here any more," so I got my whites on and got back out there. I could still bowl and I said to Nige [physio Nigel Kent] I'd be fine. It felt sore bowling but the alternative was to sit in a nervous dressing room.

'Thorpy bowled brilliantly. He was swinging it beautifully and it was like bowling with Hoggy [Harmison's former England new-ball partner Matthew Hoggard] again. It let me be ultra, ultra-aggressive and it was coming out of my hand at good pace. I'd get the odd one off the glove and he was challenging the edge and the pad. He bowled a great spell, 7-88. We bowled 46 out of the 61 overs. It was a great day and a great week.'

Breese says: 'Me and Callum had been so close because we had lived together for three years. For him to get a career-best seven-fer and me to get a hundred, it was really special. [Former West Indies captain] Jimmy Adams came to the end of that game because he'd played north-east league cricket with a lot of the guys who'd come into that team and I guess he wanted to see Durham in a position where they could possibly win a County Championship. It was just an amazing feeling.'

After Thorp took the first seven wickets, Harmison mopped up the tail as Durham spent just 55 minutes taking the five final-day scalps needed. Victory by an innings and 41 runs was confirmed at 11.44am when Kent's Martin Saggers, who hastily joined Durham from Norfolk in 1996 to cover for Simon Brown's England debut, was lbw to Stephen Harmison. His brother Ben – who had taken a first-innings 2-34, then scored 26, opening with Di Venuto – was first on the scene as Stephen was submerged by Durham players, his injured wrist poking out of the melee for protection.

Tom Moffat and Bob Jackson, members of Durham's original board, were there, as usual. 'Lord's [in 2007] was fantastic but that was better still,' says Jackson. 'I took immense pride for some of my colleagues – Tommy Moffat must have given 30 years to the minor county as a player and administrator, and there were others. I didn't think [winning the Championship] would be possible in such a short period of time.' Club president Moffat recalls, 'My wife Nancy and I left Canterbury for home when they came off the field not knowing whether Nottinghamshire had won or lost. Someone rang me in the car to say we were champions because they'd lost. I was a lucky president and it's better to be born lucky than good-looking.'

The players were on the bus by then, still in their kit, watching Nottinghamshire on TV. 'Every time a wicket went down everyone had to down a can of Stella – I'm sure that was Liam Plunkett's idea – so everyone was very drunk,' Smith recalls. 'We went into the Dartford Tunnel with Notts nine down. We came out of the tunnel, Sky came back on and it was all wrapped up, they replayed the wicket, did the debrief and the rest I can't really remember.'

Harmison was involved in one of cricket's most infamous celebrations when a very well lubricated England marked winning the 2005 Ashes with a Downing Street visit and parade to Trafalgar Square. He calls 27 September 2008, 'Arguably one of the best celebrations I've had. Normally you go in the dressing room and someone will go outside to talk to their family or go off and do something else. If you go out in town three people will end up getting lost or people will want to go to different bars but when you're on a bus there's 52 seats and you can't hide. The only thing we had to do was keep out of service stations, the state we were in. We stopped at Peterborough and again at the pub at Wetherby. No one wanted to leave the pub – the driver was going ballistic but we didn't want that bus journey to end.'

Smith says: 'Liam Plunkett went off to the supermarket in Wetherby and bought novelty gifts for as many people as he could think of. He was at the front of the bus on the microphone handing them out, silly things. He bought me a ridiculous pin-on cat mask because he said I owed it all to Kat. I had to wear that for the rest of the journey and was probably still wearing it when the bus pulled up at the Riverside with some fans and a Sky crew waiting for us. It's all a blur but other people have told me about it. A lot of people went off into Newcastle but I got a taxi to Kat's parents' in Whitley Bay so I turned up at three in the morning in my whites with this cat mask on. Kat's dad, who's sadly no longer with us, just thought it was brilliant.

I'd only really met them a few months earlier and I spent most of the next day [his birthday] being pretty ill but I think they understood the gravity of it.'

By winning the Championship, Durham achieved in 16 years what Gloucestershire had failed to in the 119 years since the first official competition, Somerset in 116 and Northamptonshire in 103. Some felt envy played its part in Durham's treatment in 2016, but Jackson insists: 'Jealousy didn't come to the fore [in 2008], the support for us did. The letters I got were from all over the country, and people involved in other first-class counties. Cricket's that kind of game, that's why I love it. I thought we could have a real period of dominance.' That Durham also won the Second XI Championship only encouraged those hopes. 'We had three or four great years where guys were still keen to play, still keen to impress, still getting good salaries and bonuses,' says Mustard.

The mood was matched in the boardroom. 'They were enjoying the success so the drum was always being beaten that we've got to keep going,' says coach Geoff Cook. 'Clive Leach always said, "Cricket comes first," and the club was trying to develop as a top-class international venue and to develop our young players. Young lads were starting to get a decent career from playing well for Durham, which was brilliant, really.' The 2009 season was better still.

11.

Unbeatable

WHICHEVER way you look at it, Durham's 2009 County Championship win was phenomenal. Whereas 2008's title was won in thrilling circumstances, Stephen Harmison calls its defence 'the biggest anti-climax going because no one could touch us'. In the two-division era, Yorkshire and Surrey had been relegated as champions, but only Sussex had retained their crown. Rain, bad light or both interrupted 12 of Durham's 16 games, yet their 47-point winning margin was a record since the table was split. The Riversiders won twice as many matches as anyone else in Division One and only once trailed after their first innings. It was not, though, a soft-touch league.

'I would argue until I'm blue in the face that the two or three years around that time were the County Championship's best standard of cricket because top overseas players were to an extent still available,' says Geoff Cook. 'There were lots and lots of top-class international players augmented by good-quality Kolpak signings and those numbers in a team meant that the remaining positions were filled by the best English players.'

Unlike Yorkshire in 2001 and Nottinghamshire in 2006, Durham continued on the path they had been on since Mike Hussey inspired 2005's double-promotion. 'I think there was just a natural belief in the squad and once you're winning things you get on a bit of a roll and you learn a hell of a lot,' reflects Graham Onions, who topped Durham's bowling averages that season. 'The belief in the squad gave us more opportunities to win. We had a brilliant team and I loved being in and around the dressing room because I felt a responsibility when I was playing for Durham and I did everything that was asked of me.'

Onions took 45 Championship wickets in 2009 despite playing just seven games because he had broken into England's Test squad. He was one of four bowlers to claim at least 40 victims. Phil Mustard's 79 Championship dismissals was more than any other wicketkeeper and he and four other batsmen averaged over 40, the benchmark of quality. Michael Di Venuto's 1,601 runs came at 80.05, the highest figures of an illustrious first-class career. Statistics can lie, but these do not – Durham really were that good.

Dale Benkenstein had resigned as captain after the 2008 title win. 'I'm pretty sure in my own mind that the time is right for me to step down,' he told my *Journal* colleague Luke Edwards at the club's end-of-season dinner. 'Whatever happens, though, has to be right for Durham. It has to be something the club agrees with. All I want to do is make sure Durham continue to progress and I think that will be done better without me as captain.'

Since taking the role, Benkenstein had pushed the case for a home-grown successor. At the start of the 2007 campaign he name-dropped Gordon Muchall as a potential candidate. That Muchall led Durham to the 2008 Second XI Championship illustrated the Newcastle-born batsman's captaincy credentials, but the fact he was playing at that level showed he had not achieved the potential that saw him selected for England's academy in the winter of 2002/03. His 2006 was not untypical, making 215 and 102 in his first two innings, but averaging 17.4 for the rest of the campaign until losing the number-three spot to Garry Park. A brilliant team man, Muchall's desire to do well for Durham was so intense it perhaps sapped the stamina to maintain his form over an entire season. Maybe it explained why he came to perform best in the shorter formats.

Instead, Benkenstein put forward the other name he floated in 2007 – Will Smith's. 'He has all the right character traits to be an excellent captain and he has the ability to become an excellent cricketer,' said Benkenstein. 'I'm not just talking about Durham. I think Will could, over the next three or four years, not only go on to play for England, but also captain them. He has the potential and I think Durham have a responsibility to English cricket to help him realise that potential.

'He's at an age where cricket means everything to him. He's hungry and he is determined. I was like that when I was 22 and made captain of Natal so I can recognise the signs. He would enjoy the job and he will do a good job. I don't quite have that hunger any more. I'm 34 and I've got three kids. I'm trying to be a parent, a captain and a cricketer. It's hard work and it has taken it out of me. This isn't something I've decided in the last few weeks at the end of a tiring season. I've been thinking about this for months.'

Cook had reservations. 'Dale was absolutely adamant that he was not going to be captain during that [2009] season,' he says. 'I'd tried to persuade Dale to stay on as captain and give Will another year to get his feet under the table a little bit. Then would be the time [to hand over].' Smith was thinking along similar lines. 'I thought Benki would keep going for a while,' he admits. 'I remember talking about it to him over the phone from Sydney [where Smith was again playing grade cricket that winter] and he said he thought I could be an unbelievable captain and play for England. Why should he keep doing it when he was towards the end of his career and I could make myself better as a player and a captain? It was testament to his willingness to see other people succeed. I wasn't convinced at first, I thought it was a bit soon after only one year doing well in first-class cricket, maybe I should get a bit more of a grounding, but the other side of me said, "How good an opportunity is this? I can't for one minute think of turning this down."'

Captaincy was nothing new to Smith. He had been Alastair Cook's skipper at Bedford School and led Durham University and the

British Universities. A popular figure in the dressing room, he could take confidence and authority from 1,476 runs in all competitions in 2008. Maybe 2009 could be better still. 'Every time I've had captain's positions in the past, my game's improved,' he pointed out. He would still have Benkenstein on hand, as well as Di Venuto, Mustard, Harmison, Muchall and Callum Thorp, plus Gareth Breese and Neil Killeen in limited-overs cricket, to name but a few.

'Geoff phoned me, probably November time in Sydney, to offer it and I said, "Great, I'd love it. See you when I get back,"' Smith recalls. 'I was always fine with the ins and outs of it but it was more a case of, "Let's not mess this up!" It was at the back of my mind that we'd got so many good, experienced players, don't get in the way of it that year.'

Durham's solitary winter signing showed they meant business. Like Hussey and Di Venuto before him, Ian Blackwell was an established star of county cricket when he joined Durham. An economical slow left-armer with 239 first-class wickets and an explosive batsman who averaged 39, his hefty physique limited him to one Test and 34 one-day internationals – the last in April 2006. 'I think they pigeon-hole you,' Blackwell commented on his arrival. 'They look at you and think you don't look right.' He had not given up hope of reviving his international career, but while England continued to overlook him Durham could bank on their all-rounder's availability in a way they could not with Paul Collingwood, Liam Plunkett, Harmison and Onions. Blackwell started his career with his home county Derbyshire before joining Somerset in 2000. He was much in demand when it became clear the Cidermen were starting to view him and his more laid-back approach in a similar light to England. Blackwell's season as captain had been ruined by injury in 2006 and by early June 2008 he had made his last one-day appearance for Somerset. After leaving, he told *The Independent* his successor, Justin Langer, was 'very regimented' and his methods 'a bit anal'.

Paul Wiseman had served Durham well, but replacing the New Zealand international with a quality spinner worth his place as a frontline batsman alone was a real coup. 'Blackwell had internationals under his belt and he was batting at six, getting wickets and winning games for us,' says Breese, whose right-arm delivery complemented his fellow spinner in limited-overs cricket. 'We probably hadn't had a match-winning spinner until then. Winning meant we were able to attract top players. When people want to play for you, that's a good place to be.' Durham milked it. 'We had a starting XI which was really quite powerful and we kept signing good players,' comments then-second-team coach Jon Lewis.

It needed more than just winning to attract stars, though. The Riversiders often offered more money than their rivals to sign the players they wanted. Australian-born British passport holder Mitchell Claydon was snapped up in 2006/07 when Yorkshire refused to meet demands 'well in excess of the club's pay structure', and Durham were thought to have offered the most from five counties to approach Blackwell. Will Gidman also arrived in 2006/07 but was little more than a squad player, joining Gloucestershire four years later without having made a four-day appearance. The influences of Ottis Gibson, Hussey, Benkenstein, Smith and Di Venuto lasted way beyond their departures, however. With the exception of short Twenty20 stints from overseas stars, Blackwell was Durham's last statement signing of the big-spending era.

'You see people putting a lot of money into clubs and you think, "They're just trying to buy the Championship," but Durham just tried to build a brand,' Mustard comments. 'They got people who wanted to play cricket and gave the young guys the best opportunity to lead the club forward. Durham's contracts were one in, all in. If someone was on X amount of bonuses, everyone else was. Diva was getting 1,200, 1,300, 1,400 runs a season and the bonuses for that were massive. Instead of treating everyone individually they tried to keep everyone happy. We were on good salaries but I don't think they were hurting, more the bonuses. To get Durham on the map, they had to do that or it would have been a bit like a Leicestershire or one of those clubs.'

Durham's spending reached its peak in 2012, when they breached the salary cap, leading to cricketing and financial sanctions. County wage bills were not allowed to total more than £2m a year, but with Harmison, Onions, Plunkett and Collingwood coming off England central contracts and back on to Durham's wage bill in a short space of time, they were £14,000 over the limit. That the Riversiders remain the only club to exceed the cap is tribute to some counties who also built squads packed with internationals but apparently avoided overspending.

The impetus came when Clive Leach became chairman in 2004, but he was not fighting against the tide. 'It wasn't just Clive, the board decided to pay the big wages and we were fined – not a lot, but it was a dent,' says director Bob Jackson. 'He was successful because we won the league but there was a hell of a risk in that as was proven in the end. It was probably the first trickle of a flawed business plan. I first had my concerns when we got past the limits of the salary cap. The risks involved in that were sadly borne out later on.'

In 2009, the gamble again paid off handsomely on the field, and with the ECB worried about the growing threat of Twenty20 to the established game, the prize money for winning the Championship had been increased five-fold to £500,000, £350,000 direct to the players. Winning was all that really concerned them. 'I've always seen the finances as not my business,' says Breese. 'We had loads of internationals and you've got to pay people what they're worth. It wasn't a case of trying to break the salary cap, but in professional sport if you don't look after the people winning the games for you they might go because you only play for a short time and loyalty doesn't really pay the bills. I think it was just a by-product of the success. OK, we broke the salary cap, but I don't think that was what got the club into debt. It showed cricket was the priority and we invested in it for the right reasons.'

Blackwell certainly earned his keep. He was frustrated to fall 51 short of 1,000 first-class runs in 2009 but averaged 40.05 and took 43 wickets at 23.53. He was named Durham's player of the year and the

Professional Cricketers' Association's most valuable Championship player. He made his first-class debut at Lord's in the traditional champions versus MCC game and marked it with 102. Blackwell scored 95 against Yorkshire on his Championship bow, then 50 against Somerset, was 39 not out as Durham chased down victory against Sussex, scored 68 versus Hampshire, 74 against Lancashire and 158 at Warwickshire before finally experiencing a batting failure. As a bowler, 'Blackie did what Ashley Giles did for England, just ran up and bowled it at leg stump,' says Harmison. 'He didn't give anybody any chance of scoring, then you had wicket-takers at the other end. I thought he was very under-rated for what he did for Durham. I remember [Nottinghamshire's] Ali Brown saying he'd never faced a bowling attack like ours at that time – me, Graham, Liam, Thorp and Blackie. That was a great attack.'

Smith describes Blackwell as 'the cherry on the top. With all due respect to Breesey and Paul Wiseman, he just added something slightly different with the ball and the bat, he was a complete game-changer in some situations. It was probably the perfect attack for him because there wasn't too much pressure on him and this unbelievable seam attack meant he could always bowl at the right times. Testament to whoever persuaded him to come, it was at the right time. He had a bit of motivation because of how things had gone at Somerset.'

Despite Blackwell's brilliant start, Durham made it to June without a Championship win. That did not tell the full story, though. The interruption provided by the 50-over competition's group stage meant they had only played three times, all draws. Benkenstein and Di Venuto scored centuries in two of them, Muchall one, and Durham had first-innings leads of 90, 474 and 17 against Yorkshire, Somerset and Sussex respectively. Although Geoff Cook started the season saying: 'With the squad we have there's no reason why we shouldn't be targeting every competition we enter,' Durham finished bottom of their Friends Provident Trophy group, sixth out of nine in the Pro40, and were comprehensively beaten by Kent in the Twenty20 Cup quarter-finals. The desire to improve on that would have consequences for Smith in 2010, but in 2009 it focussed minds on four-day cricket.

When the Championship resumed after its white-ball holiday, Smith put Hampshire in at the Riverside and saw his bowlers dismiss them for 105 and 96, Onions taking nine wickets in the match, Harmison six. It was the first of four crushing victories. Hampshire lost by an innings and 110 runs, Lancashire by 138 runs, Warwickshire by ten wickets and Worcestershire five. By the time the run was over Durham were 18 points clear at the top of Division One. Hampered by Mark Stoneman's hamstring injury, they had been 120/4 at Edgbaston yet Blackwell's century turned the tide so comprehensively the hosts were made to follow on.

For the second year running, Durham benefitted from England's lukewarm attitude towards their world-class bowler as the uncapped Onions pushed ahead of Harmison in the queue at the start of the summer. Both dismissed England captain Michael Vaughan in Yorkshire's draw at Chester-le-Street, but Onions's match figures of 8-106 earned him his Test debut at Lord's a week later, while Harmison, who would miss the start of Durham's Twenty20 campaign with sore shins, was overlooked. Onions repaid England's faith with 7-102 against the West Indies on a ground that often brought the best out of him.

Harmison was still hungry to play for Durham and few games showed it better than Nottinghamshire away in August. Although Benkenstein had told the media before the squad was even announced his fast bowler would not be in England's XI to face Australia at Lord's, Harmison had to wait until the teams were named at the toss before rejoining his county in case of last-minute mishaps. Under Championship rules, released England players could replace a team-mate nominated before the match. Durham's started 24 hours earlier than the Test and Harmison arrived during day two's lunch interval, by which time the hosts were replying to 356, based largely around Smith and Benkenstein's 193-run partnership. 'I got there about 20 past one [20 minutes before the resumption] and I remember Geoff saying just have some lunch, then bowl first change,' he recalls. 'I said, "Fuck that, I'm bowling now." I thought I should have played at Lord's so I wanted to bowl quickly that day.' He did.

Thanks to the merging of *The Journal*'s newsroom with the *Newcastle Evening Chronicle* and *Sunday Sun*'s, plus the fact Durham had competed for the Championship in Canterbury at the end of the last two seasons with the *Northern Echo*'s Tim Wellock and BBC Radio Newcastle's Martin Emmerson the only local media in attendance, the three Newcastle-based newspapers began covering Durham's Championship away games again in 2009, allowing me to watch Harmison's performance from the safety of the Trent Bridge press box. With no clean shirt, he wore brother Ben's beneath his jumper when he replaced Mitchell Claydon, who had contributed three runs with the bat, and maidens in his only two overs. Harmison's opening spell was even better – 8-7-1-1. Plunkett took 4-56 and Blackwell 3-6 as Nottinghamshire were made to follow on. Harmison then claimed a Durham-best 6-20 as they were bowled out for 83, 102 runs adrift. Nottinghamshire had gone into the game as Division One's only other unbeaten team, and Durham's closest rivals.

In the next game, at home to Sussex, Di Venuto made a career-best 254 not out and Smith 101 in Durham's 473/4 declared, only for the visitors to end day two 119/1. They lost 14 wickets on day three, six to Thorp. 'We learnt how to win games from non-winnable positions,' says Harmison. His captain Smith 'can't remember many occasions where we were actually up against it in games. We'd always get on the front foot and never relinquish it. We'd either bat really well first innings or bowl a team out cheaply. Plus, all the players seemed to understand the Riverside pitch perfectly that year even though it was still doing a bit. Diva just set the tone for everything and we always had decent opening partnerships.'

One of the few wobbles had come at Headingley, days before Trent Bridge. Durham had gone from 47/0 to 128/7 and 178 all out after Benkenstein – captaining while Smith dealt with a family illness – decided to bat first. Whereas Yorkshire had not won a four-day game since June 2008, Durham were so confident that some stern words at the end of day two sufficed to pull them around. Harmison's 5-20 limited the first-innings damage, and with Durham six wickets down, 96 ahead, they did what Paul Collingwood was doing in the Ashes opener at Cardiff and ground out a draw. Mustard's 85 and Plunkett's 65 allowed the Riversiders to declare.

'Guys had another year's experience and we still had people like Benkenstein and Di Venuto scoring 1,000 runs a season, so you're thinking, "Jesus, we've got the runs, Graham Onions is getting wickets for fun, Callum Thorp is as consistent as ever,"' Breese reflects. 'Blackwell was getting 35–50 wickets a season as a spinner, we had Mustard coming in at seven scoring hundreds at a good rate. It was just a proper line-up and, with our seam attack, teams were so fearful of coming to play at Durham. The tables had turned now so we were the predators and everybody felt like the prey. We knew if we got the weather, we would win eight Championship games at home, so if you match that with two or three away wins you've got it wrapped up!'

Durham were not to know when they signed him, but it made Shivnarine Chanderpaul's return rather frivolous, having done nicely without an overseas player for the first 11 games. With the West Indies players on strike for their Test and one-day series against Bangladesh, the left-hander initially netted against a bowling machine at his manager's house in Orlando, hoping it would be resolved before rejoining Durham for the visit of Warwickshire on 19 August. Chanderpaul started with a duck but won the game with a six in his second-innings 41 not out. In five matches he scored 472 runs at an eye-watering average of 236, but as I wrote at the time: 'Hugely impressive though it has been, his on-field contribution this season has been little more than icing on a very big cake.'

The inevitable title was confirmed at home to Nottinghamshire. Kyle Coetzer, who had won his place back courtesy of a Second XI Championship double hundred at Cardiff less than a month earlier, was out one run short of Benkenstein and Ottis Gibson's Durham record Championship partnership as he and Di Venuto put on 314 when Smith chose to bat first. Di Venuto ploughed on for 219, including 105 between lunch and tea, Chanderpaul made his 50th first-class hundred and Benkenstein became Durham's leading century-maker as Durham scored four hundreds in an innings for the first time in posting their biggest first-class total. Nottinghamshire wicketkeeper and captain Chris Read dislocated his thumb, Mark Ealham damaged his ribs running Coetzer out and Charlie Shreck limped off with a knee injury. 'I was feeling sorry for Notts,' admits their former player Smith, 'but I just thought, "I can't show any mercy here."'

The title was secured when Mark Davies, who missed the first two months of the season recovering from surgery on his left ankle, had Ali Brown caught behind on day three for a second bowling point. Nottinghamshire followed on as Plunkett took six wickets in the match and lost by 52 runs. With free admission, the final two days were watched by crowds of more than 4,000.

'It was a real sense of accomplishment,' says Smith. 'The team had helped me achieve something that not a lot of people ever get the chance to do; some people get the chance and don't get anywhere near captaining a team to win the County Championship. Since that season everything's ebbed and flowed for me and I often have to remind myself that actually happened, it was real. It's kept me driven, grounded and striving for more. I want to win another Championship – not necessarily as captain. That season seems like a real blur, which must mean it went incredibly well!'

The initial celebrations had to be more restrained than in 2008. Cook hosted a Saturday-night barbecue, but the sides met again in a Pro40 game the following day – another home win – and at 8am on Monday Durham boarded the bus to the Rose Bowl. With two games left, their target was to be the first Division One champions to go unbeaten through a season since Warwickshire in 2004.

'I remember the last two games more than any of them,' says Smith. 'Everyone deserved to celebrate and I celebrated as well but because a lot of guys had done so much I thought they deserved to relax – not that they probably did – and I felt a responsibility to perform. At Hampshire I ended up getting 150 because I looked around and thought, "I'm not sure anyone else is going to score runs here." We maybe could have set up the game in the second innings but there was no point and it finished as a draw.'

The Championship campaign concluded at already-relegated Worcestershire. Chanderpaul was 100 not out at the end of day two, Durham 34 ahead on 390/4. 'Worcester was the one point where I let go a bit and probably drank too much one night,' Smith admits. 'Day three was probably the only day I felt really ropey, I'm not ashamed to admit it now. It's not entirely professional but it was just a release of everything. I think there was a break and I was mindful we could still win the game. Shiv was going OK, on 180 or something, so I told him I'd probably declare when he got his 200. We could afford that luxury.

'Shiv hates fielding at the best of times and I think a few didn't fancy the idea of trudging around the field again having done it so much that season. He'd just get long hops he'd pat to point for a dot ball. I shouldn't have said it to him and we were trying to get his attention on the balcony but he'd never look up, it was hilarious. He loved batting and he didn't like fielding.' Chanderpaul dawdled for 81.1 overs doubling his overnight score before Smith called Durham in on 634/8 – their third-highest score.

Davies and Harmison – who had not bowled since the first day because of a 'swollen knee' (Chanderpaul was off the field with a 'bruised forearm') – dropped catches during Plunkett's 26-over final-day spell. The all-rounder took four wickets in each innings and finished one short of 50 Championship wickets. 'The guys that did bowl put in an unbelievable effort, giving everything to try to get another win,' Smith recalls. It looked like Plunkett had his milestone when Di Venuto took a brilliant catch, but the umpire could not be sure Richard Jones had edged the ball. Durham had to settle for seven wickets and a draw but Plunkett's 2009 efforts saw him called into the England squad to tour South Africa after a two-year absence.

The season ended with a 40-over game at Somerset, then a tour of Dublin's Guinness factory. 'The more experienced guys were around the ground at Taunton having a few pints,' says Smith. 'They came into the dressing room at various stages during Somerset's innings trying to put off [Justin] Langer and these guys, although in no way did it get disrespectful. After the game everyone came into the changing room, then everyone went to Dublin. It was a perfect way to end the season, really. The Guinness tour was an end goal for everyone, a reward. Benki and Diva probably started the Guinness theme because Benki's doctor told him he needed more iron in his diet. Benki took it that, "There's iron in Guinness, I'm going to drink it!"'

Alcohol features prominently in quite a few stories in this book, and Durham made a virtue of it in 2009. Four years earlier, Mike Hussey began the culture of heading to the bar at the end of a day's play to toast each Durham player's century or five-wicket haul. 'Hussey and Benks [Benkenstein] made sure we celebrated,' Harmison explained. 'They'd both come from successful backgrounds in teams who played in seasons where you only had ten or 12 [first-class] games a season so you had a week between and you flew between games. You'd celebrate and go hard at it because you didn't have to drive anywhere and there wasn't a one-day game tagged on the next day. We were very good at playing cricket but we were very good at celebrating too.'

Keaton Jennings was part of the later Durham sides that continued the tradition. 'If you've had a bad day, to enjoy someone else's happiness is quite tough at times but Durham have created an environment where that's what you want,' he argues. 'If somebody gets a hundred, a five-fer, a career-best, you go and have a beer with them at the end of the day. That for me was a big highlight because it shows it's a team game. It's the teams that win trophies.'

There was another side to it too. 'Benki just loved talking about the game,' says Onions. 'He loved a Guinness and he'd sit and talk about cricket. That's changed, people don't talk about the game as much. Blackie wasn't quite in that mould but we had Benki, Diva,

Ottis [Gibson in 2007–08] – these lads loved a beer and a chat and you learnt so much from them. I've never been a massive drinker so I've never been one to sit at the bar, have five or six beers and talk about the game, but you don't have to have five or six pints [Hussey said the toasts could be soft drinks] and I realise that now. I wouldn't be able to play the next time if I did that but I could have had three pints of water. Staying up and chatting to these guys for an extra half an hour is what it's all about.'

How sportsmen behave is usually viewed through the prism of results. 'I remember Mike Atherton saying once on TV when things are going well you look at three lads in the dressing room who are very close and work hard for each other, and when they aren't it's cliques,' Harmison points out. 'If the team and the individuals can handle it, the drinking side is not the problem. You tell The Colonel [Mustard] to stay in on a Saturday night before a Sunday League game and he wouldn't get a run. The game's completely different now – you wouldn't get away with half the things we did 15 years ago.'

Cricket's occasionally awkward relationship with alcohol was brought into the public glare by the 2018 court case which saw Durham's Ben Stokes cleared of affray after an incident while on England duty. When I asked Smith if he felt his Durham team got the balance between work and play right, he looks surprised to be asked. 'Yeah, yeah definitely,' he replies. 'That last game [of 2009] probably not. When we won it wasn't like we all went out and got steaming drunk, it was merely a case of sitting there enjoying each other's company and celebrating what other people had done. Back in the '70s and '80s people would get smashed and come in at four in the morning but it was never that. Apart from a few days maybe in that Worcester game, at no point were we unfit to take the field and give our all. Even in that Worcester game, everyone was still trying their nuts off. It was just sitting in the bar and having a chat about what we've done, having a few Guinnesses.'

All great teams have great team spirit, and from 2005–09 Durham were one of the great county cricket teams. 'We did enjoy ourselves off the field, but not in a destructive manner,' Breese stresses. 'We worked really hard on the field and in practice, but Benki was work hard, play hard. We had a culture where people felt they could be themselves but when it came to having to put performances in, that wasn't an excuse.

'Di Venuto had a family, Benki did and everyone started to socialise together, we used to have team barbecues at Geoff's house and it felt like a family, so we took people into the family and made them feel a part of it. The worst thing you can do in a team environment is feel like you're on the outside. We pulled everyone in and I felt like it was quite tight. What is under-estimated is how good the support system was when we were on the road. Benki's family and mine got on really well and a lot of the girls and the kids socialised together, they had a box at the ground. If that's good, everything else usually looks after itself.'

With young home-grown players learning from hungry, dedicated and proven performers and bonded into a unit by a strong team spirit, Durham had found a winning combination. The chemistry would never be better than in 2009.

12.

Breaking Up
Is Hard to Do

WILL Smith only lost one County Championship match as Durham captain. He was sacked before the bus got home.

The removal of the skipper with the highest Championship win ratio the county has ever had – and probably ever will – was brutal, dramatic and extremely swift. Smith perhaps tried to evolve Durham's first great side too quickly, but it was partly dismantled, partly disintegrated without him.

Durham always try to have one eye on the future, which is why Smith became captain aged 26. They began using one-day competitions as many football teams use the cups, to blood youngsters, fielding 25 players in all competitions in 2009. Although their 50-50 record limited them to sixth in Pro40 Division One, victory at Taunton made an important impression on Smith.

'It was the very last game of the season,' he recalls, 'and all the experienced guys who'd played in the Championship sat it out. Somerset could win the league if they beat us and Sussex didn't beat Worcestershire. We had a really inexperienced team with Luke Evans and Will Gidman opening the bowling. Luke Evans bowled the first over. He bowled about five wides, Marcus Trescothick hit him for a couple of fours and he got him lbw with the last ball. He'd been all over the shop then produced this beautiful inswinger to the left-hander, who fell over it a bit. We said we'd take 1-15 if we got Trescothick. Giddo bowled eight overs 1-18, he bowled unbelievably well, and we kept them to 242 in 40 overs at Taunton.'

It had a big bearing on Smith's thinking for 2010. 'I wanted to make sure we had a really good one-day unit,' he explains. 'I never wanted it to take over what we were doing in four-day cricket but maybe in not playing certain people in that one-day team, while it would have kept them fresher for four-day cricket – and that's what we always conveyed to them – it was probably just the wrong thing to do. It was probably the Somerset win with this young, fresh, vibrant team that made me think we should. Experience tells me you can't have everything. To be successful in all three formats is nigh-on impossible now, almost the nirvana.'

Ian Blackwell, not Michael Di Venuto, opened in the four 40-over games Smith captained in 2010; Dale Benkenstein and Stephen Harmison played once each as the likes of 23-year-old Evans, Gidman (25) and Ben Harmison (24) got opportunities. 'There are a lot of players who've been called "young" since I've been at Durham, and I've been here four seasons now,' Di Venuto told *The Journal*. The trouble was, Di Venuto and his fellow seniors rightly did not want to stand aside. 'I have prepared to play every day of cricket for Durham,' he announced at the start of the season but in his final four summers the Australian one-day international made just 12 limited-overs appearances.

'I don't think the senior players saw the bigger picture and they were right not to because sometimes you can change things for the sake of changing them,' Stephen Harmison argues. 'If you've got a good senior player you try to get the most out of them. If you're bringing a younger player in and you're losing, you're wasting your time. Why were Will Smith and so many other young players successful in that era? Because they were playing with very, very good senior players and all they were bothered about was winning games. Set a winning tone and the young players learn how to win. Without it, it's the blind leading the blind.'

Smith became captain on the back of a brilliant 2008. Helped by 150 at Hampshire, he made 700 Championship runs at an average of 33.33 in 2009. Four games into 2010, he had just 114 at 16.28. In their opening Championship game against Essex, Durham followed on for the first time since Headingley in 2006 and, although Di Venuto (99) and Benkenstein (98) rescued them from 4/2, their lead was only 45 with three wickets and 35 overs remaining when rain and bad light brought a draw to cheers from the stands. Hampshire were beaten at home, but it took another Di Venuto/Benkenstein recovery to salvage a draw after following on against Yorkshire. The number of points for a draw was reduced to three in 2010.

'Will was playing in a team with internationals with strong characters and opinions,' says Stephen Harmison. 'People have said anyone could captain the 2009 team but that's not the case. He had some good ideas but when you're captain you need to score runs or take wickets or the pressure comes on to your captaincy. I think he went into his shell a little bit. I don't know if he felt inferior but Will possibly worried a bit and took things to heart.'

Chris Rushworth claimed his maiden first-class wickets at Trent Bridge, and 18-year-old Ben Stokes his first century – only Nicky Peng had done that at a younger age for Durham – but losing by an innings and 62 runs left Durham eighth in the Championship, 55 points off the pace. Everyone else had at least twice as many bowling points. Nottinghamshire's 237-run seventh-wicket partnership between Chris Read and Ali Brown was crucial. 'Smith looked bereft of ideas,' I wrote, 'as he has on the wrong end of other mammoth partnerships this season.' He did not seem to get much assistance.

The new captain wrote in Durham's 2009 yearbook: 'I'm taking over a group of highly talented players who are going to want to help me out. They will put any individual considerations aside for the good of the team. We're all going to be pulling in the same direction because we all have the same aim.'

'I probably got a lot of things wrong in the first period of that [2010] season,' Smith admits when I read it back to him. 'From then on I've always been acutely aware of people's motivation, what they're doing and where they're trying to get to. I was probably too inexperienced to really know at that stage. I just felt we'd won the Championship for two years, let's go win it a third time. Why would you not be 100 per cent motivated to do that?

'It probably echoes how I became towards the end of my first season as a Durham player – a bit too intense, too willing to take on everything and be this superhuman figure by training really hard and saying things which probably didn't need to be said. It was a bit of over-thinking it and showing too much desire, which sounds a bit bizarre. Other players had probably just dropped off in terms of their desire to do certain things and I should have been aware of that.'

Smith's isolation was obvious to wicketkeeper Phil Mustard. 'I'd be stood with Diva at slip and maybe Benki,' he says. 'Although the senior guys didn't want the job, they were happy to criticise. They were very close with the coach [Geoff Cook]. It was really, really tough because I was friends with Smudger [Smith]. He would be at mid-on or mid-off captaining and then you've got Benki and Diva saying, "I wouldn't have done that," or "I think we should have done it this way." Every ten overs or whatever Diva would go up and say, "What about this? What about that?" then Benki would go up and say, "Why don't you do this? Why don't you do that?" Then Blackie would say, "Why don't you put a fielder in this position?" They were putting him under pressure, which was very, very wrong.'

Smith responds: 'He's pretty switched on so he's probably right. Whether that's purely their fault, purely my fault or somewhere in between, I don't know. I don't think people ever wanted to do it out of spite or anger. A county season is a pretty bizarre and highly stressed environment. Maybe it was just a way of people releasing their stresses.'

Cook 'was in the middle of it trying to manage a bit of unrest'. He explains: 'When people get to the top of their hill, their motivation becomes slightly different. I think one or two of the senior players were eyeing different things. Will might have been saying the same things to them but they might have been interpreting them wrongly. The senior players can be massively influential and if they aren't doing the things that benefit the group, it can stretch the group quite badly. Older players can feel threatened.'

Smith recalls: 'On the bus back from Trent Bridge, towards the end of the journey Geoff said he'd had a real hard think and he thought we needed a change of leadership. Because I was so intent on turning things around, I didn't really see it coming. I had a quick chat with him when we got back to the Riverside. I said, "Thanks for the opportunity, it's been unbelievable, I respect the fact you feel this. Whenever you need me I'll give everything."' He had been sacked just four games after an unbeaten Championship season. 'I often think back to that and it is a bit bizarre,' Smith admits. 'I think my importance as a captain was far less than making sure some of the more senior players were fully motivated. Maybe it was just a brilliant piece of management by Geoff Cook to nip something in the bud. I'd like to think I might have realised the way it was going and tried to be slightly different or tried to rectify things.'

If not Smith, who should captain? 'Although there was quite a bit of noise being made, nobody had the answers,' Cook reflects. Mustard adds: 'Benki and Diva didn't want it even though they were the back-seat drivers. Harmy wanted it but my instinct was he would be too powerful – and how much longer did he really want to play? Did I want it? No. But they asked me if I'd take it on and I said yes.'

In 2010, 31-year-old Harmison was starting a four-year contract thought to be worth £600,000, a pay cut from his England deal. Harmison played his 62nd and final Test at The Oval in September 2009, taking his 222nd wicket. Afterwards he advised the selectors not to pick him, worried his body could no longer endure the year-round treadmill, and wary of stunting Stuart Broad and Jimmy

Anderson's development. When he was Harmison's England team-mate, Darren Gough was criticised by Yorkshire members who felt he did not want to play county cricket, and shortly after his final Test he joined Essex. Durham and Harmison were keen to avoid a repeat.

'Durham gave me so much and my knees, my back, my ankles tell me I gave Durham so much back,' Harmison argues. 'I wanted four years because I knew I wouldn't want to play after that but the motivation ran out earlier.' If Harmison thought his body could no longer cope with year-round cricket, he now believes it could not perform without it. 'I was a bowler you had to bowl to the point of injury,' he argues. 'If I had a week off, it took me three days to get the ball straight again.

'On the way back from Nottingham I said I'd take on the captaincy. I didn't think Paul Collingwood had a lot of international cricket left and I said I'd do it until the end of the season. If Colly came back he could captain, or if not we could get an overseas captain. All I wanted was what was best for Durham. It would have given me something to focus on, something to train for and inspire me. The rest of my Durham career wouldn't have petered out, although I still think I would have finished at the same time.'

Cook decided against. 'While he had terrific qualities – his passion for Durham and all that kind of stuff – he was not a player in all forms of cricket and it was my subjective decision that he might have struggled to come to terms with the responsibility and the onerous nature of the job,' he says. Harmison responds: 'I can understand that a little bit but my love for the game and focus was diminishing and that would have made me switch back on to international standards. It didn't stop me from playing the best I possibly could and it wasn't like I was all over the shop but it wasn't up to the standards I'd set. I didn't have a problem with Colonel doing it, though.'

Mustard's unorthodoxy and Jack-the-Lad persona perhaps denied him due dressing-room respect. 'Great ideas, you just weren't sure what was going on inside that head,' says Harmison. 'But people can't underestimate how good Philip Mustard was for Durham County

Cricket Club – he was an unbelievable player, person, character.' Smith acknowledges: 'Colonel would set certain fields or ask certain bowlers to bowl at certain times and it just flew against convention but it would work. You would either think it was complete luck or sheer genius and probably a bit of both! I imagine Geoff was hoping it would put the emphasis and responsibility on players to perform and be self-motivated. To a degree it probably did.'

Mustard felt, 'I was always under the pump from the day I accepted it for who I was, what I did. Was I tactically aware? Not really. Once you start getting one or two players saying, "That's a crap decision," and you lose the respect of the dressing room, you're fighting an uphill battle. The senior guys were trying to put their stamp down for their next job but they probably hurt a lot of younger people. Having [since] captained Gloucester without being the keeper, I look back now and think it's an impossible job for a keeper to captain. Then I thought, "It's easy," but there's not enough time in the game to do everything. It's great being an assistant leaving the captain to do his job and getting the fielders to do theirs. That's what I believe is a wicketkeeper's role.'

Nevertheless, Mustard scored two Championship centuries as captain in 2010, four years after his previous two, and was voted Durham's player of the year by members and team-mates as they finished fifth in the Championship. Nearer the top than the bottom in points terms, they had more fifties than in 2009, but fewer centuries and five-wicket hauls. Durham beat champions Nottinghamshire but lost to relegated Kent and drew twice with bottom-placed Essex.

Neil Killeen retired but Di Venuto went into the 2011 campaign aged 37, Benkenstein and Callum Thorp 36, Gareth Breese 35, Collingwood 34, and Blackwell and Harmison 32. After a 40-over defeat to Nottinghamshire in July I noted that: 'Emerging from a lengthy post-mortem, one player mentioned the word "desire" when asked where things were going wrong.' Breese admits: 'The edge wasn't there. We had won trophies three years on the trot and there was all the talk about whether we could win the Championship for a third year. It was still a formidable team with proper players turning good teams over.'

Cook says: 'Winning games got a momentum going. That almost took away the need to motivate individuals. It was only when the success had to be strived for and people became a bit more vulnerable professionally and emotionally that things got a little bit more stretched. That's when you had to try and evolve a different unit. I felt Blackwell was always going to be a temporary addition – a brilliant addition, but because of the type of person he is, short-term. But I think it had to be a staggered dismantling of the team.' Durham were the only county without an overseas player in 2010, but Cook could see talent coming off his production line which needed accommodating. At times it meant taking decisions not in the team's short-term interests.

Scott Borthwick made his Championship debut as soon as the 2010 title was secured. That Essex's James Foster hit the leg-spinner for five consecutive sixes in a one-day game ten days earlier – the next ball went for four wides, confirming Durham's defeat – did not deter Cook. Although his cap was mistakenly sent to Ireland, Borthwick did not look out of place at Hampshire, making 26 not out and taking 3-95.

When John Windows watched Borthwick captain Durham's under-15s against Cumbria, he was sufficiently impressed by one of the opposition to invite him to the Riverside nets. New Zealand-born Ben Stokes moved to Cockermouth aged 12 when his father Ged began coaching Workington's rugby league team. Of the two all-rounders, he blossomed quicker, playing for Durham's academy at 15 and making a century against Lancashire on his second-team debut aged 16. He hit 100 against India at the 2010 Under-19 World Cup and when he made 81 not out at more than two runs per ball on Durham's pre-season tour of the United Arab Emirates, they picked him in the champions versus MCC match, where he scored 51. Like Borthwick, Stokes had been dipped into the 2009 one-day side, dismissing Mark Ramprakash with his third ball in senior cricket.

He followed his Trent Bridge century with another in his next game, 161 not out in front of the television cameras at Kent, and topped Durham's 2010 Championship batting averages.

Stokes started the next season with 6-68 at Hampshire – immediately passing his 2010 four-day wicket tally – and in May became the first teenager since Denis Compton to score five Championship centuries. More thrilling than his 313-run stand with Benkenstein against Lancashire was a partnership with Blackwell which became a hitting competition. Stokes twice cleared the pavilion – something only Kevin Pietersen had done – with slog-sweeps whereas the best Blackwell could manage was striking a hospitality-box window. Stokes bludgeoned 185 as previously unbeaten Lancashire lost by an innings and 125 runs. Although his progress was rapid, it was not always smooth. Pencilled into England's one-day squad to face Sri Lanka, he dislocated his right index finger dropping a catch offered by Paul Horton later that day. 'Where once there was a joint, there was none,' he wrote in his autobiography. It took three operations before he could bowl again.

Opener Mark Stoneman was a flamboyant talent too, and although the 20-year-old made his debut in 2007, it took some time to cement his place. When he followed his second-team 282 with 118 against Durham University in May 2010, it ended Kyle Coetzer's Championship career at Durham. The Scot, who had featured in all three major trophy wins, played 40-over cricket for Durham, Scotland and Northamptonshire in 2011, joining the latter permanently after a loan.

Apart from ten Twenty20 games (selected more for his fielding and occasional bowling) and two 40-over appearances, Smith spent the rest of 2010 in Jon Lewis's second XI after his sacking. 'I spent quite a bit of time with him because I felt he was in a very difficult situation,' Lewis says. 'He's not the most expansive emotionally so I wanted to know he was all right. He handled himself with a lot of dignity. I tried to get him to play golf a few times but he just wanted to work hard. I thought he was not giving himself the chance to nurse a few wounds. He refused to bear a grudge or take an "I'll show them" attitude. He said he wanted to move on but he was probably looking forward to the end of that season.' Smith's contract expired in 2011.

'I was just trying to do everything I possibly could to set a good example,' he explains. 'Like Gibbo [Ottis Gibson] says, don't get bitter, get better. I think I'm quite a level character but it seems everything has been quite extreme in my career. I love being in a successful team environment where people are enjoying each other's company and winning so I just wanted to be back in that. It took me until the start of the [2011] season to get back in the team, through Rocky [Stoneman] breaking his finger at the Rose Bowl in the first game. I felt like a youngster coming back into the dressing room and a lot of people were great towards me.' Smith scored more first-class runs than in any Durham season to date and did not miss another Championship game until joining Hampshire.

'At the end of the 2011 season Diva and I were having a beer in the changing room with everyone else,' he recalls. 'He said he'd loved playing with me. Whether he meant it or he'd had too many beers I don't know, but he said I was the toughest cricketer he'd played with. Coming from Diva, that was special. I think he appreciated how I'd kept my decorum. I've learnt an unbelievable amount from that time – about myself and other people, about how to be aware of other people. I wouldn't have had the enjoyment and experience and achieved some of the things I have done without it.'

In 2011 Durham took some of the weight off Mustard by making Benkenstein their first specific limited-overs captain. He also deputised when gout ended Mustard's 99-game run of consecutive Championship appearances in April. Durham started the season so well that in late June I wrote they were 'threatening to turn [the Championship race] into a procession'. Their five-wicket win over second-placed Lancashire opened a 23-point gap, albeit having played a game more, while unbeaten scores of 83 and 60 took Benkenstein past Lewis as Durham's leading first-class run-scorer and made him only the second batsman to 1,000 for the English season. Not for the last time, I was wrong.

Twenty20 ruined Durham's momentum. 'All the travelling, the distorted cricket, the shortened format – the guys start to play silly shots and it tends to disrupt the flow of things,' Blackwell explained. With Stokes nursing his dislocated finger, Durham lost three of their first six 20-over games. On his return Stokes played just four competitive county matches as a specialist batsman but ten for England and England Lions. In September the Riversiders were hammered by Somerset in the 40-over semi-final, as they had been in all but one knockout game since the 2007 Lord's final.

Durham went top of the Championship by defeating Worcestershire in their last game but Warwickshire were closing in on a draw to clinch second place, Lancashire the victory which secured their first outright title in 77 years. Durham suffered the same number of defeats as the top two, claiming more batting points and as many bowling as anyone in Division One. There had been England debuts for Stokes and Borthwick, and 50 four-day wickets for Graham Onions on his return from career-threatening injury.

Liam Plunkett only played one Championship and 14 limited-overs games in 2011, then remodelled his action in the winter, when Mark Davies joined Kent. In July 2012 Plunkett was caught going to an all-night garage while twice the legal limit and received his second driving ban in just over five years. In October he joined Yorkshire, where Jason Gillespie restarted his international career by encouraging him to stop over-thinking and return to bowling fast.

In 2011 Durham released Ben Harmison. 'I didn't enjoy how that went and it wasn't just Ben, Kyle went as well,' his brother Stephen says. 'I couldn't understand why they did that but it was the best thing for Ben to get away from Durham [like Davies, he joined Kent]. Something in me just left that winter. The game just got to me and I was starting to pick up injuries. I had seven or eight years where I hardly had any, then they all came at once. I think it was because I was having long periods off. If I wasn't bowling I was losing fitness, I was striving for consistency, I'd have an injury again, then the season would finish. Coming back was soul-destroying.'

Harmison missed what should have been the first appearance of his contract after trapping a nerve in his back warming up for Essex, then injured his ankle in May. In July he had 'badly skinned toes', and he ended the season with a torn foot muscle. 'He's going to have to do some serious work to get his general conditioning right,' Cook warned. Harmison was the non-striker when Mustard's drive broke his arm in 2011's opening game, and when he stood on a football preparing to face Sri Lanka A in July, shortly after Ben's release, it ended his season. 'We were on the bus back from Taunton, where I was all over the shop, and at the service station I'd asked Geoff to play in that game,' he recalls. 'Every time I came back to bowl I had problems in the back of my ankle, I couldn't understand what it was. I might have been close to being fit for the last couple of games but there was no point because the team were doing quite well.'

Harmison lost a stone and a half that winter but on the second day of pre-season snapped ankle tendons standing on a cricket ball. For all his misfortune he was not always helping himself. 'Steve may be sulking,' an unnamed Durham source told *The Mirror* in September 2011. Harmison now accepts: 'I probably should have gone overseas in the winter but one of the reasons I didn't want to play for England any more was my body couldn't do that [at international level] so why would I do it for someone else? It was to my detriment. Having to spend a lot of time in the indoor school training, the love for the game left my body. I was still on a contract I tried to work hard for but I found motivation very, very difficult. People will ask did I feel guilty because I was getting a lot of money and there was an element of that, but when I played in 2005–09 I wasn't getting paid by the club [because he was contracted to England].' In return for Harmison's four-year deal, Durham got 19 first-class appearances and 57 wickets.

Time was also catching up on arguably Durham's greatest batsman. In 2011 Di Venuto scored 935 first-class runs at 38.95. With the exception of 2004, when he was injured, it was the first English season of the 21st century in which he failed to reach four figures and average at least 45. After a winter's club cricket and coaching, then representing Italy in March's World Twenty20 qualifiers, he sounded refreshed in the Lord's rain in April talking about his hunger to play 'game-shaping innings' and earn a new contract.

Three weeks later Smith opened with Di Venuto at Taunton. 'I remember facing Craig Overton and there was a bit of a gap in one of the sightscreens at a funny angle and a funny height,' says Smith. 'I found a few hard to pick up but I had a slightly squat stance so it was OK, but for Diva it was coming straight out of that. He batted three yards out of his crease against a bowler of Overton's pace. Maybe that was him saying, "I'm going to go out taking a step forward, being tough, and if it's not there, it's not there."' Despite Di Venuto's 96 and Smith's 100, Durham lost by five wickets.

An Achilles injury kept Di Venuto out of the Twenty20 Cup but back-to-back 25-over second-team games against Northamptonshire were more to test his appetite than fitness. He made 156 not out from 80 deliveries in the first, opening with Keaton Jennings. 'They had a left-armer, a young lad [Christian Davis], and he was bowling back of a length to Diva, who just kept smacking him out of the ground,' Jennings recalls. Shortly afterwards, Di Venuto retired from cricket.

'I was ready to go,' he told me when he returned to Chester-le-Street as Australia's batting coach in 2013. 'I was always told one day you'll wake up and you'll just know it's time to retire. I didn't understand how you could love playing cricket so much, which I did, then one day turn around and say, "I'm done." But I had two days like that in a row at Somerset and that's when I realised I'd had enough. My batting was fine and I loved the contest of facing the new ball, but it was everything else… I didn't want to become that bitter and twisted older player in the dressing room.' Smith says: 'A lot of people would just potter on and pick up the cheque.'

Di Venuto was not the only worn-out senior pro playing that day. 'If I'd been an overseas [player] I probably would have done what Diva did,' Harmison admits. 'I think he was similar to me in that if he wasn't playing every game it made it harder to get going and the body would feel old, it gets tired.' Only Stokes was averaging more than Di Venuto for Durham that season, and for five days after Mark Ramprakash's retirement he was the world's most prolific first-class batsman still playing. On top of losing their best batsman, Durham were losing matches. Opening 2012 with a 114-run defeat at home to Nottinghamshire set the Championship tone. A narrow loss at home to Lancashire left them worse off than when they started thanks to a four-point over-rate penalty. They had seven batting points after eight games and no wins.

'You know when you haven't performed,' says Mustard. 'I knew I wasn't the right man for the [captain's] job. I'm not the world's best speaker to individuals, I'm not a leader. I hadn't even wanted the job, I'd just given it a go. Was it the worst decision I've made? No. I really enjoyed it and I learnt a lot about the game of cricket. Now I've got a different perspective on leaders and how hard it is when your leader's saying something and your fielders are saying different.

'The biggest upset for me was the relationship between me and Geoff has always been strong. He was under pressure too because everyone was expecting us to do well but I was really, really disappointed with the way they did it. I gave him the chance on three or four different occasions when I asked, "Am I getting the sack yet, Geoff?" Instead of saying, "Colonel, let's go and have a chat," like he normally did, I was in the house, he rang me up and said they were relieving me of my duties. That was it. All through my career we'd had a talking relationship so why couldn't he do it the right way? That hurt me a lot. But I didn't get dropped like you normally do so I was still a big part of the Durham team. I didn't hold any grudges.'

Ten games into the Championship campaign with Durham 23 points adrift at the bottom of Division One, it was obvious what would happen next. Tim Wellock had even written in Durham's 2012 yearbook: 'It seems that any possibility of Paul Collingwood taking over will have to wait until his T20 globe-trotting days have ended.' Unlike David Boon's, Collingwood had been openly adjusting

Mustard's fields. 'I think in retrospect, Philip knew he was only a stop-gap but there was a bit of fragmentation,' says Cook. 'It didn't reflect well on myself or what the club was trying to achieve that in two out of three seasons we'd decided to change captain halfway through.'

Collingwood immediately addressed the Harmison issue. 'You had an international-class bowler and I felt his standards weren't as high as they should and could be so you've got to have some honest conversations,' he says. 'I wasn't making an example. I wanted Harmy close to 80, 90 per cent but I felt he was only 60 per cent of his true potential. He no longer had the ambition to play international cricket so he had to find that motivation to do those extra yards you need. We fell out over it because he felt he should be playing. We get on fine now and he's said to me since I probably made the right decision.'

Five days into Collingwood's captaincy it was announced Harmison was joining Yorkshire on an 'initial' one-month loan. Harmison, who by his own reckoning 'was about two stone overweight', claimed he found out from Michael Vaughan. The loan ended with a side strain after three games. Harmison's Durham contract included a 2013 benefit year, and after five weather-hit early-season second-team games he played it out with Northumberland League Ashington.

Blackwell was eased out too. A 2006 operation on a torn shoulder muscle failed, so in 2009/10 he had that repaired, plus a second tear in his supraspinatus. It didn't stop him taking as many wickets in 2010 (43) as 2009 but he needed a couple of injections to get through 2012's initial games, and after back spasms before Lancashire's Championship visit in May Blackwell never played competitively for Durham again. Despite top-scoring with 62 and taking a career-best 7-52 against Australia A in August, he was loaned to Warwickshire, where in four Championship games he averaged 53 with the bat, took six wickets and won another title. When he underwent more winter surgery, ruling him out for six to eight months, a pay-off was agreed and he retired.

Benkenstein's body was also starting to let him down. He detached a tendon running out Anthony McGrath in April 2010 but played on until hernia and knee operations in August. It was a poor season by his high standards, but having started 2011 expecting to concentrate on limited-overs cricket he ended it as Championship Division One's third-highest scorer and signed a two-year contract extension. In May 2012 Benkenstein dislocated his left shoulder in a fielding drill with Lewis, popped it back in and rushed back too soon, making only 523 Championship runs that season.

When Benkenstein dislocated his shoulder again at Surrey almost a year to the day later, he was told he needed an operation on the rotator cuff and aimed to return in September if needed. Illness delayed the surgery so it became season-ending and he tried to put it off, but a Second XI Trophy appearance against MCC Young Cricketers made him see sense. 'At certain stages in my career a 70 per cent Benkenstein was good enough, but we're playing such good cricket at the moment I don't think a 70 per cent Benkenstein will do,' he admitted.

He was being groomed as Cook's successor but the picture changed completely in 2013. Benkenstein's wife Jacqui and three children returned to South Africa when her interim job as Durham University's women's hockey team coach was not made permanent. On 20 June, Durham's management were due to plan the Twenty20 campaign. 'I was very keen on moving aside and allowing a specific white-ball coach to come in,' says Cook. 'Dale was coming to the end of his career, hugely respected and a good tactician.' Cook had a heart attack that morning, so by the time the meeting took place the issues were rather different. 'It was one meeting round the boardroom table with Dale, Jon Lewis, Alan [Walker] and Paul [Collingwood],' explains David Harker. 'The coaches decided to go with Jon moving up from second team to first team.'

Collingwood stresses, 'They were circumstances that would never occur in cricket again. I'm a big believer that you've got to make sure people understand where they sit in a team and it's the same with coaches. If you're on the next rung on the ladder how can someone jump into that position? I was quite strong on that. I didn't believe

Benks should be coaching in the T20s, which he obviously disagreed with. Benks said he'd discussed with Geoff being Twenty20 coach but I hadn't heard that. I still wanted Benks as a player and I didn't see why he should leapfrog Lewis, Walker and Killer [Neil Killeen].' Lewis insists: 'Splitting [coaching duties] never got mentioned to me. That is the first I've heard of that, I swear – I don't doubt it, though.'

In September Benkenstein became Natal's batting consultant and in February Hampshire coach. 'It looked like a lot of people fighting to jump into Geoff's position, which is shocking, really,' says Graham Onions. 'The club had always been a happy family and for once it just seemed unstructured. It needed a strong person to take hold of the situation.' Collingwood did.

'It was sad it ended that way,' says Smith, who joined Hampshire in 2014. 'But Jon had been second XI coach for a long time, he'd been captain of the club. If you'd kept Benki there, what would he do? Equally Benki would never take away from an environment.' Harmison's sadness was that, 'Durham didn't have the money to have both [Lewis and Benkenstein], it would have been a good combination.' Cook simply says: 'I thought [Benkenstein] would do a fantastic job and I was disappointed when the club went in a different direction.'

In little more than three years the team had changed dramatically. Effectively pushing out legends like Harmison and Benkenstein needed silverware to justify it. Durham did not have to wait long.

13.

Climbing the Mountain

W E WERE on the Riverside outfield waiting for Durham to receive the County Championship trophy when I heard a shout from high over my shoulder. 'Stu!' a grinning Mark Wood yelled from the balcony. 'I told you so!'

If he looked justifiably pleased with himself then, Wood's expression had been one of shock when I turned my recorder off on more or less the same patch of turf three weeks earlier. 'Wow, I've said it now, haven't I?' he gasped. Durham's next game was away to the Division One leaders, 25.5 points ahead with three matches left to Durham's four. 'If we beat Yorkshire, I fancy us to win the league,' said Wood.

If he had seen it coming by late August, not many others had when Durham sailed dangerously close to the wind that spring. Money was so tight, their pre-season tour was to the rain-swept Midlands. It snowed in Chester-le-Street before the opening first-class game against Durham University and because it was Easter even the council-owned indoor training facilities were closed. As in every season since 2010, Durham had no Championship overseas player, this time not even in Twenty20. Michael Di Venuto, Ian Blackwell and Liam Plunkett had left, Mitchell Claydon was on loan at Kent, and Stephen Harmison in exile.

'[Paul] Collingwood will do well to keep them up,' wrote the *Daily Express*. 'Little preparation and a weak squad, it's hard to argue that they'll survive,' agreed the *Daily Mail*, tipping Durham to finish bottom and Surrey, who actually suffered that fate, as champions. They were overlooking the on-field revival captain Collingwood had started.

The all-rounder returned to Durham at the end of his international career in 2011 full of uncertainty. 'It was trepidation about playing cricket full stop,' he recalls. 'Form-wise I was shot to bits and you've got to make that decision about whether to continue playing. International cricket to me is the ultimate, the whole reason why you put in all those hours as a kid. I wanted a long, hard think about whether cricket was still the thing I wanted to do. It was a difficult decision.

'I thought that by giving up on Test cricket I could focus all my energy on the white-ball game for England and the [international] captaincy. The next [Twenty20] World Cup was 18 months away but we only had six T20 games before that so I thought I would really be able to get my teeth into that… but then I got sacked. I never retired from white-ball cricket but I knew that was it. That hit me seriously hard. That initial period was about seeing if I could get my form back and my juices flowing but it wasn't until I got the [Durham] captaincy that I was really 100 per cent switched on.'

Collingwood was due to miss the start of the 2012 county season but after a poor Big Bash, Rajasthan Royals – overloaded with ten overseas players – released him from the Indian Premier League. The Riversiders saw little benefit – with only one Championship fifty and no addition to the century in his first post-England appearance – until he became captain and finished the summer with three more half-centuries and a hundred.

Despite leading England 55 times, Collingwood always painted himself as a reluctant captain. 'I didn't really want it but it was the right time for Durham, for Phil Mustard, and for me to get my teeth into something,' he says. 'I became like a juggernaut coming in with ideas, telling Geoff [Cook] we should have more coaches, ideas I'd brought from England. I think Geoff was probably, "Whoa! This is not what I expected!" I was accountable and as soon as that's the case you want to do the best job you possibly can. In Test cricket Straussy [Andrew Strauss] had brought this real patience game which was successful and I think I utilised that very well. We were going to go at two-and-a-half runs an over and suffocate the opposition.'

Between returning from his career-threatening back injury in 2011 and the end of 2013, Graham Onions took 180 Championship wickets and Callum Thorp had the best bowling average of his career in 2012, but more was needed to fill the gaps left by Harmison and Blackwell. Chris Rushworth was yet to make a real impact since rejoining in 2010. 'He was capable of bowling really good first spells, possibly really good second spells, but he battled a little bit for the strength to bowl three spells a day,' explains then-second-team coach Jon Lewis.

Rushworth's career took off with 5-31 in June 2012's televised 40-over game against Nottinghamshire. 'I remember thinking, "Make sure you keep your spot" and I pretty much did,' he recalls. 'The more you play, the more you relax and the more your natural ability takes over.' His man-of-the-match display earned a first Championship appearance of 2012 against Warwickshire two days later. Rushworth started with five maidens in six overs and finished the innings with another career-best five-wicket haul. Two more followed that season as he took 38 Championship wickets at 16.39. It was the first of four summers where Rushworth took more scalps than previously. 'There was probably a period where Rushy and Callum were similar in what they could bring to the side, but Colly wanted bowlers who could bring him control so suddenly the two of them in the same side was fine,' reasons Lewis.

'Colly didn't do a great deal in terms of telling me where to bowl or what plans to have, he was just very confident in our abilities and kept you calm under pressure,' Rushworth explains. 'It was all just about containing, and if me and Callum were going at under three an over we would take wickets. When a bloke that played 68 Tests and nearly 200 one-dayers says, "Rushy, you're the man," it gives you a massive boost.'

Not that things were left to chance. 'We studied opposition at length to provide us with the blueprint to counter them at home and away,' Mark Stoneman reveals. 'We thrived on the fact that opposition teams hated coming to the Riverside – their batsmen couldn't trust the wicket and more often than not opposition bowlers felt they just had to turn up to get wickets. We knew we had some outstanding seam bowlers, and as long as we kept the mental resolve when times got hard with the bat then we would give ourselves every chance of winning.' Onions says: 'A lot of times under Colonel we didn't necessarily have a plan and lost a session or a game. Colly knew so much about his game at that stage it probably allowed him to think about other people's games, whereas Colonel probably needed to think about his own game more.'

Keaton Jennings, handed his debut by Collingwood, was impressed by his man-management. 'He kept guys energised, relaxed, wanting to play for each other,' he explains. 'He was very good at knowing what needed to be done at the right time – whether it be technique, fitness, skills – and imparted that quite nicely to the younger guys. I remember him saying that as an older guy if you're going to continue giving energy to every other guy, it's going to be draining, but if he knows you're going to take it on board he doesn't mind.'

When Collingwood addressed the media before his supposed first game as captain, at Worcester, he revealed he had not fully recovered from a broken hand. The leadership fell again to the reluctant Dale Benkenstein and with only 166 overs bowled as Britain got the rain out of its system before the Olympics, Durham were still winless when Collingwood returned for the two-wicket defeat to relegation rivals Sussex at Arundel. 'It was such a tight game I came off thinking, "We're close,"' he says. 'I knew we'd actually found something very quickly that would work. We steamrollered everyone after that. We were winning so many close games.' Durham won five of their final six matches, drawing the other in the Aigburth rain. Champions Warwickshire only won six all season.

Durham were determined to play two spinners to accommodate Scott Borthwick in 2012, but one wicket and only two 20-plus scores under Mustard had not justified it. Twelve Twenty20 wickets lifted Borthwick, who took four at Worcester, four at Hampshire in a 40-over game, and made his first fifty in 13 months at Arundel. Sixth-placed Durham had the division's most bowling points but only bottom-placed Worcestershire earned fewer batting bonuses. Collingwood was Durham's top-scorer with just 697.

Stoneman's biggest contributions were his first three one-day centuries. 'It was the key year in turning my career around,' he reflects. 'It was a very wet summer and a lot of the four-day wickets were quite spicy. I made some telling contributions as we fought off relegation and took confidence and a sense of belonging. I'd finished the 2011 season in strong form, having spent a lot of time in second-team cricket after breaking my hand in the first game in Hampshire. Everything was starting to come together from the experiences I had already had at first-class level, some frank conversations with the likes of Benki and Diva and a pretty key discussion with Jon Lewis, who was second XI coach, about the differences he was seeing from me between the two levels.

'White-ball cricket offered a sense of freedom and I was able to find a rhythm alongside The Colonel, who would often get us off to a flyer, allowing me to provide the platform. Once Diva retired it was a case of not only having to pick up some of the slack but also a sense of freedom to carve out a role in a manner and style that would work for me and no longer be judged according to the performances of the senior partner. My game-management and matchplay evolved rather than taking the lead from Diva.'

Collingwood wanted to recruit a batsman for 2013, Benkenstein a 'death bowler', but Jacques Rudolph was unavailable until June, Junaid Khan turned Durham down, and money was so tight £2.8m was borrowed from the county council at seven per cent interest in

March. Durham started the Championship season 2.5 points back for breaching the 2012 salary cap, plus quarter-point penalties in 20- and 40-over cricket. While Yorkshire, Hampshire, Derbyshire, Northamptonshire, Nottinghamshire and Warwickshire went to Barbados for pre-season and Essex practised in a huge heated transparent marquee, Durham's games at Loughborough University and Worcestershire were abandoned.

Collingwood had surgery on his right thumb, chief executive David Harker was talked out of resigning, and even ever-bullish chairman Clive Leach spoke about 'a transitional phase'. 'I remember sitting in the house with Usman Arshad looking at the odds to win the Championship and I think we were 33/1 – I think we were bottom,' Jennings says. Collingwood publicly ticked off the points until relegation was avoided. 'I didn't want to put any pressure on my players,' he explains. 'If you want something too badly, it restricts you. I would rather sound more on the cautious side than over-confident.' Easter's snow forced Durham to be creative, climbing Beinn Dubh in Scotland. 'It was two feet of snow going up, horizontal winds, ice coming in,' says Collingwood. 'We did it all together, it was a hardship thing, it was fantastic.'

Will Smith calls it 'probably the best pre-season anyone's ever had. You want to play some cricket but it was brilliant in getting the team together. We played a bit of golf, climbed a mountain, did a bit of fishing, then got together on a night, had a bit of food and a few beers. If we'd done badly they would have said we should have gone away and played but it definitely helped.' Jennings recalls: 'An email went out and you had to reply to make sure you were there. Two players [Borthwick and Jamie Harrison, plus strength and conditioning coach Mike King] hadn't replied. They still came but they had to jump in the lake when we arrived. It just took the edge off it.'

Next came what coach Geoff Cook called a 'micro-pre-season' – two days of outdoor practice and a three-day match against Durham University before the Championship opener at home to Somerset 48 hours later. Ben Stokes, Jennings and Smith made centuries,

Borthwick 99 (and 6-76), as six of the top eight spent more than 100 minutes at the crease. Fortunately the students improved on 2012's 18 all out to take the match the distance.

Rushworth began 2013 with another career-best – 6-58 – to defeat Somerset, but Collingwood's unbeaten run as captain ended at Edgbaston. Set 413 to win, Durham were 94 all out. They lost their third game too, despite Stoneman's first Riverside century in six years. A hailstorm which took 70 minutes out of day three accelerated Collingwood's declaration and he set Yorkshire 336, a ground-record run-chase. Durham thought Stoneman ran Joe Root out from the point boundary on 88, and that a reverse sweep Collingwood caught on 93 had come off bat as well as pad, but by the time he was dismissed for 182, the scores were level.

It was a good way to lose. 'We only drew twice that year, which shows the kind of cricket we were playing,' says Rushworth. Collingwood joked: 'Next time I'll set a target of 450 and probably get criticised for that too!' and when hail interfered with the next home game he did err too far on the side of caution and had to settle for a draw.

By then, though, Durham had shown their courage with a remarkable victory at Trent Bridge. Smith's 153 set it up, but was in keeping with a plodding match which briefly caught fire on day three. 'Woody got it reversing and suddenly ripped through them,' Smith recalls. 'I was at short leg for most of it and all of a sudden the switch just flicked and his pace and control were phenomenal.' Final pair Ajmal Shahzad and Graeme Swann doused the flames on day four, batting together for 22.3 second-innings overs. Durham were entitled to feel worn down, having been woken by fire alarms at 1am and 2.30am – all except Phil Mustard, fast asleep with his phone off until eventually being roused. Some players moved to another hotel, others slept on the bus.

When Borthwick finally trapped an unconvinced Swann lbw for 57, Durham needed 183 off 23 overs. I rang the office to tell them not to leave too much space for my report of the draw, but Durham promoted Mustard to open and won by six wickets with 2.4 overs to spare. 'Stuart Broad was coming back from injury and wasn't quite all there,' argues Smith. 'Because they saw us reversing the ball I think their plan was to basically bang it in as short as they could to try to get one side scuffed up, but in 20 overs is it going to happen? If they hadn't had Broad saying that, they might have set better fields and been a bit more effective in where they wanted to bowl. Instead they kept banging it in and Colonel and Rocky kept smashing it into the stands.' Mustard made 72 from 54 deliveries, Stoneman 69 from 38.

'I used to enjoy giving the boys little motivational things so before the final innings I said, "If we do this, I'll take you all to Hooters. There's a team meal on me!"' Collingwood reveals. 'Lo and behold we're in Hooters an hour after the game. I think I ended up paying about £320!'

Another season-defining decision came on the journey down. 'We stopped at the services and Colly told me if I was playing I would be batting at three,' said Borthwick. 'It was a mixture of worry and excitement.' A top-order batsman in his youth, Borthwick scored his maiden Championship century from his now-customary eight in the Edgbaston defeat but was a luxury there, bowling just 125.4 Championship overs in 2012. Using a first-innings nightwatchman, then a limited-overs batting order in the run chase meant Borthwick did not bat at three until the next game, at Surrey, but he was Durham's top-scorer in 2013 with three centuries.

Gareth Breese had side and shoulder problems ahead of the trip to The Oval, where Surrey produced a pitch to suit Gareth Batty and Gary Keedy – spinners with a combined 74 years and 1,145 wickets – so Durham asked Ryan Buckley to join them after the second-team game in Nottingham. Picked ahead of Ryan Pringle, who played in the previous night's one-day match then drove home in his new car to make a 100-ball 124 and take 9-31 for Hetton Lyons, 19-year-old Buckley had not claimed a wicket in the 2012 Second XI Championship or Trophy. 'I travelled straight down to London on the train,' he revealed. 'I caught a taxi to the wrong hotel, so I had to get another taxi to the right one. I didn't have a room so I ended up on a sofa bed in [bowling coach] Alan Walker's room!'

The off-spinner was thrown the ball in the 21st over and his 30.2-over spell was broken only by a change of ends. 'I don't think I've bowled 30 overs in one day!' he said afterwards. Buckley dropped a simple caught-and-bowled chance in his second over, but dismissed Vikram Solanki in his third. His 4-4 in 16 evening-session deliveries completed the first five-wicket haul by a Durham debutant since Liam Plunkett. Borthwick claimed a second-innings 6-70 as 14 Surrey wickets fell to spin, seven Durham.

Stoneman top-scored in both innings of what, but for Root, would have been a third consecutive match-winning performance once Dale Benkenstein defied his dislocated shoulder to send Durham top of the Championship. Somerset had been beaten on a green seamer, Nottinghamshire a flat pitch and Surrey a raging turner. 'There was a sense of something special beginning to build,' says Stoneman. 'I remember Paul Collingwood speaking to the team about how, historically, Durham teams had struggled in London and that regardless of what pitch we played on if we kept our focus for the full four days we could achieve something special and set up our season.' Stoneman provided inspiration too, telling the final-morning huddle Durham had never won at The Oval.

Although Benkenstein made just 233 runs in 2013, he was one of only two Durham batsmen to have scored 1,000 in a Championship season – and Collingwood had last done it in 2005 – so his injury ought to have been a real problem. Instead, Geoff Cook says: 'The standard of the English game was just starting to diminish a little bit so those players who were given a chance could play match-winning roles a little bit more easily, and they did.' Another decisive performance at home to Warwickshire meant Stoneman, who had taken his hero Di Venuto's shirt number and adopted his habit of facing the opening delivery of Durham's first innings but not their second knock, passed his 2012 run tally before the Championship broke for the mid-season Twenty20 competition, which ought to have derailed them because of Cook's heart attack.

When Cook collapsed on his early-morning run, another jogger tried to resuscitate him, then called to the builders working on a new stand for the Ashes to ring an ambulance. The nearest paramedic was a few hundred yards away and rushed Cook to hospital in Durham City, where he spent five days in an induced coma. 'He always seemed incredibly fit so it was a huge shock,' Rushworth recalls. 'For most of the guys, he'd been around for a lot of our career. To not have him there for a huge part of the summer was like losing an arm or a leg.'

It stirred unpleasant memories in Smith. 'In 2009 my father-in-law was working down south and he'd had a heart attack playing squash, so I drove Kat, her mum and her sister to London not knowing what we might encounter,' he explains. 'As the weeks went on it was clear he was beyond recall, he'd lost consciousness and breathing for too long and he was basically in a vegetative state. He sadly passed away towards the back end of that season. When I heard Geoff had lost consciousness and stopped breathing, I thought, "Oh God! That's not good."'

Jennings comments: 'He was a father figure to many of us but if you have a fight with your girlfriend or a bad night's sleep you need to go on to the field and score runs or take wickets, as pragmatic as that is. The Colonel's got a phrase: "Just get on with it," and he literally does. That's what the team did.' According to Jon Lewis: 'Everyone knew they had to be bang on and do a bit more – players, chief exec, coaching staff, physios, everybody. It was credit to Geoff's coaching style that he made players quite independent so, while his absence was deeply concerning, he'd created a dressing room that could handle itself quite well.' With Lewis as interim head coach, Alistair Maiden moved from academy to second-team coach, assisted by Neil Killeen, and Collingwood became Twenty20 captain.

In the pre-match huddle before Durham's 40-over game against Hampshire, stand-in skipper Stoneman told his players: 'Geoff has shown a lot of pride in this county and we need to show we are proud of wearing the Durham shirt.' Lewis admits: 'I was crapping myself because in the second team you don't live and die by results, but we chased the runs down quite comfortably [winning by six wickets on the Duckworth-Lewis Method].'

With the team now coached by his close friend, Collingwood's authority was strengthened. 'They had that relationship built in,' says Smith. 'Jon's a fairly down-to-earth character, he tries not to get too up or down but equally has the passion and the desire to succeed, which was prevalent in so many characters in the club.' It was yet another example of Collingwood's view that 'Although everything went against us, in the cricketing sense everything went for us.' Lewis had captained Collingwood, Onions, Mustard and Breese, while everyone else played second-team cricket under him. 'It was very much about stability,' he explains. And for Jennings, familiarity: 'A lot of the younger guys had worked with him from the age of 17 or 18. You knew what he was about and how he was going to react.'

Cricket was a release for some. 'When you were actually playing you were almost not thinking about what you were doing cricket-wise, you just let things happen,' Smith argues. 'Often you play your best when you take the emphasis and the real focus off thinking about doing this or that – you let all the practice and the thoughts you've had previously play out.

'Colly has an unbelievable cricket brain and an unbelievable ability to channel his will to win a game of cricket or succeed in a particular situation. Some of his decisions and the way he manoeuvred things in games, what he'd say to a certain player at a certain time, I learnt a huge amount. Without him as captain there is no way we would have won the Championship. That's not taking away from what a lot of players did, but they probably felt they were in an environment where they could put in performances like that.'

Even Collingwood was soon missing, lacerating his thumb taking a return catch during a maiden Twenty20 campaign for Pringle, Wood, Michael Richardson and future *Love Island* contestant Max Morley. Stoneman, who only made three 20-over appearances prior to 2013, captained for the remainder of the competition and the next Championship game.

As if being without their coach, captain and vice-captain against Derbyshire wasn't enough, England called up Durham's leading wicket-taker Onions to not play at Trent Bridge. Nominated to stand down had Onions been released, Rushworth took a first ten-fer on his 27th birthday. Jennings followed his first-innings 93 with a maiden Championship hundred, and by the time Durham won by 279 runs Cook had left hospital. 'By all accounts it wasn't that great but Geoff being the incredibly resilient, bloody-minded character he is, he just somehow forged his way out of it,' says Smith. 'I can imagine Geoff just lying there going, "Right, I'm going to get back from this."' With the title race on, Cook was happy to just watch. 'The team was playing well and you get a sixth sense,' he reasons. 'I don't think they were missing me too much.'

Not that it was all plain sailing. A Championship defeat at Lord's was the first of four in five games across different competitions, and in the only win Onions broke a knuckle. 'I really thought I was playing in the Ashes at the Riverside,' he says having been named in England's squad. 'Before the game [coach] Andy Flower asked me about the wicket because he said I always bowled well there and I found him quite a difficult bloke to talk to normally so I thought, "This is great." So when he told me I wasn't playing I thought, "Why not?" I was getting a bit fed up of England. They told me I could stay, have some lunch and just chill but I went to play for Durham at The Grange, bowled brilliantly and then the ball fractured my hand.'

In his absence Jamie Harrison made a first Championship appearance for 14 months and Usman Arshad made his debut against Surrey. Harrison took 5-31 in the first innings, where Arshad was on a hat-trick, Wood 5-44 in the second. 'A bowler would come in and take five-fer, and then another one would come in and do the same,' says Smith. 'It was a revolving door of people coming in and out but always performing when they were in.'

Smith warmed up for Wood's Scarborough title decider with an unbeaten 79-ball 120 against a weak Surrey 40-over team. Joe Root's involvement in the Twenty20 international at Chester-le-Street mitigated Onions's absence and crucially Ben Stokes was overlooked. From 5/2 after winning the toss, Durham claimed their first maximum batting points of 2013. Stoneman made 122 of the first 195 runs, 98 in boundaries. 'It's certainly an innings I look back on very fondly given the importance of the match as it then felt and as it turned out, but also the feel of festival cricket and the partisan Yorkies,' he reflects. 'It summed up the season on a personal and team level that we found ourselves under pressure but we maintained our manner of play and took every opportunity to throw pressure back on to the opposition.'

Stoneman was not the only one rising to the occasion in front of a four-day crowd of 18,500. Dropped by Adam Lyth on 92, the second half of Stokes's first Championship century since June 2011 came off 45 deliveries. Playing as a specialist batsman at eight, Richardson was on 33 when Wood was eighth out yet reached a maiden first-class hundred. Excluding debutants, it was Durham's sixth career-best performance in seven days of cricket.

Yorkshire's reply began with a full-length, two-handed catch by fourth slip Stokes. 'You don't see many of those in a lifetime,' Michael Henderson wrote in *The Times*. Soon, though, Yorkshire were enjoying batting too. 'We fielded from just after lunch on day two until tea on day four,' Jennings recalls. 'It was horrible. I remember fielding near the stands getting so much abuse.'

The hosts began day three 182/3 in their first innings, with Kane Williamson 76 not out. Stokes removed him for 84 and when Yorkshire were 274 all out, Collingwood had little choice but to enforce the follow-on, even with Wood's game ended by a side injury. 'I remember Stokesey bouncing the hell out of Jaquesy [Phil Jaques] who was trying to belt anything short,' Collingwood recalls. Jaques ended day three unbeaten on 151, Williamson 90, from 276/1.

'I remember walking to the chippy quite distraught because we'd put a hell of a lot of effort in and it was kind of slipping away,' Collingwood continues. 'I had a pint and fish and chips with Stokesey and I said we'd got to get back to disciplined bowling, putting it in an area where they're uncomfortable. On flat pitches you've got to do it from both ends time and time again; it's not like the Riverside, you're going into Test-match mode to put them under pressure and as soon as you get that sniff you're into them. That was probably the first time I'd really had to get hold of Stokesey to focus him. He had everything, but sometimes his emotions controlled his game. That was a really good learning curve for him.' Smith is full of admiration for the way Collingwood 'had the wherewithal and the balls to rein him in but in a way that said, "You're still going to win this game for us."'

Most of those I spoke to highlighted Scarborough as when Durham believed they would win the title, but some were more specific. 'I set a gully field to Williamson and he was caught there because he was after his hundred,' says Collingwood. 'As soon as we got that mistake, it was amazing. Everything made you think, "Wow, this is happening here!"' On taking the brilliant catch off Stokes's bowling, Smith 'just thought, "Yes, we're winning this game!"'

Stokes had clearly decided he was not prepared to allow anything other than a Durham win, and had Jaques caught behind in his next over. As well as a side who had only lost one of their previous 30 Championship games, Durham were battling a flat pitch. Stokes bowled 33 outstanding second-innings overs from the Trafalgar Square End, Borthwick 38.2 from the Peasholm Park End. Borthwick had 0-134 until 3-0 from his final 17 deliveries ended Yorkshire's innings on 419. Stoneman was out to the first ball of the chase but Stokes finished it with a six and a four.

'It was like a Test match,' says Collingwood. 'My senses were heightened because it felt like pure quality – there was a crowd in, there was an atmosphere, a proper pitch with pace in it, the work we had to put in to win that game with Woody going down and Scotty Borthwick having to bowl from one end. There was also the realisation that you've got to do things as a team to win those games.'

Rushworth recalls: 'The changing rooms at Scarborough are like a tiny wooden box so when we started singing our team song [the Blaydon Races], you probably would have heard it from two towns away! I remember Will Smith saying to me, "We're going to win the Championship this year." He was convinced.' Smith admits: 'Some of the younger players were probably thinking, "Oh my God, what is he saying?" It was in a bit of a jokey way but I had complete conviction because we had such youthful naivety.'

Durham paid a high price for bowling 206.1 consecutive overs as Harrison suffered an ankle problem to join Wood in missing third-placed Sussex's visit. Stokes was on England duty, a hamstring injury ended Callum Thorp's season at Lord's and Ruel Brathwaite had joined Hampshire. Even with Onions back, Durham lacked bowling options for their game in hand. Having called for 'a bit of magic' on the third evening at Scarborough, Lewis rang an amateur magician.

Mitchell Claydon had not played for Durham since August 2012, and was seeing out his contract on loan at Kent, where he had four Division Two wickets at 56.5 runs apiece. At lunchtime the day before Durham played Sussex he was heading to play golf in Cardiff when Lewis asked him to drive to Chester-le-Street. Claydon had to wait for team-mate Ben Harmison to bring his car. He made 18 not out from 245 before Joe Gatting shouldered arms to his second ball, which kept low and sent off-stump cartwheeling for the first of three wickets in each innings. The recalled Arshad also took six wickets and made 30 and 34 as Durham won by 285 runs to go top. 'It could have been easy for Mitch to say, "I'm getting released, do I really need to put in a massive effort?" but he bowled his backside off,' says Rushworth.

'The international had been on the week before and we used the same pitch so it was drier than normal at the start and it became the sort of pitch Mitch would bowl well on – it wasn't by design,' insists Lewis. 'He's a better bowler on dry pitches because he bowls a line which hits the stumps more than Rushworth and he's good at reverse swing.'

The ridiculous wins kept coming. Day two at relegation-threatened Derbyshire was rained off and by the fourth morning Durham were still in their first innings, with only two batting points. They made the 43 needed for a third, but did not push for more and were 325 all out, 27 ahead with less than five hours of cricket remaining. Meanwhile at Hove, Yorkshire negotiated to chase 300 in 64 overs and narrow the gap to 1.5 points.

'There's absolutely no way we should have won,' says Onions, 'but me and Rushy were a great partnership and we just got on a massive roll.' Unhappy with his line, Onions adjusted his run-up at lunch and took 5-4 in 41 deliveries. With three for Rushworth and two for Arshad, Derbyshire were 63 all out. Durham knocked off the 37 needed for the loss of Stoneman, and bad weather in Sussex held Yorkshire to a draw.

Three days later Nottinghamshire became the only visitors to bat first at the Riverside in the 2013 Championship. Collingwood felt he should bowl but did not want to change a winning formula. Fortunately, Chris Read won the toss. 'We had Rushworth and Onions and it didn't matter if they bowled first or second, so we rolled them over for 78,' says Lewis. Durham were 74/6 until Collingwood, with a season's-best 88, added 121 with Mustard (77). Desperate to play, Stokes took 5-61 in a floodlit one-day international at Southampton the night before the game started, went for a morning scan on his hamstring, then drove up to join in.

Durham began day three 7/0 chasing 69. Rain delayed the start until 1.30pm but 57 minutes later Stoneman struck the winning four through the covers. 'I remember being not out overnight and thinking of being there at the moment we got those runs and what that would mean, having been involved in previous Championship wins but not with the contributions I wanted, and everything that had come and gone in the years since, all the hours of practice and training, the highs and lows as a group and as an individual, and that when that moment would come how it makes it all worth it,' he says. 'I don't think I slept that much but I do remember getting up in the morning feeling incredibly relaxed – excited but calm. When that moment came it was great to have my very good friend Will Smith at the other end.' Stoneman had passed 1,000 Championship runs for the season at Derby minutes before Borthwick, who had never previously reached 500. Rushworth hit his pre-season target of 50 wickets in Nottinghamshire's first innings, while Onions finished with 70.

Presenting Championship trophies to Durham's senior and under-17 teams was Bob Jackson, the only director throughout their first-class history. 'David Collier, the ECB chief executive, rang me and said, "Bob, we're tied up, can you present the trophy?"' he recalls. 'I was the proudest man in this region by a distance. The number of home-based players enhanced that Championship win and set the bar.' Stoneman argues: 'There was a strong identity of what we were about and who we were representing. I do believe that gave us an edge.'

Nevertheless, there were signs of trouble brewing. Three-time champion Thorp and four-time winner Smith were released as Durham, who used fewer players (18) than any first-division side in 2013 and were the only one without an overseas player, slashed their wage bill by a third. Smith was a Championship ever-present, top of Durham's Twenty20 and 40-over bowling averages and 40-over batting. 'He never once bemoaned his position and carried on like the great professional and bloke he is,' says Stoneman. Smith's departure, like Thorp's, was confirmed in two sentences at the end of a post-season press release four days after Hampshire announced his signing. Eleven days earlier I had broken the story, keen that members at the season's final game could say goodbye.

'I found out three-quarters of the way through the season,' Smith reveals. 'We'd had a meeting in May/June when there were the first mentions of financial issues. That was the first time I thought, "That's a bit odd. I'm out of contract here, that's not great." From a club's perspective you want to give the impression that every decision is being made because they want to but I think there were decisions they didn't want to make.' Onions says: 'It's just horrible. You say to these lads, "Oh, I'm really sorry," but you've still got a contract. Just because the club's been run badly why should they lose their job?'

Cook's heart attack wiped his memory of the first half of the season, yet Lewis 'felt it was still Geoff's decision [on contracts] because to me it always felt like he was coming back'. Collingwood insists: 'We didn't want to lose someone of Smudger's quality in the dressing room. When you're being told you have to cut the wage bill by such-and-such, it was "Jesus!" Naturally players are going to want contract extensions and pay rises after a good year. That's when you think, "Something's not right here."'

That it could not stop Durham's on-field success only added to the fairy tale.

14.

Life's a Breese

SPORT can be so good at throwing up fairy tales sometimes that the unlikely feels inevitable.

When it was announced Gareth Breese's 11th Durham season would be his last, the Riversiders were in danger of heading out of the 2014 Royal London One-Day Cup, but as he tried to withdraw his bat from a Chris Woakes delivery at Lord's in late September, it was no surprise the ball disappeared for the runs that won Durham the trophy. Yet again, they had backed themselves into a tight corner and wriggled out of it.

Breese's goodbye had been a month in the making. The all-rounder took a pay cut to stay at Durham for his benefit year (shared with Gordon Muchall) but for an increasingly cash-strapped club, just 11 Championship appearances in his final seven seasons (with one to come) was a luxury they could no longer afford, even from someone who gave so much in limited-overs cricket and off the field. A month and a day before the Lord's final it was revealed 2014 was Breese's final season at the Riverside.

'There are going to be times when you might not be in favour in all formats, but there's a competitive part of you that thinks leaving might be the easy way out,' he said on that grey Chester-le-Street morning. 'I've never lost my one-day place so I was playing the majority of games if not the majority of days.' When I asked about a dream Lord's send-off, Durham were still waiting on the following day's results to qualify for the quarter-finals. Even being in contention was an achievement.

It had been a difficult summer for Durham. Their Championship defence never got out of the blocks, losing one and drawing six of their first seven matches of a soggy season. Mark Stoneman and Scott Borthwick made slow starts, ninth and tenth in the county's batting averages at the start of June, although both would pass 1,000 Championship runs for the season again, Borthwick setting a new career-best three times. Twice in a fortnight in May he chipped bones in separate fingers on his right hand. The second occasion, at Taunton, was symptomatic of Durham's luck there. Having thinned their squad, Sod's Law dictated those remaining would suffer injuries.

Mark Wood had taken a brilliant first-innings 5-37 which had England selector Angus Fraser jumping in his car to watch the second attempt, but when he arrived in Somerset Wood was off the field with a sore side, and Jamie Harrison had a bad knee. It exposed debutant off-spinner Ryan Pringle to Marcus Trescothick, and the left-hander smashed 133. Pringle dismissed him but had figures of 17.3-1-94-2 as the hosts won by seven wickets. Chris Rushworth was also over-worked, delivering 165 overs in Durham's opening five games, only one of which they finished with 11 fit players. 'It's getting a bit annoying,' said an exasperated Paul Collingwood.

Defeat marked the end of 11 days in which Durham travelled 1,300 miles for Championship games at Hove and Taunton, sandwiching a Twenty20 home game. The first bus journey caused Graham Onions and Usman Arshad's backs to give way in the first innings at Sussex. Surgeons drilled into Onions's spine to free a nerve in November, after just one more Championship appearance.

Durham signed Australian bowling all-rounder John Hastings for 2014 but had to wait for him to play in the Indian Premier League – or rather not. Hastings featured in one of 16 Chennai Super Kings matches, and reaching the knockout stages ought to have ruled him

out of Middlesex's early-June Championship visit, but he was desperate
to play having avidly followed and commented on Durham's games
via Twitter from India, where he had a box of red Duke balls sent out
to train with. Hastings made his debut the morning after landing,
fortunate the Riversiders batted first and posted 411/4 on day one.

Having gone without an overseas player outside of Twenty20
cricket since Shivnarine Chanderpaul in 2009, Durham used three in
2014. It emerged during the opening game that Kumar Sangakkara,
a veteran of 122 Tests, 369 one-day internationals and 56 Twenty20
internationals who had just retired from the latter format with a
World Championships Final man-of-the-match performance, was
joining to warm up for the England versus Sri Lanka Test series, but
by the time he arrived he could only squeeze in two games, making
14 runs, taking a catch and dropping another against Yorkshire, then
scoring 159 at Hove.

Although Hastings topped Durham's batting averages and was
second in their bowling, the Riversiders finished sixth in the nine-
strong Twenty20 northern group. They beat Lancashire narrowly
and Sussex crushingly in consecutive home games to break their
Championship duck, but went into the 50-over competition on the
back of what Jon Lewis – given the head coach's job permanently the
previous winter – called a 'kick up the arse' at home to Warwickshire.
Durham lost 17 final-day wickets, five for ducks, and were 113 all
out following on 301 behind for their first innings defeat since May
2010. Only Nottinghamshire's one-wicket win over Lancashire kept
the champions out of the relegation zone as four-day cricket went on
hold after 11 games.

The change of format brought no instant relief. Mothballed at
county level after 2009, 50-over cricket was new to many Durham
players and they lost three of their opening four games under
Stoneman. The left-hander made just 12 appearances in his first five
limited-overs seasons, but having filled in after Dale Benkenstein's
career-ending injury in May 2013 he was confirmed as white-ball
captain in March 2014. 'It was an incredibly proud moment, having

worn the Durham badge since playing for the under-11s, through the academy up to first-team level,' he says. 'There were certainly big boots to fill, but having the full support of the coaching staff and dressing room made it a very exciting challenge and one I know made my parents and partner very proud.'

Initially it seemed the responsibility was hampering him. Although Stoneman had found his feet in four-day cricket, he went into the game against Warwickshire without a limited-overs half-century for a year, and only two double-figure scores in nine matches. It was Durham's first home game away from Chester-le-Street since 2006, played at South Northumberland to celebrate the Newcastle club's 150th anniversary. It started on a Thursday morning and Durham's bus only got back from their floodlit game in Kent and a second defeat in as many 50-over matches in the early hours of Wednesday. That the players got social media grief for playing golf that day clearly rankled with the sometimes prickly Stoneman because he mentioned it in his post-match interview.

Durham's eight group fixtures were squeezed into 19 days. The away games were in Taunton, Canterbury, Hove and Cardiff, with only South North between them. Hastings took a career-best 5-46 there, including bowling centurion Jonathan Trott with a slower ball, and from 213/3 after 40 overs, Warwickshire were 264 all out – a score Durham lost five wickets passing. Stoneman made 50, Collingwood 77. Soon Durham were back on the road and beaten again, by five wickets at Sussex.

Each defeat saw an opposition bowler improve his career-best batting score. Lewis Gregory hit 105 not out (and James Hildreth an unbeaten 146) as Somerset went from 106/5 to 315/5 and victory, while Calum Haggett made 36 as Kent scored the 97 needed in the final 16 overs. 'We had Sussex beaten – they were dead, they were done,' says Lewis. 'Then Will Beer got [a career-best] 45 not out and [Yasir] Arafat 55 not out. So we lost three games we'd played really well in.'

Collingwood argues that '75 per cent of the game we were dominating, we were doing a lot right', but as Rushworth says: 'If you lost three, more than likely you were not going to get through.' It was not looking great for Breese. 'I was just thinking, "Jesus, my last season is going to fritter away,"' he admits. 'The turning point was at Glamorgan. It wasn't a great wicket [Glamorgan were docked points for it] but we managed to get a score on the board [185] and Graham Onions got four wickets.' Durham stayed over after their televised 52-run Friday-night win. It was, says Breese, 'a big night out in Cardiff. Everybody was out together.'

Stoneman believes: 'The momentum we managed to build on the back of an horrendous start proved unstoppable. There were some fairly frank conversations as we simply didn't turn up at times, but when we clicked we did some outstanding things. We got into a position of knockout cricket fairly early on, but I think that brought the best out of us and by the time we reached the knockout stages we were accustomed to the pressure and began to excel.' The home game with Middlesex was rained off but Ben Stokes, who made a duck in it, smashed the century he cited as the turning point of his 2014 at home to Nottinghamshire the next day, adding 150 for the third wicket with Stoneman (86). Against Surrey in Durham's final group game, Keaton Jennings was the unlikely star.

Despite four one-day fifties in six South African domestic games, Jennings did not play limited-overs cricket for Durham until 2014. They used him as a Twenty20 bowler and fielder, not facing a ball in four appearances but delivering 13 overs (4-103). In 50-over matches, Durham exploited his versatility, sometimes a pinch-blocker to head off batting subsidence, others looking to pepper the boundary. He made 45 from 43 balls at Taunton, batting at six, 26 not out from 16 at nine in Canterbury, and top-scored with 70 from 67 at five in the rain-affected win over Surrey.

'You just learn to adapt,' Jennings says, matter-of-factly. 'I suppose that's where my one-day cricket has grown because I've been able to assess conditions quite quickly. It's tough when you're playing in the four-day side as an opener and you're batting ten in 20-over cricket. As a young player you question what you're actually doing, but it was good to have three strings and know you needed to work on all three. To trust a young guy like me who hadn't played much cricket to calm things down was awesome. There was so much trust in individuals in that campaign.'

Finishing their group matches six days before their rivals, Durham did not know if the Surrey victory would suffice for the quarter-finals. 'Rocky said it could be my last game at Durham, did I want to go in [ahead of Hastings with six runs needed], but I said, "No, it's not about me, let's just play properly and if I'm not seen here again, that's fine,"' Breese recalls. 'It turned out to be one of the best decisions of my life because I ended up having another game at Durham in the semi-final against Notts and I got to say bye without it being fabricated, then I got to say a proper goodbye at Lord's.'

When Surrey beat Somerset via the Duckworth-Lewis Method, Durham were confirmed as finishing fourth in a nine-strong group which provided all the semi-finalists. Belief was growing. 'I remember Johnny Hastings at the start of the season saying, "We're winning this!"' says Collingwood. 'We lost three of the first four games and he was still absolutely adamant. I don't know if he'd had a vision or something!' Collingwood's tongue is firmly in his cheek but perhaps he is closer to reality than he realises. 'I remember very clearly a dream I had before the quarter-finals,' Stoneman reveals. 'When I woke up I told my wife I'd just dreamt we won the Lord's final and we were singing the team song. From that moment it felt there would be no other outcome.'

Stoneman's 112 against group A winners Yorkshire was his first as captain. His concentration was tested when the game was suspended for 31 minutes after a home spectator received CPR which failed to restart his heart, and Stoneman felt Durham's 237 was about 30 short. 'Yorkshire were doing well when we got [Kane] Williamson out with a nice bit of planning to get him to nick off wide and full, and Rushy produced a spell to turn the game a bit,' explains Lewis. Thanks to Rushworth's 3-23, Durham won by 31 runs despite dropping five catches.

Next were group B winners Nottinghamshire at home – and a Stokes masterclass. It had been a difficult 2014 for the all-rounder. His performances in Durham's title-winning season and Trott's mental struggles led to a Test debut in the 2013/14 Ashes. Stokes was England's sole centurion and one of only two bowlers to take five-wicket hauls in the series, then won his first England man-of-the-match award in the fourth one-day international. Yet when he slammed his hand against a locker in frustration at a golden duck in March, the broken wrist ruled Stokes out of a dismal World Twenty20 campaign and on his return it felt like he was still to win England's trust.

In February 2013, a little over a year after being arrested for obstructing a police officer, Stokes and Matt Coles were sent home from the Lions tour of Australia for 'ignoring the instructions given to them around their match preparation'. Even with Graeme Swann retiring in Australia and Kevin Pietersen dropped, England resisted giving Stokes a central contract. Rather than rush him back for the Sri Lanka Test series, he was asked to prove his fitness while England lost without him. When he returned – after his maiden ten-wicket haul, against Sussex – it was to bat at eight and nine in the first two Tests against India. Ducks in all three innings saw him dropped. To Durham's immense good fortune, Stokes was left out of the Twenty20 side too. 'It was hard to know which was more unbelievable, Ben Stokes's 164 on Saturday, or the fact he was not considered good enough to play for England the next day,' I wrote.

'When we lost the toss on what looked a slightly green pitch at the Riverside under overcast skies you know you're gonna be under pressure, but I think the way everybody played that day was on the back of the work we'd been doing in the build-up,' reflects Stoneman. Phil Mustard missed the preceding Championship game, also against Nottinghamshire, with a knee injury and was having a poor season but played after an injection.

'White-ball cricket started to become Colonel's identity so it was a bigger thing to remove him from that side, although he wasn't happy to be left out of the red-ball [matches],' Lewis explains. 'The great thing about Colonel was form was irrelevant. Because he'd scored a hundred the week before didn't mean he was any more likely to score runs this week; because he hadn't scored a hundred for three weeks didn't make him any less likely to score an 80-ball hundred. That gives you the optimism to persist with a bloke who's not scored runs for a while and he was a big personality, which you need in the knockout stages of the cups.'

Mustard produced an uncharacteristic but brilliant innings, stabilising Durham after three wickets in 6.1 overs. Recognising Stokes's form, Mustard largely dropped anchor for 89 from 111 deliveries, cutting loose only in the batting powerplay. There was nothing reserved about his team-mate. 'The way Ben played just highlighted his high class combined with brute force and undying competitiveness against very strong opposition,' says Stoneman.

Dropped on 12 by England's best wicketkeeper Chris Read, standing up to Steven Mullaney, Stokes smashed 18 fours and six sixes in a 113-ball 164. Durham's 353/8 was 30 more than any limited-overs team – county or international – had made at the Riverside. 'I remember thinking if we got 250 we'd have done well and we'd reached it by about 30 overs!' chuckles Lewis.

Nottinghamshire recovered from the loss of three wickets in the opening 15 overs to equal Durham's score after 30. They too had a player mystifyingly overlooked by England but James Taylor's 114 from 112 deliveries could not match Stokes's late-innings pyrotechnics, so Durham won by 83 runs. 'It felt tighter than it looked in the scorebook,' says Lewis. Not from the press box. 'I want to be playing for England but I looked at it as a great chance to get Durham to a final,' a beaming Stokes commented afterwards. 'It's quite good because I reckon we will be having a decent night tonight.'

Rushworth could scarcely have had a better build-up to the final. He was offered the chance to sit out the previous Championship match, at home to Northamptonshire but, still somehow short of his 50-wicket benchmark, wanted to play. The seamer appeared to have no luck all season until it all came at once. 'That's still the most incredible game of cricket I've ever been involved in,' he says. 'The first day was washed out, we batted for the whole of day two and it was over by tea on day three! It literally felt like every ball I was going to take a wicket. Some days you feel good but you end up with none or one-fer, other days you can get five or six and not feel as good but that day everything clicked and luckily I got the rewards. There was a lot of hard work and consistency throughout the season to finally get those rewards. I would never expect that kind of game again.'

Durham posted 392 thanks to centuries from Collingwood and Scott Borthwick, then bowled Northants out for 83 and 90. Rushworth was only denied ten first-innings wickets by an embarrassed Stokes, and took six in the second. His 15-95 beat the club record set by bowling coach Alan Walker, the first to shake Rushworth's hand when he came off. If Lewis wanted his premier seamer to rest, he need not have worried – Durham bowled just 40.2 overs in the match.

There was good reason to wrap Rushworth in cotton wool. Onions, top of Durham's group-stage bowling averages, picked up a season-ending abdominal injury in August, and Chennai selected Hastings for the Champions League. 'He was devastated,' says Lewis. 'He was a big member of the side, a big personality, and I was more sorry for him than for us.' Hastings offered to fly back from India after Wednesday's match against Kolkata Knight Riders and return for Monday's against Dolphins, but coach Stephen Fleming would not entertain the unrealistic plan. Hastings bowled two wicketless overs and did not bat as Chennai won the last Champions League before it was scrapped. 'I was having nets in the morning in Bangalore and the game came on later that night,' he recalled. 'It wasn't live but I was following the scores live and I rang the guys when they were singing the [victory] song. It was shattering not to be there.'

Fearing Championship relegation, Durham signed Varun Aaron to replace Hastings but were safe by the time he arrived and the Indian was ineligible for the final against Warwickshire. Peter Chase, a 20-year-old Irishman, became only the fifth player to take five wickets on his Durham Championship debut at home to Nottinghamshire in August/September – and would have been the second after James Brinkley to take six had Collingwood not dropped a catch – but Durham gave the new ball to Sunderland-born all-rounder Paul Coughlin at Lord's. The 21-year-old had never played there, was making only his seventh one-day appearance, and had a stress fracture in his back, the injury that wiped out his 2013. When Stoneman won the toss, Coughlin bowled the second over on a day so gloomy the floodlights stayed on throughout. 'I remember walking out next to Coggers,' says Rushworth. 'I wished him good luck but his face was white, he was shaking. He said, "Rushy, I'm absolutely crapping my pants here."'

Nerves clearly brought the best out of Coughlin. When he came out to bat at 184/8 against Lancashire in June he told Mustard, 'I cannot grip my bat properly,' then made 85, the highest score by a player making his Championship debut with Durham since Nicky Peng's 98 at Surrey in 2000 and the most by a Durham number ten in four-day cricket. He followed it with 3-42. Coughlin's cup-final bowling was better than his figures suggested, and 8-0-30-0 looked pretty decent. 'He bowled amazingly,' says Rushworth. 'He set the tone.'

Durham were firm underdogs, only Breese, Collingwood and Mustard having experienced a Lord's final. 'Warwickshire expected to win,' says Lewis. 'They'd won the Twenty20 Cup and there was a suggestion that before the final they'd asked for a photo with both trophies. I don't know if it was true or not, but I perpetuated it and it was something we talked about – not dwelt on, but it certainly got mentioned.'

It was a bowler's morning – it would be a bowler's afternoon too – and Rushworth's reward for a day's work which included two maidens was the scalps of openers Will Porterfield and Varun Chopra. 'Stokesey bounced out Laurie Evans and went straight through Rikki Clarke, then Calum MacLeod took a great catch,' recalls Lewis. 'Turning and running when the ball goes over your head was something he'd been talking about with Colly in the weeks leading up.' MacLeod's catch running back at mid-on after seemingly losing the flight of the ball brought the first of Breese's three wickets.

'Because I'd never been a star player I always wanted to try to make sure that right up to the end I wasn't carried,' Breese insists. 'I wanted to go back to Lord's and do a bit more than in 2007 when I didn't bat, I didn't take a catch and I bowled three overs for 21. In the Notts game when we had a wobble in the group stage I was not out 68 and we won by one wicket so I felt like I played my part to get us there, but in the years after that there was a little bit of frustration because I always wanted the team to get back to Lord's. Sometimes in life dreams come true!'

Warwickshire were 165 all out in 47 overs. Stoneman set about the target in a hurry, hitting 31 off Chris Woakes's first 20 deliveries and shrugging off the loss of Mustard and MacLeod for ducks. In the 12th over, Chopra threw the ball to off-spinner Jeetan Patel. 'At the halfway stage I thought Woakes was the danger but he didn't get it right early on to Rocky, then suddenly, it's turning – shit!' says Lewis. 'We didn't honestly think this was the pitch for Jeetan Patel, but he's a very, very fine cricketer and we had a lot of left-handers, so he made it interesting.' Collingwood was waiting to bat: 'We thought it was done and dusted then when the first couple of balls just ragged we thought, "Oh God! This could be trouble!" It was tense and you wondered who was going to get you over the line.'

Pushed up the order along with Borthwick, Jennings was batting with Stoneman when Patel came on. If Rushworth went into the final on top form, the opposite was true of left-hander Jennings. 'I'd come off a pair at Lord's [in the Championship, then another duck at home to Northamptonshire] into a high-pressure situation in a final and I walked in at 12/2,' he recalls. 'As a 22-year-old who hadn't played a whole heap of cricket, you're like, "How do I actually go about this?" I remember walking down the stairs feeling OK but when I got out [lbw in Patel's first over] and I was walking back up those stairs I was a mess.

'There's a big centre console in the dressing room and I sat behind that looking away. I couldn't watch. Eventually I sat next to Alan Walker at the console. I went to get up and he grabbed me and said, "Sit down!" because we were playing quite nicely at that stage. Everything about the game was more tense being out of it than being in it. I don't think we ever believed the game was over but to bowl them out for 165, you think you're in the pound seats. Suddenly you're 12/2 and you're going, "Are we?"'

Patel trapped Stoneman, for a run-a-ball 52, and Borthwick lbw. Collingwood and Stokes added 31 before Oliver Hannon-Dalby removed the elder statesman for 21, and Gordon Muchall became Patel's fourth lbw victim. With 36 needed, Breese joined Stokes, again rising to the occasion. 'For Stokesey to play as he did was awesome,' says Jennings. 'Someone said, "I hope he doesn't reverse sweep," and two balls later he took on Jeetan Patel with his reverse sweep. That's Stokes to a tee – he wants to take you on and beat you.' Stokes was 28 not out when the under-edge narrowly missed his stumps and bounced off wicketkeeper Tim Ambrose's ankle for four.

'If we hadn't had Breesey or even Stokesey's experience we might have struggled,' Collingwood admits. 'They kind of calmed everything down until Stokesey's reverse sweep. I think every other decision he made was spot on.' Lewis stresses: 'It was probably a big day for Stokesey because he was impressive in a very high-pressure situation. It was great to see how important it was to him. Seeing [Stephen] Harmison win County Championships and what that meant to him, and seeing Stokesey that day when these guys have so much bigger games, you can't deny victories for Durham are genuinely important to them.'

The script, though, was written around Breese. 'We didn't talk about it much [beforehand],' Lewis insists. 'We didn't want to send him off at all but we didn't dwell on that too much. But it was good that it worked that well. It was great for him and he was hugely popular. Winning dressing rooms at Lord's are about as good as it gets, so it was a nice place to be after he left the winning runs! It was a big evening for Gareth but we got him back to the hotel in one piece.' Stoneman points out: 'There was motivation at every angle,' yet still, 'it felt like the script was written for Gareth to be there at the end and the icing on the cake was for him to hit the winning runs and run off to his family.'

As the ball crossed the third-man boundary, Stokes leapt into the air, then Breese's arms. On to the field ran five-year-old Savannah Breese and her brother Max, not yet two, shouting: 'Daddy win!' Breese embraced both, then his wife Celia. 'If there's a guy you want to do something for, it's Breesey,' Jennings grins. 'He's the first guy to pick you up if you're in trouble or do something for you. So if you can't find it for yourself, to do it for him was quite cool.'

It was massive from a team perspective too. 'Fifty-over cricket's the toughest format and I don't think anyone was banking on us winning a one-day trophy that year,' Rushworth argues. 'To have only used 13 players [in the whole tournament] shows what a huge effort it was.'

The following week Collingwood was named player of the tournament after averaging 53 with the bat and taking 14 wickets at 22.85. He was the most economical bowler to take ten wickets or more. Although his leadership was crucial in the 2013 Championship, Collingwood only contributed two fifties, but his 113 at Somerset in 2014's opening one-day game started an Indian summer which put the then-38-year-old's retirement plans on hold until 2018. He was Durham's leading Twenty20 wicket-taker, and although he just missed 1,000 Championship runs for the season, his first-class batting average was above 40 for the first time since 2007.

Collingwood had been assistant coach as Scotland missed out in the World Twenty20 qualifiers, but jointly with Craig Wright he led them to the 50-over World Cup. He was England's fielding coach in the West Indies and the 2014 World Twenty20 Championships, learning as much from those he coached as they did from him, and making a slight technical change to hit the ball harder and open up the off side.

It was no one-season wonder. Durham's player of 2014 started 2015 with his first Championship five-wicket haul in ten years at Somerset, and made 109 not out. In 2016 he topped the county's

Twenty20 batting averages with 69.50 and in 2017 he was their only batsman to 1,000 Championship runs. It was after his England career that he claimed Durham's first Twenty20 hat-trick and century, and made his career-best one-day score. 'He not only tried to keep pace with the game but to stay one step ahead,' says Geoff Cook.

'I felt I was improving technically,' Collingwood says. 'I had more areas to score in and I probably erred more on the aggressive side. I probably wanted to play in more of a free manner because after ten years of grafting my tits off at international level there comes a point where you just have to go out there and enjoy it, and try to put the bowler under pressure rather than yourself. In some ways I was a better player than when I played international cricket.'

It was not quite the end for Breese either. With Jamie Harrison awaiting surgery, Usman Arshad, Gavin Main and Coughlin suffering back injuries, and Stokes (England), MacLeod (Scotland), Chase and Stuart Poynter (both Ireland) rested by their countries, Breese played at Edgbaston three days later in Durham's final Championship match of 2014. So did Mark Wood, despite being, in Lewis's words, 'probably ten days off being fit for a game of cricket'. Breese made 26 and seven and did not take a wicket, but enjoyed Ryan Pringle's unbeaten 63 in his first post-Taunton first-class outing. Jennings finished the summer with another duck as Warwickshire beat Durham by an innings and 13 runs.

I always felt it a shame Breese had not bowed out at Lord's. Did he? 'Sometimes I do,' he admits. 'But do you know what? It was still a perfect end for me. Over my last six years at Durham my main contribution was in one-day cricket and for a couple of years I'd wanted us to compete a bit harder in one-day cricket so to sign off with that, there's not much which could have spoiled that, having my family there and being able to do it one last time for the guys on the balcony. I'm getting a bit emotional even now!'

After consecutive trophy-winning seasons, 2015 was Durham's comedown. Their cup defence ended with a damp squib of a quarter-final they again scraped into. It was reduced to a virtual Twenty20 game by a near-five-hour rain delay, and Nottinghamshire triumphed by 49 runs. Durham won four of their five games over the full 50-overs-a-side in 2015 but lacked explosiveness with bat and ball for shorter contests.

In all three competitions their small squad caught up with them. They won four of their first six Twenty20 matches, but only one of the last eight. Compensating for poor first-innings batting with good run-chases, they sat drinking beer on the Arundel outfield celebrating a 178-run win over Sussex top of the Championship. Halfway through the competition, they had already won as many games as in 2008 but their next victory came in the final match.

Muchall's mid-July century was Durham's last of the 2015 competition, and afterwards he told me he had been warned not to expect another contract. Jennings, MacLeod, Mustard and Graham Clark were dropped in the Championship and no one convinced as Stoneman's opening partner. Borthwick made 11 Championship fifties but only one century, playing on for 99 in his final knock, although he hit half-centuries in all bar one of Durham's five successful run-chases. The exception was Worcestershire, where he scored a first-innings 103. Collingwood was unable to continue his excellent start when he moved up to four to try to paper over the batting cracks.

The fielding was sloppy, the bowling ineffective when the ball went soft, and Hastings, carrying a shoulder problem, looked dead on his feet by the end. Until injuries to Shane Watson and Nathan Coulter-Nile brought an unexpected call-up to Australia's one-day squad in September, he had not missed a Durham game in 2015. The series against England finished in time to face Worcestershire and reach 500 runs and 50 wickets, seasonal milestones only Manoj Prabhakar and Ottis Gibson had simultaneously passed for Durham, but by then he had succumbed to injury.

Rushworth was a shining light, taking 100 wickets in all competitions, including 83 in the Championship. 'It was incredible,' he says. 'You don't go out looking for targets but when you get close it's always in the back of your mind, and I remember thinking I was going to break Gibbo's [80-wicket] record, then having a game where I only got one or two and it was just getting later and later. To finally do it at the Riverside was nice because it's been good to me and it was nice to do it in front of my family. Hopefully it isn't broken for a long time or, if so, it's me again!'

Rushworth ought to have been recognised with an international call-up when James Anderson's injury left England a swing bowler short for the Trent Bridge Test. 'I remember the selectors telling me I was in the frame so that was hugely exciting,' he admits. 'When the squad was announced I was keeping an eye on my phone and I was nervous. My dad sent a message to tell me I wasn't in it. I didn't really think much of it for the next few hours but when I thought about it a little bit more I was a little bit sad. But to come from being released and get that close, it was still an incredible feeling.'

Durham's fourth-place Championship finish flattered them considering they only avoided relegation in their final session of the season (they sat out the last week), and their 26 batting points was easily Division One's lowest. Next season would be tougher, with Somerset the only county not playing at a Test ground in a division which would be reduced to eight for 2017.

Durham's financial troubles were beginning to bite. Harrison played the final two games back-to-back days after Collingwood said: 'When Jamie's been playing I've felt as though he's been in too much pain and I wasn't comfortable sending him out time and time again. When we're 50 years old, if he turns around to me and says, "I can hardly walk," I will be very upset.' Harrison was sent for a knee operation that winter, and never played Championship cricket again.

Between them Hastings, Rushworth and Onions bowled 1,454 Championship overs in 2015 when no other seamer managed 120, and injury prevented the Australian returning. How much longer could Durham defy the odds?

15.

Failing the Tests

O N 30 May 2016, Chester-le-Street witnessed a significant moment in English cricketing history. As Alastair Cook's drive trickled to the midwicket boundary a huge '10,000 Test runs' banner was unveiled on the Riverside's north-east terrace. The first Englishman to the milestone, Cook was the youngest of the 12 worldwide and the only one still playing.

With Lumley Castle over its shoulder, the stand which previously stood at the 2012 Olympic beach volleyball tournament often attracts photographers. As they snapped the banner, the sea of empty blue seats beneath it highlighted what a commercial disaster the second England versus Sri Lanka Test was. Only 2,759 fans were in the ground watching England's nine-wicket win. When the day started it seemed unlikely Cook and England would have to bat again to clinch their series victory and the weather was not the best, but still it was embarrassing and hugely costly for Durham.

Cook's landmark was one of the last acts of the final Test at international cricket's most northerly ground. For a part of the world which had done so much in recent years to staff England's team, it was hard to take but, after that response, difficult to argue. From the start of their first-class journey, Durham planned to host internationals but the scale of their ambition made it the only way to pay the bills.

Staging their most lucrative and glamorous Test in 2013 – despite not asking to host the Ashes – burdened them with games they could not afford and accelerated their financial meltdown.

The Riverside's first international was a women's one-day game between England and New Zealand, who wrapped up a 3-0 series victory there in June 1996. In August it hosted Durham versus Pakistan – where Simon Brown's 7-107 was not enough to add to his only Test cap, won against the same opposition a fortnight earlier – and South Africa A against a TCCB XI featuring Jimmy Daley alongside future England captains Adam Hollioake and Mark Butcher. Two years later David Harker and Mike Candlish, whom the former succeeded as chief executive, carried out a financial analysis on the benefits of international cricket. 'I cannot remember one member of the board not supporting seeking Test cricket,' says director Bob Jackson.

'The money in cricket was around international cricket so the board accepted that, having made the commitment to develop the stadium, if we were going to make ends meet then international cricket was the way to do it,' Harker explains. 'It became the mission of the club to secure regular international cricket. There was significant European grant money at the time so I think there was an element of, "If we're going to do this, now's the time and let's make a statement."

'I think people saw international cricket as a bit of an ego-trip for certain individuals, but I don't think that was ever the case. Once you'd set your stall out to develop this [stadium], it was very difficult to go backwards because what you've built is already in place and costing you money. As far as I ever saw it, it was only ever motivated by the desire to finish the job of building the stadium and try to make the best of it.' A member of the TCCB's working party who assisted Durham's first-class bid, Steve Coverdale says, 'I don't think the Riverside being a potential international venue played much of a part [in their elevation] but I think they needed that sense of ambition. That was very important to attract potential sponsors.'

There was an ideological element too. 'The club was founded as a first-class club to give opportunities to local kids, and to give local cricket supporters the chance to see international cricket on their own patch was consistent with that story,' Harker points out. 'Paul Collingwood would have been 15 years old at the time we became first-class and seen an opportunity to pursue a career in cricket.'

Durham academy director John Windows's job relies on the enthusiasm of north-east youngsters to play cricket. 'My son is ten, just coming into it, and you probably don't realise the effect cricket has until you see it first hand,' he argues. 'I couldn't believe how keen he was to come to the Twenty20 because he was absolutely desperate to see Chris Gayle. You can see him on the telly but, close up, he's in awe of him. He likes cricket because I'm involved and he'll follow Durham but he wants to see Woody [Mark Wood], [Ben] Stokes and Chris Gayle; he wants to see superstars in the flesh.

'I used to go to the Callers Pegasus matches. I remember thinking, "Cor, they stand a long way back." When you went to Jesmond and played a club match, you thought, "Jeez, our wickie stands there and they [the internationals] are 30 yards back." That's why international cricket has to keep coming. It was really far-sighted from the Caller brothers to have done that.'

The Riverside hosted two 1999 World Cup matches – Pakistan beating Scotland by 94 runs and Australia defeating Bangladesh by seven wickets. On 15 July 2000, England played their first one-day international (ODI) there, comfortably beating the West Indies by ten wickets in front of a 15,000 sell-out as part of a triangular tournament. Sherwin Campbell's century the next day could not stop Zimbabwe inflicting a second defeat on Jimmy Adams's side. The following June, Australia and Pakistan were due to play a 50-over game but, with all 12,000 tickets sold, it was abandoned at 1.55pm without a ball bowled. In July 2002, Collingwood became the first Durham player to represent England at Chester-le-Street but again the weather won, 12.3 overs into England's reply. Collingwood had taken 1-48. According to Tom Moffat: 'The first day we had an international game a man I knew came up to me on the steps of the pavilion and threw his arms around me and said, "Thank you, we all know how much we owe to you for all of this" – but the real ambition was Test cricket.'

Lancashire chairman Bob Bennett warned from the start: 'We have to be careful we don't have too many stadia which cannot be filled.' Old Trafford was part of the status quo, along with Headingley, Edgbaston, Trent Bridge, The Oval and Lord's. The Riverside joined in November 2001, accepted as the first new English Test ground since Sheffield's Bramall Lane in 1902. Globally, Chester-le-Street became the 87th venue and, until Gros Islet in 2003, the only town. Durham hoped to stage a Test every other year, with one-day internationals in between. Although it has not quite worked out like that, England have been back every year since 2005 – a sequence due to continue until at least 2024.

Zimbabwe were the first Test visitors in June 2003, when Stephen Harmison won his seventh England cap. 'It was a great day for the club, for the people at Durham, for the board members, for the likes of Don Robson, Geoff Cook, Bob Jackson, Tom Moffat, the Caller brothers, David Harker and Mattie Roseberry, to see the recognition of their hard work,' says Harmison. 'We were always going to get a Test against a team not in the top echelons but Zimbabwe were not a bad side.

'Being from the north east it meant a hell of a lot to me. Not many people can say they've played in the very first Test their home ground hosted. Once it starts it's just another Test match – the stumps are 22 yards away and you just want to beat the guy at that end. The crowd, the sledging, it's just background noise wherever you are in the world, but walking out beforehand and seeing so many familiar faces – not just family and friends but members and people who'd worked so hard to get it – that was special.'

With Andrew Flintoff injured, England needed an all-rounder but Collingwood, still uncapped at Test level, dislocated his left shoulder at Old Trafford in April, so the honour fell to Anthony McGrath, who had made a half-century and taken 3-16 on his Test debut at Lord's a fortnight earlier. 'You could tell what a big deal it was,' he told me in 2013. 'It's a fantastic location and a great club, so for them to get a Test was brilliant. Everyone there really enjoyed it.' England were 156/5 when McGrath joined Alec Stewart, but his 81 turned the game from contest to cakewalk. Harmison claimed two first-innings victims as the tourists were 94 all out in swinging conditions, then 4-55 – including the wicket which clinched victory by an innings and 69 runs – on day three.

Harmison was not Durham's only representative. When I ask Windows about his stint as a substitute fielder he bursts out laughing. 'The home ground had to provide 12th men but the first team were away and the third day was a Saturday,' he explains. 'Geoff [Cook] was in charge of it and, when we could see it was going to go to Saturday, we were sorting out our academy side for the weekend and everyone was playing club cricket. So we went through the teams for Saturday and I'd been sort of half-playing for the academy, helping out. So Geoff said, "Well you do 12th man, you and [Graeme] Bridge, you'll be fine. Duncan Fletcher [England's coach] is a nice fella, just turn up and introduce yourself." It was £110 so I got roped into it and I had to come in at half-eight to meet Nasser Hussain and Duncan Fletcher. It was only because Geoff hadn't thought about who would do it but it was the best thing.

'I was involved in the warm-up and I'm thinking, "What am I doing here? This is ridiculous!" Bridgey went on the first few times and, because England were winning, he said, "We'll have a bit of fun now." When I brought the drinks on he said, "You stop on, no one will notice." Harmy had just taken a wicket, so I'm standing behind [wicket-keeper] Alec Stewart with Harmy ready to bowl and I had to shout, "Oi, Stewy! Where you do want me?" Then I shout, "Harmy, Harmy, stop!" and I'm thinking, "What am I doing here?" So they put me in at short midwicket to Heath Streak. It was crackers! It was embarrassing!

'Afterwards everyone goes around and gets things signed. I never got anything signed, did I? Everyone frittered away at about half-past six and I thought, "What do I do?" So I went to watch the end of the academy game at Maiden Castle. That was a massive line in the sand I was part of, but at the time you're not really aware of the gravity.'

The Riverside's next Test, against another minnow, was just as one-sided. Michael Vaughan wrote in his autobiography he was 'looking for another two-day win' over Bangladesh to follow the one at Lord's as England tuned up for the 2005 Ashes. The former have improved greatly since, but in the mid-noughties Andrew Strauss wrote that games against Bangladesh and Zimbabwe 'are as close as you can get to a foregone conclusion'. Harmison took 5-36 as England won by an innings and 27 runs, but Bangladesh made Vaughan wait until the third morning to pop the champagne corks.

Chester-le-Street's one-day internationals in that period were just as unsatisfactory, but it was England who were the lambs to the slaughter in that format. The 2004 match against New Zealand lasted just 50.1 overs after the hosts were 101 all out. Harmison took the three wickets the Kiwis lost passing it. The 2005 pre-Ashes one-dayer was more notable for the fun at Shane Watson's expense after Australia's all-rounder thought he saw a ghost at Lumley Castle before England lost by 57 runs. The following year new-ball bowlers Harmison and Liam Plunkett produced combined figures of 15.2-0-101-0, and Collingwood also went wicketless, as Sri Lanka secured an eight-wicket win 46 balls early. The north-east terrace showed its boredom with a few Mexican waves and the odd conga before plenty headed home early.

Every international seemed to be dogged by bad weather, a poor team or both. One of the car parks was so boggy it had to be closed on the Saturday of the 2007 West Indies Test. With the start delayed until 2pm and the finish brought forward to 5.30pm by bad light, only 40 overs were possible – but it was 40 more than the opening day. The tourists were a sorry sight too. Ramnaresh Sarwan replaced Brian Lara as captain after the latter's post-World Cup retirement, only to dislocate his shoulder in the second Test. They had lost the four-match series by the time they arrived in Chester-le-Street. At least Shivnarine Chanderpaul was in good touch, the first to bat more than 1,000 minutes in Test cricket without being dismissed, making an unbeaten 136 out of 287.

Collingwood made history too, the first Durham player to score a Riverside Test century. 'Not that I knew about it,' he says. 'When you're playing, a lot of the time you're in such a bubble. It might sound silly but you don't feel like you're at home, you're just playing. You've got this travelling circus going around the whole of the world to different venues with the same people. The only thing about coming here is you've got to get about 40 tickets, so it's actually a ball-ache. In many ways it's more stressful. But once we were playing I obviously knew the wicket pretty well and I was facing Fidel [Edwards], [Daren] Powell and Corey Collymore. It was, "My God, this can't get any better." You've got all your family and friends there. They weren't the best in the world but I would have taken it against anyone. It was a magnificent week.' His 128 came on the Monday, and a seven-wicket victory followed on Tuesday. On Wednesday, Collingwood was part of the Durham side that reached their first professional-era Lord's final and on Thursday he was told he would be England's new limited-overs captain.

Although Collingwood made 64 and took 4-15 in his first Riverside international as skipper, a 2008 ODI against New Zealand, he was overshadowed not so much by Kevin Pietersen's first 50-over century since the previous year's World Cup as the 'switch-hits' which decorated it, and England's 114-run win. August's Twenty20 international against South Africa was rained off.

Durham's addition to the international map presented the England and Wales Cricket Board with an opportunity. 'I went to the media centre of one of the grounds in 2007, went to the toilet and a rat followed me out,' recalls chief operating officer Gordon Hollins. 'It was a disgrace. Investment was required but, like the railways, there was a lot to catch up on.

'The competitive process drove up standards of facilities beyond recognition. The customer won. Joe Public and the media got better facilities, but it did put financial strain on some of the venues. Durham started to chase Test-match cricket but, as soon as Birmingham and Manchester got their act together, they were always going to struggle to compete against most of the criteria for high-profile matches, other than on geography – but not on seating capacities, facilities, transport infrastructure, hotels, diversity of populations, population sizes...'

Harker says Durham joined the international roster by 'going down to Lord's to meetings chaired by Peter Anderson of Somerset and eventually persuading Tim Lamb that there was a case for having some international cricket in the north east'. Soon, though, the authorities realised they could benefit from a competitive environment. 'I was on the Test-match grounds working party,' says Steve Coverdale, 'and from the moment I stepped into cricket management [he became Northamptonshire's chief executive in 1985] I was very conscious of the tensions between the Test grounds and the non-Test grounds. It's having an impact even now. One of the things we opened up was the potential for clubs to develop their stadia and bid for international matches.

'We talked about staging agreements but counties would also have to bid to stage international matches. I don't think we saw the mammoth investment counties would make in their Test grounds, and the fact that some were going to really overstretch, which Durham did. There's now just not enough international cricket to go around. Having to pledge large sums seemed sensible at the time but there is only a finite amount to be made out of these games.'

Cardiff was controversially awarded a 2009 Ashes Test, and in 2011 Southampton's Rose Bowl took the number of British Test venues to nine. They were not even fighting over seven Tests a summer because The Oval was guaranteed one and Lord's two. As each ground upgraded, its rivals had to respond without knowing if their investment would be rewarded with fixtures. 'If the TCCB genuinely wanted Durham to have a stadium capable of staging international cricket, the other side of the bargain was that there either should have been [a guarantee of] international cricket, or the funds from international cricket to support that stadium,' argues Harker.

In the late 1990s, Lord's spent £5.2m on a new media centre, while The Oval's £22m Vauxhall End Stand opened in 2005. Headingley's £21m pavilion, built jointly with Leeds Metropolitan University, opened in 2010, just as Old Trafford was undergoing a radical £60m redevelopment and Edgbaston's pavilion was being rebuilt for £32m. Trent Bridge was also transformed. Unless the Riverside kept pace, Durham had a white elephant. England venues are required to have 15,000 permanent seats but the Riverside has never got close to filling that many for county cricket. It was obvious which way the arms race was heading. 'It is a miracle no one has yet gone bankrupt, but surely it's only a matter of time,' I wrote in 2014.

The ECB seemed happy to milk it. In 2008 they replaced blind bidding with fixed-price packages of matches. They broadened their criteria to include infrastructure, operations and 'legacy', but it remained cripplingly damaging to county bank balances. Big games centred on the southern grounds with greater capacities and richer catchment areas, narrowing the spread of top matches while increasing the number of venues. Disgracefully, the 2015 Ashes series did not venture north of Nottingham, even though six of England's 13 players were born in the north and eight played for their clubs.

'Initially the guys literally sat around the table with a chairman and decided between them pretty much who would get what,' says Harker. 'It sounds sort of archaic but actually probably worked quite well, and there were programmes to compensate people who didn't have matches. Competition was brought in to try to ensure the maximum returns were generated on behalf of the wider game. Having never had international cricket, the opportunity to get any sort of game and make any sort of money was a plus so we were forced to compete quite hard, not necessarily to receive a fair return but to earn a return that was better than no return. There was a lot of money generated on behalf of the game but, instead of that being ploughed back into the venues, it was pretty much all spent on Team England.'

Bob Jackson felt 'there should have been a shared risk rather than a bidding process. I still believe strongly that taking international cricket around the country is important but, when you realise the returns that Lord's and The Oval can bring to the ECB, it's a double-edged sword. The [competitive] intensity was far, far, far too heavy and the money lost to the game so these other grounds can develop is sad.'

Durham built a new media centre in time for Australia's 2005 visit and added a replay screen in 2009, when £3m was spent extending the south-west corner to retain category-A venue status. In 2012, 2,500 further seats were added. Durham lost the right to host the 2011 domestic Twenty20 Finals Day because they had no permanent floodlights and, although they take place during the day, they would have lost their 2019 World Cup games too had they not overcome local objections to rectify that in 2015. The ECB at least covered the cost of a high-tech drainage system for all Test grounds in 2009/10.

The plan was for a five-star hotel and conference centre by 2011. Capacity would have been raised to 20,000 by a stand sweeping from the old scoreboard to the gym, plus a second replay screen. Chairman Clive Leach announced in 2007 he was looking to raise £5m. More than a decade on, the club is still hoping to build the hotel.

'In 2008 you had the credit crunch [starting with the collapse of Northern Rock, Durham's 2003–08 shirt sponsors],' explains Hollins, Durham's commercial manager from 2001–07. 'The north east got hit disproportionately harshly so Durham were spending money and, at the same time, there was pressure on ticket sales, ticket prices and a declining hospitality market which meant the revenues weren't keeping up with the expenditure. They were banking on a hotel/conference complex to sort everything out but the economic realities were such that the anticipated inward investment wasn't available.' The situation was made worse when regional development agency One North East closed in 2012.

The competition to host international cricket spawned all manner of irrational decisions. In 2008 Durham were awarded the second

Durham's 'A directors' were the driving force behind the county's admission into first-class cricket. Secretary Ian Mills (far left) is pictured with (from left to right) Bill Milner, Mattie Roseberry, Don Robson, Neil Riddell, Bob Jackson and Tom Moffat, in 1991 **(courtesy Tom Moffat)**

	DATE	DETAILS	INVESTED £	WITHDRAWN £	BALANCE £	2
01						
02	23DEC86	007 013 CHQ	7506.75		£29254.04	
03	22JAN87	011 001 CHQ		2000.00	£27254.04	
04	1APR 87	11 OON EG IT	679 95		£27 933 99	
05	1 APR 87	11 OON EG TRF		27933 99	NIL	
06						
07						
08						
09						
10						
11						
12						
13						
14						
15						
16						

Please produce this passbook for every transaction and check that all entries are correct. See also the important notes at the end of the passbook.   3

In April 1987, Durham had £27,933.99 in the bank. They had to increase that to £1m to be granted first-class status in 1990

The inclusion of 16-year-old schoolboy Neil Killeen on Durham's first overseas tour, to Zimbabwe in 1992, highlighted the county's commitment to developing its own players. Like the policy, Killeen remains at the club **(courtesy NCJ Media)**

Durham chairman Don Robson had a well-earned reputation as someone who could get things done. Here he oversees the start of work on the Riverside in February 1992, with John Ward of Tolent Construction **(courtesy NCJ Media)**

Durham's original squad blended experienced imports such as (front row, left to right) Paul Parker, David Graveney, Ian Botham, Wayne Larkins and Dean Jones with local talent such as Andy Fothergill (second row, second from left), John Wood (third from left) and John Glendenen (leaning forward) **(courtesy Press Association)**

Geoff Lovell (left) and David Graveney toss up before Durham's maiden first-class game as Simon Hughes takes a photograph **(courtesy Dave Whitlock)**

Paul Parker (left) and John Glendenen walk out to make history as Durham's first batsmen in first-class cricket, as team-mate Steve McEwan watches on **(courtesy Dave Whitlock)**

As a Durham player, Ian Botham could rarely escape the prying lenses of photographers – not even team-mate Simon Hughes's **(courtesy Press Association)**

At times in the 1990s Simon Brown almost single-handedly carried Durham's attack. In the first one-day game at the Riverside he was given an introduction to the pitch's unpredictable bounce in its early years **(courtesy NCJ Media)**

Future coach Jon Lewis felt his ability to make gritty 30s and 40s more so than big scores made him well-suited to opening at the Riverside **(courtesy Getty)**

Australian captain David Boon had a big impact on Durham's mindset – most tellingly that of Jon Lewis, Paul Collingwood and Stephen Harmison **(courtesy Getty)**

King Letsie III and Queen Masenate Mohato Seeisso of Lesotho with Durham CCC chairman Clive Leach CBE (right). Durham became much more ambitious once Clive Leach became chairman in 2004, and it ultimately led to glory and financial problems **(courtesy Getty)**

Ottis Gibson traps Kevin Pietersen lbw in the 2007 Friends Provident Trophy Final. Durham's first major trophy capped an incredible year for the veteran bowler **(courtesy Getty)**

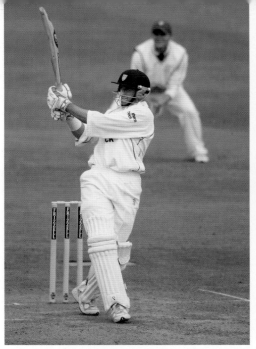

Mike Hussey (top left), Michael Di Venuto (top right) and Ian Blackwell (left) arrived as established county stars with wage packets to match, and were key figures in Durham's glory years **(all courtesy Getty)**

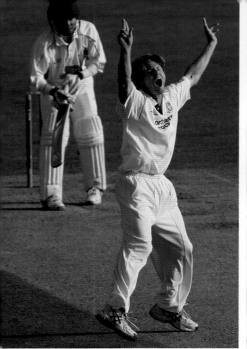

Callum Thorp (left) and Stephen Harmison (right) took the decisive wickets at Canterbury as Durham clinched their first County Championship title by beating Kent in 2008 **(courtesy Getty/Press Association)**

Geoff Cook joined Durham in September 1990 and shaped its development until his retirement in 2018. Graham Onions soaks him with champagne to celebrate their first Championship title **(courtesy Press Association)**

Will Smith (centre) found himself isolated as captain in 2010 when he tried to build on the success of winning the 2009 Championship without losing a game **(courtesy Getty)**

Dale Benkenstein, Durham's greatest on-field signing, heads back into the Aigburth pavilion after hitting the runs which sent them top of the 2011 Championship and made him the club's highest first-class run-scorer. Hosts Lancashire came out on top in the title race, while Paul Collingwood eventually overtook Benkenstein **(courtesy Press Association)**

Paul Collingwood (left) replaced Phil Mustard as captain in 2012 and led Durham to their third Championship title in a remarkable post-England career **(courtesy Getty)**

Released in 2005, Chris Rushworth had four summers playing league cricket, working in call centres and selling satellite subscriptions door to door before returning to be a key bowler for Durham **(courtesy Getty)**

Ben Stokes, a decisive figure in Durham's 2013 title win, jumps for joy as they follow it up with the 2014 One-Day Cup **(courtesy Press Association)**

Gareth Breese celebrates Durham's 2014 One-Day Cup win at Lord's with children Savannah (left) and Max **(courtesy Getty)**

Scott Borthwick (right) and Mark Stoneman decided to join Surrey as Durham's financial problems began to mount in 2016 **(courtesy Getty)**

The packed Riverside when Stuart Broad bowled to Peter Siddle in the 2013 Ashes (above) was in stark contrast to the empty seats as Alastair Cook became the first English batsman to score 10,000 Test runs there in 2016 **(both courtesy Getty)**

Mark Wood played against Surrey when not fully fit in September 2016 to try to save Durham from Championship relegation but they were demoted for financial rather than cricketing reasons **(courtesy Getty)**

Sir Ian Botham, pictured receiving a silver cap from ECB chairman Colin Graves (left) to mark his 100th Test appearance, returned to Durham as chairman in 2017 **(courtesy Getty)**

Durham supporters make their feelings towards the ECB known as Keaton Jennings walks out to start their 2017 season in Championship Division Two **(courtesy Getty)**

Graham Onions leaves the field after breaking the Durham record for most first-class wickets. It was his final Riverside appearance before leaving to join Lancashire **(courtesy Alison Sutherland)**

Durham's Twenty20 captain Paul Coughlin left for Northamptonshire in 2017 after a good campaign personally, but a difficult one for the team **(courtesy Getty)**

Paul Collingwood bowls at the start of his first full season as a Durham first-teamer, against Derbyshire in 1996 (left), and versus Middlesex in his final game before retiring aged 42 **(courtesy Press Association/Getty)**

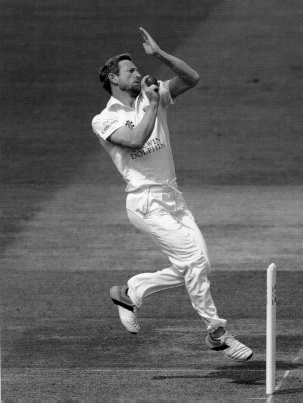

of two Tests against Zimbabwe for the following May, even though the Africans had been suspended from Test cricket since 2005. West Indies somewhat reluctantly took their place. Conditions were bitterly cold and visiting captain Chris Gayle did nothing to help ticket sales, flying in with his Indian Premier League colleagues 48 hours before the first Test at Lord's and telling the media he would not mind if Test cricket died. His side's feeble performance in London was no great advert for it. A power cut wiped out the new scoreboard for three-quarters of an hour on day three and trapped some spectators in lifts. Collingwood made an unbeaten 60 and filled in as wicketkeeper on the Sunday, while Graham Onions – selected ahead of Harmison – took three wickets as England won by an innings and 83 runs.

In 2010 England's Chester-le-Street one-day international against a Pakistan side tainted by match-fixing allegations followed back-to-back Twenty20s in Cardiff, the second watched by fewer than 6,000. Nevertheless, the Riverside sold all but a few hundred seats. Initially Durham had not been due to host any international cricket in 2012, but they swapped one of their 2011 ODIs, against Sri Lanka, for a 50-over game featuring Australia the following year and gained a Twenty20 double-header of England Women against West Indies and the men versus South Africa. The night before the Australia game the sheets covering the square were floating above it but, after the groundstaff stayed up until 1.30am clearing water away and returned three hours later to finish the job, fans were treated to 97 overs and 401 runs.

Kevin Pietersen missed the start of the build-up to England's World Twenty20 defence amid the fall-out from 'textgate' and, without him, England posted their third-lowest 20-over score. The Riverside audience was split, with fewer than 9,000 at each 2012 game. Durham appeared to learn their lesson, handing back a 2014 Twenty20 international against India and a 50-over match against Australia the following year because they already had one-dayers against New Zealand and Sri Lanka respectively for those years, and deemed the cost prohibitive.

The money-maker was the Ashes. The ECB therefore ramped up the price and packaged its games with less attractive fixtures. Traditionally played in each country every four years, England hosted three series in six summers, plus extra limited-overs games in 2010, 2012 and 2018. Overlooked in 2005, heavily indebted Yorkshire sat out the competition for 2013 and 2015. In 2006 Durham unsuccessfully bid for a 2009 Ashes Test, and decided against asking to host in 2013 – but got one anyway.

Years of spending on the team and the ground against an increasingly difficult backdrop were starting to take effect. 'In 2011 they put Ashes tickets on sale two years before the game,' Hollins points out. 'They needed the cash.' Harker does not deny it. 'Clubs and even the ECB use the boom years – Ashes summers and years where there is a broadcast deal with India – to fund the lean years,' he explains. 'With the possible exception of Surrey, I don't know of a county that doesn't. The ECB do it, we did it, everyone does it.'

With finance for the new stand and hotel still elusive in 2013, a very temporary-looking permanent stand was hastily erected. Even that was only possible after March's county council and local enterprise partnership loans. 'We were very close to having difficulties with our cash situation,' Leach admitted in October.

Lancaster-born Simon Henig became a Chester-le-Street councillor in 1999. Having been runner-up in the contest to be Labour's candidate to succeed Tony Blair as Sedgefield MP in 2007, he became leader of Durham County Council the following year. It was the first to come under Labour control in 1919, and has remained so ever since. A plate on the wall of Henig's County Hall office commemorates Durham's entry into first-class cricket. 'I enjoy going to watch cricket but, probably like most of the north east, I'm more of a fanatical football fan,' he says. 'I was well aware of the importance of the Ashes to the region and clearly it was in some doubt. My personal view was that had we lost the Ashes Test it would have been a disaster, not just in terms of cricket and Chester-le-Street, but also the capacity of the whole region to have a big occasion like that.'

·

'We agreed some of that loan and made sure the local enterprise partnership was involved because one of the points I made at the time was that it was not really fair this should all fall on Durham, because clearly it was an asset for the whole region. The idea – and it might not quite have worked out like that – was that whatever assistance Durham put in would be matched by the region. It was critical we did all we could. The informal discussions went right across the party spectrum.'

Leach, who claimed 'the publicity the north east got from the Ashes Test would cost £100m', insists it was never in doubt. Henig says the council loan 'wasn't general running costs, it was about specifically enabling that [game] to go ahead'. Though he adds: 'I can't remember how direct the threat [of the match not happening] was but I'm pretty sure it was there in the background.' The seriousness of Durham's situation was undeniable.

England went into the game having retained the urn in a soggy Old Trafford draw but looking to win a third straight Ashes series for the first time since 1956. By day four victory looked unlikely. Set 299 to win, Australia's first century opening stand in 35 Ashes Tests helped them to 147/1, before Stuart Broad exploded into life. He had taken 5-71 in the first innings, but set the tone when he came out to bat on the fourth morning with Ryan Harris on a hat-trick. Although Broad only made 13 from seven deliveries, Graeme Swann and Tim Bresnan joined the fun as England went from 250 to 300 in six overs. Broad had 0-30 until bowling opposition captain Michael Clarke for the first of six wickets in 45 deliveries. Fuelled by a noisy and energetic crowd, match figures of 11-121 were his Test best, and England won by 74 runs.

'The BBC's Jeff Brown argued that Ashes Test was one of the greatest sports events ever held in the north east and, while I don't go back that many years, I agree,' says Henig. 'For England to clinch the series in County Durham, you would have pinched yourself a few years ago. Just to have that event in the north east was a massive thing, not just for County Durham or Chester-le-Street, but for the whole of this region. People were talking about how well we'd done it – the involvement of the town, the volunteers we had.'

Broad bowled too well for Durham. The Riverside was the only 2013 Ashes venue not to sell out day four in advance, and there were a few hundred empty seats amongst the 17,500 available. 'If the game had started on a Thursday [it was the only match of the series to begin on Friday], I think day four would have been sold out,' Harker insisted. The £75 ticket prices did not help but, with the joint-smallest capacity of the series (with Trent Bridge), Durham had to charge more to extract the same return. They calculated that between 2008 and 2015 they earned £700,000 a game less than average from hosting England Tests.

Broad's wickets forced an extra half-hour and with umpire Aleem Dar ostentatiously looking at his light meter, he was briefly forced out of the attack as the sun hid behind clouds. When Jimmy Anderson caught Peter Siddle to clinch victory it was 7.45pm. One former employee told me how 'distraught' some of Durham's senior figures were when they realised they would miss out on around £250,000 by not having a fifth day.

To host the Ashes, Durham also had to buy a 2016 England–Sri Lanka Test for £952,000. 'You bid for a package of games over a five-year period [2012–16],' Harker explains. 'There would be six, seven, eight different packages, and you bid for your preferred order. They came with a fixed tariff so we weren't blind-bidding the way we were before. I think the package we asked for was all one-day cricket if I remember rightly, or there might have been one Test. We were told we'd been unsuccessful with our first, second, third choices or whatever, but we were going to get this particular package – and the good news was it included an Ashes Test. We were quite aware the other games didn't really make sense to us.

'We didn't bid for an Ashes Test that year. We took the view that, over the course of five years, if you weren't going to make enough money off the other ones then the value of the package was less because the cost of it was so much more. You don't know when the games are going to be played and how they fit within the schedule. Sri Lanka in July with nothing else around would have been fine but Sri Lanka in May on a back-to-back with Headingley was less than fine. So, although the price was fixed, you had to make certain assumptions around the income.'

The Riverside's Sri Lankan Test was the second of three and again the audience was split, Chester-le-Street's game starting eight days after Headingley's. Visiting captain Angelo Mathews described his side's performance at Leeds as 'embarrassing', only rain taking it into a third day as England recovered from 83/5 to make 298 in their solitary innings. Only once since being raised worldwide from 150 to 200 had a lower follow-on mark been enforced. A combined 37,863 attendance watched the mismatch. Nobody gave Sri Lanka much hope in the second Test. Even the road signs approaching the ground only warned of cricket traffic between 27 and 29 May. After the first couple of days they were changed to include up to the 31st.

'International cricket… locally sourced' was Durham's marketing slogan for tickets, alongside pictures of Mark Wood and Ben Stokes. Wood missed the Test summer with ongoing ankle problems, while Stokes had an operation after his knee locked in Leeds. Add in miserable weather and the fact that England's footballers made a rare trip to the north east on the first evening to play Australia in their final pre-Euro 2016 friendly 13 miles away at the Stadium of Light, and Durham were taking one for the ECB.

'The sense of putting those two games at Yorkshire and Durham… there isn't any sense,' says Harker. 'I attended a meeting at Lord's where their consultants went through what they felt was the sweet spot for ticket prices and what they felt we should expect in terms of attendance. They felt the sweet spot was around £30, £35 and then we should expect to sell 30,000 tickets [over the course of the game]. If you netted that down it came to about £900,000, which was a little bit less than we were paying for the game so, in other words, if their own experts were right and we did exactly what they said – which as it happened, we did – you were still going to lose money. That's when the whole absurdity of the situation becomes apparent.'

Now-chairman Sir Ian Botham is typically forthright. 'We had the gun put to our heads,' he says. 'Why on earth we accepted the Sri Lanka fixture I don't know because we were competing with football, we had the weather [to combat], we're the most northerly [professional] club in the country – it just didn't make sense. We were always going to run foul of that. That won't happen again.'

Durham's sixth Test was their last of that allocation – and it was clear which way the wind was blowing. 'It is no exaggeration to say this could be a "use it or lose it" opportunity,' I warned that week. I was fortunate to attend the Test and the football and, for a lover of both sports, the contrast was painful. The Stadium of Light was officially sold out and, although small pockets of empty seats were visible, it was nothing compared to the 10,000 at Manchester's Eastlands when the Three Lions were there the previous weekend. Very unusually, the only north-east-based player was at the football, albeit Newcastle United winger Andros Townsend was booed off the bench at Sunderland. Earlier, just 6,218 were at the cricket, where the weather was so gloomy the floodlights were on until after lunch. The conclusion was obvious: 'Persuading them [the ECB] to come back for more Test matches could be like Friday's cricket – a very hard sell.' Even on a much brighter Saturday, only 11,688 attended.

When Sri Lanka batted, they became the first team in 58 years bowled out for under 120 in three consecutive Test innings, and followed on again. As the bowlers tired, the batsmen belatedly found some fight, led by wicketkeeper Dinesh Chandimal's first Test century outside Asia. The game dragged into Bank Holiday Monday although, with Sri Lanka starting 189 behind on 309/5, it seemed Cook's milestone would have to wait for more fitting surroundings at Lord's. He began the summer 36 shy of his 10,000, and made 16 at Headingley and 15 in Chester-le-Street's first innings before Dimuth Karunaratne's brilliant slip catch. When Sri Lanka were finally bowled out for 475, Cook produced the inside edge then the four needed. He was 47 not out when England's 100 per cent Riverside Test record was maintained.

Cook's team was watched by 103,691 in the drawn dead rubber at Lord's. It really was another world. The average attendance for the four-match Pakistan series there, at Old Trafford, Edgbaston and The Oval was 82,577. 'There was a general consensus that Test matches would be supported well by the region's public but they never were,' says Jackson sorrowfully. 'I don't know if it's because of the strength of football here but the bottom line is Test cricket does not pay at the Riverside. It's better for us to have an attractive 50-over match, or a Twenty20 match as successful as the West Indies one in 2017, albeit it was in September under lights.'

Hollins agrees. 'What's [cricket's] objective in the north east?' he asks. 'To me it's different to that in the bigger cities because you're trying to grow the game and increase the audiences. So do you stick your growth product – your white-ball, short-form game, which has a wider popularity – in those locations?'

Botham insists: 'We don't need Test cricket because we've got one-dayers, including the 2019 World Cup, and Twenty20 internationals. You could play Test cricket here, you could play any live cricket here, it's just a question of what's most productive for the club.' Harker's successor Tim Bostock believes 'The traditional grounds should get all the Test cricket, quite frankly. All we should get and hope for is guaranteed one-day international cricket. If we can have a minimum of one, hopefully two [games] a year, that would be great.'

And at the end of all this madness? When England's 2020–24 home schedule was announced in 2018, the only venues hosting what is now six Tests per summer (plus six one-day internationals and six Twenty20s) were the 20th century's big six. Southampton and Cardiff were awarded franchises for the 100-ball competition, and Durham were the big loser. To quote the headline of George Dobell's Cricinfo article: 'Was it worth the millions?'

16.

'We Just Can't Keep on Pushing Water Uphill'

A S far back as 1998 Bill Midgley was asked to fight the financial fires threatening to engulf Durham but they were still burning when the empty seats at the 2016 Sri Lanka Test helped trigger a meltdown.

When David Harker became financial controller in 1991 Durham had raised huge amounts of money at astonishing speed, but by the time he was made chief executive in 2000 the picture was very different. 'We always had the bank looking over our shoulder and they were regularly asking what we were going to do about things,' says Tom Moffat. The answers cost thousands of pounds to supply, in the form of regular reviews by outside consultants.

'It started to become apparent that we weren't able to make ends meet around the time Bill Midgley got involved [joining the board in 1998],' Harker explains. 'Don [Robson] identified Bill as his successor with one eye on someone from a financial background. About that time or just prior to that the club committed to the second phase of the stadium development, which is basically all the stuff in the north-west corner. There was European money available but it wasn't going to meet the whole cost. Don had hoped to bring in money from

Scottish and Newcastle Breweries but that wasn't forthcoming, at least not to the extent he'd hoped. It was probably from about that point on that the club took on more debt from the Co-Op Bank and it was really a struggle financially. That was quite early in the club's [first-class] genesis. It wasn't that the club had money, then suddenly didn't – we never had money.'

When Midgley became Durham's chairman in 1999, the Newcastle Building Society chief executive adopted a very simple approach, says Gordon Hollins: 'Durham did not spend anything they did not have.' Clive Leach's ambitions were more expensive, and they borrowed £4.3m from the county council in two tranches, in 2009 and 2013. Breaching the 2012 salary cap was therefore not a good look. 'They might say by only a few quid [£14,000] but the fact they were even close wasn't in line with the reality of where they were,' argues Hollins, then the ECB's managing director of professional cricket.

'I felt the salary cap was unjust because when it was introduced we said it was something we were likely to breach because of the contractual commitments we had,' Harker argues. 'Most of our salary was taken up with [former] international players who were home-grown. There was an argument which said if we produced these players and there was a risk of us going over we should release or not replace them but that was entirely counter-intuitive to what they were telling us we needed to do. It was another well-intentioned initiative badly executed by ECB.

'I met with the financial director at ECB and I'd said we'd have to present to the panel. He told me when the meeting was and it was going to be really difficult for us – I think either myself or the chairman was away. We wanted to bring the lawyers down and make our case.

'He told me they'd decided on this date because it was very convenient for the ECB and the panel and if we asked them to change it, it wasn't going to help. He said not to worry about it, it would be fine, because it was such a small breach and they understood the circumstances, nothing would come out of it. We took him at his word and didn't attend.

'I got a call from the chairman of the panel to say it was good news. It would be a £2,500 fine which would just come off our distribution [of ECB funds] and it was only a 2.5-point [Championship] penalty. I said, "Hold on a minute, we've gone from there won't be any sanctions to this." I think both of them acted in good faith but you could tell they didn't understand the implications of the penalty. With hindsight we'd have said, "We're going to be there, you have to change the date."'

Durham were paying for retaining Stephen Harmison, Paul Collingwood and Graham Onions after their England careers. 'We wanted to try to give something back,' says Onions. So congested is their calendar that England players who appear in all formats are essentially full-time internationals. It explains why Collingwood was lukewarm towards Durham between 2006 and 2010, plus how the Riversiders won Championships in 2008 and 2009 when Harmison was more out of England's team than in, and 2013 before Ben Stokes, Mark Wood, Keaton Jennings and Mark Stoneman's Test debuts. Year-long central contracts pay England players so counties do not have to, but Stokes won 34 caps before receiving his. The salary cap is judged over a 12-month period starting in April, whereas central contracts are awarded in September.

'We have a system of performance-related payments paid on certain criteria,' Harker explains. 'The payments for England representation for 2017 earned us £260,000. Yorkshire topped the league with £376,000 and the next best after us is Middlesex with £148,000. But you get the reward months after the end of the season and the amount is typically less than you were paying the player. If you were being rewarded you would think you would earn money over and above the cost of the player you employed and you'd have that money in place to recruit a replacement. If you don't replace them or provide cover, the consequence of producing England players is relegation. When we were regularly losing Ben Stokes to England [before he was centrally contracted] the compensation [about £2,000 per appearance] was less than his salary and it wasn't a super-dooper salary, it was kind of the going rate.' Those payments have increased in new County Partnership Agreements between the clubs and the ECB.

Moffat believes the main responsibility lies with Durham, however. 'The troubles were self-inflicted to a large extent,' he argues. 'When I finished as president [in 2008] I was almost immediately put to one side as yesterday's man and they kept other people who weren't really cricket people. I think I was quite successful building up the county's finances and I was always thrifty so I like to think I would have asked the awkward questions when we were overspending.'

Durham particularly struggled to keep their head above water in 2007 and 2013 – ironically trophy-winning seasons – and had grown weary. 'When we got to 2016 we reached the point where we said, "We just can't keep on pushing water uphill,"' says Harker. By 2015, their wage bill had dropped to around £850,000 – well under half the 2012 figure – but the cuts were starting to hurt. Wood needed protecting because his rare talent to bowl fast sat within a fragile frame, but with Durham again unprepared to stretch to the cost of a marquee, England sent him to do 2016 pre-season training at Bristol, The Oval and Loughborough for the grass practice his ankles needed. While others prepared in the United Arab Emirates or Caribbean, Durham went no further than Canterbury.

In February, Emirates Airlines extended their sponsorship of the Riverside by seven years and in March Foster's agreed a five-year shirt sponsorship, but it was not enough. Durham had written to the ECB in November 2015 outlining their difficulties. 'I think they understood the problem, had desire to support but weren't clear how they best could without causing them problems elsewhere,' says Harker. 'That's the other part of our experience – the politics and the fear factor at Lord's in terms of, "If we do this for Durham, what are the others going to say?" We'd been speaking to the ECB about different ways of funding the game probably since 2007. You'd always get so far and think you'd cracked it – this is also colleagues from other counties having meetings and working parties and coming up with recommendations – and nothing happens. That was frustrating.'

When the ECB's annual reports were discussed at a board meeting on 10 May 2016, Derbyshire chairman Charles Green accused them of being 'overly prudent' in accumulating reserves of more than £73m while the counties struggled. Kent's George Kennedy requested clarification of county cricket's financial future, Yorkshire's Steve Dennison details about the next four-year funding cycle. MCC chairman Gerald Corbett asked accountants KPMG to look at the situation. The ECB agreed to give an extra £300,000 annually to the counties.

Days later, when I interviewed Harker for *The Journal*, he spoke of a '£5m–6m debt', commenting: 'As much as I'd like to reduce it, it doesn't worry me unduly.' It ought to have. When Durham's accounts for the financial year up to September 2015 were published – late – in September 2016, they showed borrowing up £700,000 to £7.5m. Servicing it cost £1m per year. In July Harker assured me: 'We're not afraid we're going to lose players we would prefer to keep for a lack of cash.' I was sceptical, writing: 'Every summer Durham dodge death by a thousand cuts, makes you wonder if it will be the last.'

In 2016 a number of senior playing contracts expired, including Stoneman's. 'Being captain of the white-ball sides yet having my contract run into the final year initially raised alarm bells as to why, when in previous years the club had been proactive in securing me on medium-length deals,' he says. 'This time they paid no attention until I submitted my 28 days' notice [allowing him to speak to other counties] on 10 April to try to stimulate some discussions. At that point they only came back with a standard two-year offer and no interest in negotiation. After declining the offer and doing a little more digging I discovered the club was looking for a buyer and that there was a considerable amount of instability.'

Harker sees it differently. 'We were happy with Mark and wanted him to stay,' he stresses. 'We had no sense there was an issue. We'd made it clear to his agent at the end of the [2015] season we wanted to renew Mark's contract, and the fact he was away for the winter made it less of a priority. There was nothing that should have given Mark any cause for concern. We wanted to keep the core of the best players and we made serious contract offers to Scott [Borthwick, whose deal also expired in the winter] and Mark. Throughout this period the over-riding priority was securing the future of the club. A player can only put in 28 days' notice once the final season of his contract is underway, and an offer was made to Mark early in April. A two-year offer to me is not a bad offer and I've never, ever opened negotiations with a player where it's been "take it or leave it".'

Durham had hoped to buy time with a £1.35m short-term ECB loan, to be repaid with four per cent interest. Clive Leach believed he had a buyer and solicitors began drawing up a final sale and purchase agreement but the money could not be paid until October. 'Even in the final throes Clive was very confident he'd bring another investor in,' says director Bob Jackson. 'If Clive's optimism had been absent I think we would have gone to the ECB a bit earlier. I think we went a year too late. The longer it took, the more stringent it [the terms] became.'

In a letter to Durham County Council in October 2016, the ECB claimed: 'The only third party which has expressed any provisional interest [in buying the club] is backed by an individual who would not pass the ECB's fit and proper person test.' Harker says: 'One guy in particular never took the test and had he I'm sure he would have passed it. Sadly for all of the time he spent talking to us, looking at us, suggesting things, when push came to shove he wasn't prepared to put his hand in his pocket. Looking back, I'm not sure he was ever going to. He will have spent money on due diligence and all the rest of it so I really don't understand the mentality. If he was genuine in his intentions why didn't he get more involved sooner?'

Once CR Financial Solutions, which bought Durham's £788,000 debt from the Co-Op Bank, responded to Britain voting to leave the European Union by calling the loan in within 30 days, and once the damage of the Sri Lanka Test was absorbed, the club could not make it to the end of the 2016 season alone. 'There was talk about an investor but we didn't see any evidence,' insists Hollins, who became the ECB's chief operating officer in 2014. 'We wanted to turn the crisis into an opportunity and say, "Can we get this club, which has a strategic importance, back on track and ensure it is there for the long term?"' It started a process which ended with Sir Ian Botham being installed as chairman.

One person I spoke to had another word for Hollins's 'opportunity': 'power-grab'. 'That's the last thing I needed in my life!' he responds. 'The scenario that materialised at Durham was a nightmare for us. There's absolutely no upside. It costs the game a lot of money and takes an awful lot of resource that could be doing other stuff, so I don't get people saying it was a "power-grab". What have we grabbed? We don't own any of it, all we've got is debt.' What appeared to be grabbed was an unspoken hold over Durham when the ECB were trying to push through an unpopular plan for a franchised limited-overs competition. While many counterparts were sceptical, Botham was supportive from the start, but he also bridles at talk of power-grabs. 'That's bullshit, quite frankly, there's no other word for it,' insists a man rarely accused of toeing lines.

For as long as television pundit and newspaper columnist Botham is chairman, Harker's successor as chief executive, Tim Bostock, believes Durham will always get their views across. 'He's in the media and he's one of the greats of the game so he's always got a voice people will hear and he knows lots of people in the game who will get the message out,' Bostock argues.

On 26 May 2016, ECB chief executive Tom Harrison wrote to Durham outlining their 'conditions precedent' – the terms on which they would help. From October Durham were to pay 44 monthly £20,977 instalments to cover the fee for hosting Sri Lanka. They had to give up their 2017 South Africa Test and 2019 one-day international against Pakistan, and would not stage Tests for the foreseeable future. Durham were required to produce a written restructure plan acceptable to the ECB and become a community interest company – able to pay no more than 35 per cent of profits back to the sort of investors Leach sought. An ECB-approved cost-cutting and 'core business consolidating programme' would have to start immediately, with weekly updates to chief financial officer Steve Scott. No capital developments or new signings would be allowed without ECB consent. The £415,000 loaned to Durham by its directors (principally Leach, Frank Curry and Lord Stevens) in 2013 could only be repaid after the governing body, and Leach must resign to be replaced by a Lord's-vetted chairman. When the board agreed on 23 June, Leach quit. Even had his investor found the money, there was no longer anything to sell.

Phil Mustard was the first player to leave. By 2016 the greatest wicketkeeper-batsman in Durham's first-class history was on the wane in four-day cricket. His glovework was poor in 2014, which ended with a knee injury, but he returned at the start of 2015. Initially pushed up to bat at five, he made 51 runs in his first seven innings. 'I was on the bus back from Edgbaston and I got a phone call I didn't know how to react to, so I went up to Colly and Judgey [Jon Lewis] and said a family member had taken ill, did they mind if I missed the next game?' he recalls. 'They said it was no problem and I never played a four-day game again. I just got the sense that, "That's made our job a lot easier." I think every decision they made for three or four years was financial.'

Mustard ended the 2015 season on loan at promotion-chasing Lancashire when Alex Davies injured his knee. He remained a limited-overs regular in 2016, but Michael Richardson kept in the Championship. Third-choice Stuart Poynter was in his third Durham season, still awaiting his competitive debut. 'I asked if it was a financial issue,' says Mustard. 'They said no, so I said, "OK, so you're trying to tell me I'm not good enough." They were still picking me for the Twenty20 and one-dayers. I knew and they knew it was a financial decision.' On 15 May, hours after being formally told he would not get a new contract, Mustard became English Twenty20's all-time top-scorer. He was the country's leading wicketkeeper in the 2016 competition and comfortably Durham's leading scorer.

Two days later, Gloucestershire keeper Gareth Roderick broke a finger against Essex. 'I was looking for my next job,' says Mustard. 'I wanted to play all forms and I think I'm best suited to four-day cricket. I'd been awarded a benefit for 2016 but I knew in 2015 what was coming. I'd worked my nuts off, I'd got runs in the second XI [averaging 57 in their Championship] and I still wasn't getting picked, then I looked at who took over my role [Richardson] and if they're saying he's better than me it's the biggest bull I've come across.

'I was still playing Twenty20 and one-day cricket so we came up with "The Colonel's Last Stand" for my benefit game [Durham's final limited-overs home match of 2016]. They were still keeping me hanging on about four-day cricket but I knew I wasn't going to play it again. Gloucester had a really good Twenty20 year and Durham looked down and out, never going to make the quarter-finals. Gloucester said they'd sign me on a two-year deal from 2017 but they'd like me to play Twenty20 in 2016. All I had to do was play one group game to qualify for the quarter-finals. I thought long and hard about it then I went down to the ground and cleared out my locker. It was a case of, "You're happy for me to go, I'm happy to go, it's been like this for a year and a half, thanks very much."'

Mustard missed his benefit game and the quarter-finals after Durham improbably qualified to play Gloucestershire. The highlight of his old side's 19-run win was Richardson's outstanding catch. 'We didn't feel right saying no when someone offered him an opportunity if it was only for a small part of our season,' explains Lewis. 'It was not easy to say to Phil – an absolute stalwart and a bit of a legend – that he wasn't going to be retained, but he had an opportunity to give his career some legs.' Mustard made a Championship century and three fifties for second-division Gloucestershire in 2016, averaging 55.87 with the bat, but was released after one more season and played for Northumberland in 2018. 'Colonel was gutted when he went and it was so unfair,' says Graham Onions. 'Because it's such a young club, I think that's an issue Durham have still got – they don't know how to deal with people who are getting older and Colonel deserved that respect.

'Breesey will always get a lot of credit because he was a bit of a crowd favourite and he hit the winning runs at Lord's, but people like Muchy [Gordon Muchall] and Colonel didn't even get a mention [not strictly true, although more should have been said], which is unfair after what they gave for the club. I know it's their job and they got paid for it, and if Joe Bloggs left his job at Burger King he wouldn't get a massive round of applause, but these guys gave everything and it would just be nice for the club to say well done. Jon Lewis was an ex-player, an ex-captain of the club, and should have known what it was all about but he didn't handle those situations particularly well.'

The day after Mustard's departure, to Lewis's surprise, Stoneman announced he was leaving too – for Surrey at the end of the season. Surrey were coached by his idol and mentor Michael Di Venuto. 'It was one of the hardest decisions I've had to make,' Stoneman says. 'Leaving everything you'd ever known and believed in was incredibly difficult, but I felt that those at the top were willing to lie about the perilous situation the club was in and jeopardise my future, that of my family, and the ability of the team to continue the success I had been part of. I very much felt like there had been a discussion where they decided that at least three or four quality players on decent wages had to go and everyone was played off against each other.

'The only time any issues around the financial situation were discussed with the players was after I announced my decision to join Surrey. David Harker addressed the players to say that the club was in no financial trouble but they were seeking to restructure and any such rumours were simply the work of agents to try and get more money for their players or earn commission on signing elsewhere.

'The hardest discussion was telling Jon Lewis, who was not only head coach but a very close friend. We had worked very closely together. Once I had done that, the weight was lifted off my shoulders and I knew I could finish the season strongly and leave with my head held high. An hour later when in my mid-season appraisal Dave Harker said the club wanted to issue a statement immediately saying I had turned down a contract, I knew I'd made the right decision. I asked them to wait until the next day so I had a chance to tell as many players as possible in person.' Durham agreed to delay, but wanted news out before they played again, against Warwickshire two days later, because they had decided to take the limited-overs captaincy off Stoneman. Confirmation of Collingwood's latest contract extension was rushed out.

Harker denies lying to the players or keeping them in the dark, but says: 'One of the big challenges was that we couldn't be certain of how things would eventually pan out. We had to meet with the players to tell them where we were and what we were trying to achieve. Certainly at that time we shared with the players everything we knew. Why would I address the players if I was trying to make out there were no problems? I couldn't go into details about the potential sale of the club because of confidentiality agreements but [playing] contracts weren't at risk. If anyone was at risk it was the creditors, which is why you couldn't say too much in public because you don't want a "run" on the club. I was very frank with the players and answered a lot of questions during and after the meeting. With regards to Mark, we didn't get a response from him or his agent to our April offer until June.'

Chris Rushworth says: 'People knew we weren't quite as flush as we'd been but things started to come out in the press and in the meeting; I think people were a little bit shocked about how bad it was. You want to be kept in the loop a little bit but you don't want to be told things that will distract you on the field. I guess the people in charge were just trying to do the best for the club.' According to Mustard: 'That's when it all came to a head that the club were in more shit than we thought. That's when things started turning sour.'

Stoneman wanted to be kept informed. 'Whatever was known should have been shared and solutions discussed to better manage the fall-out,' he argues. 'The sackings and departures of players in 2016, followed by players opting to use release clauses [in 2017] decimated a very strong and productive county through no fault of the players, yet those who chose to leave were portrayed as traitors jumping ship. It felt like we had been lied to while doing everything we could to make the club successful, and many players were released who had given fantastic service with very little recognition, which I felt was very poor. It seemed to me that the lines coming out of the club when I made my decision to leave were designed to give the media and fans the impression it was merely players leaving for financial reasons, but my motivation was to further my career.' Harker insists there was no attempt to portray Stoneman in a bad light.

Despite four prolific seasons, neither Stoneman nor Scott Borthwick were among the more than 70 players on England's 2016/17 winter programmes, but Stoneman started 2017 well at Surrey, England batting coach Graham Thorpe's former club, and made a career-best 197 against Essex. By June he had the England Lions call-up Collingwood had demanded for years, made his Test debut in August, and won another Championship in 2018. 'I would argue he would still achieve what he did [internationally] if he'd stayed, he would argue it's because of where he's gone,' says Lewis. 'There are no ill feelings and I still speak to him regularly but it was tough to take.'

Stoneman made a first one-day fifty in 16 innings in the game after his decision, a four-wicket win over Warwickshire at South Northumberland. 'Not knowing where your future lies in a very uncertain sport does make things very hard,' he reflects. 'Thankfully I had incredible support from my wife and family, which allowed me to think things through properly. Losing the captaincy hurt massively as I felt that, although I was leaving, my commitment was unquestionable. The lads were very good about it in the dressing room. There was the odd sly comment and some elements trying to portray my choice to leave as simply chasing money, which was hurtful and disrespectful to everything I'd put into my career at Durham.'

Lewis argues: 'There's always a question mark over whether someone who's going to leave will be able to lead as well as someone who isn't.' Collingwood adds: 'We needed Rocky to play out the rest of the season but we may as well give someone else that [captaincy] experience. It wasn't a punishment, it was just to better Durham. It wasn't difficult to play with him. You wished him well.'

The season started with doubts about whether Durham would renew Keaton Jennings's contract – now retaining him was crucial. The opener was dropped in July 2015 after averaging 23.65 in ten Championship games and having not scored a competitive century since June 2014. 'I remember a members' forum in pre-season and they were asking what we were going to do about the opener's position,' Collingwood recalls. 'I said Keaton would be opening with Rocky. They were saying he couldn't do it. I remember thinking, "I hope this guy proves them wrong." I'd told him to go away that winter, find what his strengths were and work on them. I thought it was a mental thing more than anything else.'

Every winter Jennings works in the nets with the dad he calls 'coach' and in 2015/16 he also leant heavily on his uncle, Dr Ken Jennings, a sports psychologist who had worked with South Africa's rugby union and cricket teams. His equilibrium was further helped by buying a house in Durham and, shortly before the 2016 season started, qualifying to play for England. Starting the campaign with three career Championship centuries, he scored two more in its opening two days and seven in all, including two doubles, making 1,548 runs at an average of 64.50. At one point he spent 922 minutes at the crease without being dismissed. When Collingwood's calf tightened during July's televised One-Day Cup game at home to Yorkshire, the ex-South African Under-19s captain led Durham to victory. Jennings top-scored at Twenty20 Finals Day and was the Cricket Writers' Club's player of the year, as well as picking up five of Durham's end-of-season awards. Rewarded with an England Lions winter tour, he was quickly called into the Test team after Haseeb Hameed's broken finger, making a debut-innings century in Mohali.

I ask Jennings how close he was to leaving. 'Fairly close,' he replies. 'When you move into the last year of your contract you've got to consider things. You've got a mortgage to pay, you need opportunities, you have to balance off a lot of things. It was down to three things – continuation, because I'd had a good year in 2016 and I wanted to try and back it up; we were in [Championship] Division One; and I was happy. My mates were in Durham and the lifestyle was good, I enjoyed playing at the Riverside, I enjoyed the environment. Despite Rocky leaving, despite what was happening, I wanted to be a part of it. Captaincy didn't come into it. I like to think I'll always be involved in leading a culture, even if it's only leading myself, and having the title of captain doesn't necessarily mean you're a leader and vice-versa.'

Jennings skippered Durham in August's Championship game at Taunton and the announcement of his new four-year contract – negotiated without an agent – was released to bury the bad news that their unbeaten start to 2016 was over as they and the pitch crumbled. With Collingwood fit again, they fell by an innings and 80 runs at Lord's. Durham lost 27 wickets to spin over the two games, while Borthwick had taken one and off-spinner Adam Hickey two. They had done remarkably well to reach the Twenty20 final, and although they did not qualify for the One-Day Cup knockout stages, it was only on net run-rate with the top six equal on points. However, they failed to win a Championship game in the nearly two months between Stoneman and Borthwick deciding their futures. While Paul Coughlin was used conservatively, Brydon Carse was over-bowled in an exciting start to his debut season, breaking down after his sixth straight Championship game. Injury restricted James Weighell's availability too, while Ireland had first call on Stuart Poynter.

Gordon Muchall retired shortly after Stoneman's announcement. He had been warned mid-season in 2013 and 2015 not to expect new contracts only to survive, but when Bow School offered a permanent job after three winters working for them, the 32-year-old took it. 'When I was left out of the team [which faced Warwickshire in the

One-Day Cup], I must admit I thought, "I've had enough of it, it's the right time to move on,"' he said.

'It was a horrible distraction,' Collingwood says of Durham's off-field issues. 'Rumours were coming through that we might not get paid at the end of the month. We had to lose players we didn't want to simply balance the books. When players are deciding to leave because they feel opportunities are going to be better elsewhere, that kills me. There was uncertainty around the club but I would have loved those players to have seen us out the other end.'

For Jennings, losing team-mates meant gaining opportunities. 'Rocky's a good mate and there was a bit of sadness that he was leaving, a bit of excitement too that he was moving on to new things,' he reflects. 'I didn't hold it against him. I got called all sorts on social media when I decided to leave in 2017 but that's the excitement of being in the public eye to a certain degree.

'I remember captaining against Somerset and Rocky was part of the team. That was tough for me because here was a guy who had helped me so much and I respected him as a player and a friend but I could see he was being pushed out. At the same time it gave me an opportunity to get involved in new things, just like opening on [Twenty20] Finals Day wouldn't have happened had Colonel not left, and playing in 2013 wouldn't have if Diva was still there. Emotions are part of the team ethos and it was tough to see a guy like Colonel, who was such an important part of it, move away and I've got his spot. You wonder how you're meant to feel about it. But cricket's a business and the last few years have taught me to look at things very pragmatically.'

Durham went into 2016's final two games, against Surrey and Hampshire, with relegation a real danger. Mark Wood needed pain-killing injections to take 2015's Ashes-clinching wicket, but rather than operate England decided to push him for as long as possible. He went to the United Arab Emirates to face Pakistan, but did not see the tour out. Wood was having problems with the front and back of his left ankle, but the ECB decided to deal only with the sharpest pain, at the front, in November. When he resumed pre-season training, the back inflamed and he went under the knife again. He struggled for fitness all season.

Wood begged England to let him play the final two games despite being only 60 per cent fit. 'I really wanted to keep Durham up,' he told me. 'People say I was stupid but I couldn't have sat back and not done anything.' Wood bowled 35 overs against Surrey before being diagnosed with a stress fracture of the ankle. If the rumours were true that the ECB had already decided Durham would be relegated, they had needlessly exposed Wood to injury ahead of England's winter tours of Bangladesh and India, but Hollins insists: 'As soon as the season started Durham needed to complete that season for the good of the game. If they go out of business in June it damages your media deals, your sponsorship deals, other counties don't get home games they've budgeted for, players are unemployed, it's chaos. So the decision was made to try and get them through the season, and if and when we had something to manage – because they were still trying to sell it – we would deal with it.

'The ECB board considered its options on 28 September after the season had finished and informed Durham of the outcome within 48 hours. They were still trying to sell the business at the start of September. Informal discussions took place throughout the season – we didn't just create it in one day, we talked over a period of time about what type of sanctions the club would face in return for financial assistance. There would have been talk about lots of things – whether it was straight relegation, whether there was no relegation, relegation plus points, do you leave the T20 alone, etc.' Collingwood says: 'It sounds like everybody else knew before us. I don't know how I would have taken it if we'd found out mid-season. We battled hard right to the end, fighting to stay up, but it was all in vain. That period was gut-wrenching and you didn't know who to blame. Who do you believe?'

Wood's England team-mate Stokes was equally desperate to face Surrey. 'I read the email sent to Durham and it said I could play as a batter with a limited amount of overs but it didn't set a limit,' he smirked after bowling 47 in the match. 'I did bowl off-spin [for an over!]' Surrey went into the final session needing 113 to win with six wickets in hand, including first-innings centurion Jason Roy's. Wicketless at tea, Stokes had Roy caught down leg side for 96 with his next delivery and finished with 4-54 as Durham won by 21 runs to escape relegation – they thought. 'Rarely can a maximum-points win have been so tight,' I wrote.

The day before the game Borthwick told his team-mates he too would be playing for the opposition in 2017. For weeks there had been two pieces of paper in his kitchen, one listing reasons to stay, the other to go. 'It's purely a cricketing decision,' he insisted. 'The Oval's a fantastic place to play cricket, to bat and to bowl leg-spin.' His father continued to watch Durham but had his car 'keyed' at a game early the next season. Hampshire signed 19-year-old seamer Asher Hale-Bop Hart, while Jamie Harrison, Calum MacLeod and leading second XI wicket-taker Gurman Randhawa were released.

Final-week hosts Hampshire were not safe from relegation, and Durham could earn £27,000 by finishing fourth. Michael Richardson made a first-innings 99, his best score as wicketkeeper, as Durham recovered from 186/7 to 361 in reply to 411, and Ryan Pringle more than doubled his summer's Championship wickets with match figures of 10-260.

'We had a fourth-day run-chase on a turning pitch and the two guys who were leaving got all the bloody runs!' says Lewis. 'After the game the first thing the Hampshire guys did was invite us into their dressing room to have a beer. They were dealing with some pretty sore wounds but they were impressive. It's been asked if they knew what was happening – I've got no idea.' Will Smith, who made 90 for Hampshire, says: 'I don't think any of the players knew but I think within some of the hierarchy there might have been inklings.'

Set 296 in a minimum of 78 overs, Durham got there with ten minutes left thanks to Stoneman's 137 and Borthwick's 88. 'That was a massive day for me and for the club,' says Stoneman. 'My commitment was there until the very last day and to finish my last game for Durham knowing the club were still in Division One was very important. We sang the team song that last time and it felt the perfect way to sign off.'

That same day, 23 September, Durham's board approved the changes demanded by the ECB. With a gun to their head, they signed a blank cheque. Two days earlier Steve Scott had written to say there would be further unspecified conditions. Their severity came as an extremely unpleasant shock.

17.

The Wider Wake

'**B**ETRAYED, cheated but not defeated' – the banner at the Riverside left no one in any doubt how supporters viewed Durham's treatment. 'ECB it's not cricket' read the T-shirts of fans applauding Keaton Jennings and Steven Cook on to the field to start the club's 2017 season.

Durham's fate had not been uppermost in my mind when their kneecapping was delivered on 3 October 2016. I was in Scarborough at the funeral of family friend Stephen Drury knowing a decision was imminent, but not when exactly. It was clear they would be punished for getting into unmanageable debt, but the scale surprised most observers. Having finished the season 45 points clear of relegation, the Press Association reported the expectation was that 'any points deduction would only apply to next season's Championship, meaning Durham will start their Division One campaign at a disadvantage – but crucially still in the top-flight.' Rod Bransgrove was vocal in calling for demotion, arguing: 'Those of us who were playing Durham while they were being propped up were probably being put at a disadvantage,' but then he was chairman of Hampshire, who finished in the second relegation spot.

On Friday 30 September Durham's directors were summoned to the Danubius Hotel, across the road from Lord's, where the ten conditions of assistance were confirmed. There had been plenty of rumours, but leading figures insist this was the first indication they would be relegated from Championship Division One after a record 11 years. It was take it or leave it.

They would also start life in Division Two on minus 48 points – effectively a 94-point penalty which made it extremely unlikely they would return at the first attempt. There was a four-point deduction in the Twenty20 group stage, and a decisive two in 50-over cricket (one win in each). Durham were forced to work within a salary cap 60 per cent smaller than their rivals for three years, prevented from making signings or ground developments without ECB permission, and stripped of Test cricket.

Still, at least their debt was cleared. Except it was not. The ECB offered half-measures, 'assisting' with a £1.8m loan but withholding prize money until it was repaid, and writing off a further £2m of debt – though we only found out why later. When I left the funeral wake and switched on my mobile phone to be confronted with the punishment – because the 'assistance' was a punishment – I struggled to comprehend its cruelty, even before realising how little of Durham's £7.5m borrowing had been cleared.

'The game had a strategic decision to make,' the ECB's chief operating officer Gordon Hollins explains. 'The ECB had to decide should they intervene financially and potentially set a precedent or let them go? It was not a straightforward decision. The ECB's come in for a lot of stick for being harsh and brutal, but the reality was in the middle of 2016 we were staring at long grass, paint peeling off the media centre, padlocks on the gate Ayresome Park-style [a reference to Middlesbrough Football Club's voluntary liquidation in 1986]. If it had been football, they'd have gone. The ECB took the decision that strategically a first-class county club in the north east was an important thing to have.'

Former Northamptonshire chief executive Steve Coverdale believes: 'Had Durham been a non-international ground it would have been much easier to say, "Sorry, but we can't help you." Durham also has access to a big population. I think it had become too big to fail.' They had, though, been made an example of. 'I thought the savagery came in the second tranche of points deductions which they carried forward to 2017,' says director Bob Jackson, who served on the ECB management board from its inception until 2014. 'I had some strong words to the deputy chairman of the ECB about that. I was bitterly disappointed.'

Condemnation of the sanctions extended beyond the county. 'If it is the brutality of the ECB's decision to punish Durham that strikes first, it is the inconsistency that follows close behind,' wrote Cricinfo's George Dobell. 'You can bet that the next club in need of financial assistance will call Wonga before it calls the ECB.' *Wisden* editor Lawrence Booth argued: 'To punish them doubly, triply and more, felt like cricket's version of the postcode lottery.' In *The Times*, Michael Atherton wrote Durham had been condemned to 'cricketing serfdom'. Mark Nicholas called the punishment 'needlessly cruel', adding: 'Ambition is the centrepiece of sporting dreams and all of us cricket folk are dreamers in one way or another.'

Former captain David Boon 'found it quite distressing that a club who in a relatively short period of time had become so successful and strong could have that happen to them. I thought, "Oh no, all those years the club has worked so hard, please don't let it go down the drain and fold." I look on from a long way away and think some of those decisions were made with every good intention but were they right?'

However, Jackson points out: 'Not all the counties were very supportive of the view that the punishments were harsh.' Were some envious of Durham's rapid rise? Then-chief executive David Harker 'would hesitate to say there was jealousy because you just wouldn't expect professional, grown-up people to have those thoughts, but it's difficult to argue against the theory there were certain individuals who weren't sorry to be able to pull Durham down a peg or two.'

At least there was no need for another funeral. Advancing £1.294m – half Durham's annual ECB fee payment – allowed them to pay their tax bill, wages and settle their debt to CR Financial Solutions, so there would still be a club. It could have been worse. One county wanted Durham expelled from Division One for five years. Although only ten were awarded, although injury had kept him out of five-day cricket since October 2015, and although England had introduced supplementary limited-overs deals that year, Mark Wood received a Test-match central contract, keeping him – like Ben Stokes – off Durham's payroll. Wood only played two Tests in 2017, but perhaps it was a tacit admission of England's mismanagement of his ankle since sending him to the United Arab Emirates in 2015 when surgery appeared a much better option. It was a crumb of comfort.

That Durham's contribution to the game ran deeper than international level was demonstrated when they won the 2016 Second XI Championship (with Ian Blackwell umpiring the final against Middlesex). South Northumberland were national club champions, and Blagdon Park Young Bulls were Under-19 Twenty20 Club of the Year. All 11 players in 2016's final match at Hampshire had come through Durham's youth set-up, and five were England internationals, with Mark Stoneman to follow. Jimmy Adams was the opposition's only Hampshire-born player, and they responded to their relegation reprieve – they, not Kent, who finished second in Division Two, were awarded Durham's spot – by signing South African internationals Kyle Abbott and Rilee Rossouw, two of 14 new Kolpak signings rushed into county cricket in 2017 before Brexit. Official overseas player Ryan McLaren was making his final Hampshire appearance alongside Zimbabwe's Irish passport-holder Sean Ervine, Gareth Berg, a South African with an Italian passport, and South African-born Scotland international Brad Wheal. Hampshire were only doing what Durham once had, but it was clear who was contributing more to English cricket's health now.

The Riversiders had over-reached but their ambition was encouraged by the allocation of international matches, and where the bar was set before awarding first-class status. 'Durham would say they'd done exactly what the ECB had asked of them: shown ambition, got Test matches here and ticked all the boxes from the start,' Paul Collingwood argues. 'Now we're getting penalised for it. If you speak to [some at] the ECB they say it should have been harsher, that was the severity. It's somewhere in the middle, who knows where?

'I don't think we should be losing players we don't want to and getting into a position where they're saying we're not sure you're going to get paid. It sounds like what's cost us is getting Test matches here, apart from the Ashes. The ECB get all these TV deals on the back of Ben Stokes and Mark Wood – what kind of reward are we getting? We've got a great conveyor belt of international-class players. This is a vital cog in the ECB, so don't try to take that cog away.' Tom Moffat, a driving force behind Durham's first-class application, calls the punishment: 'An arrow through my heart. It came from people at ECB who should know better. Everybody in the world of cricket knows what Durham did for England and for the TCCB, only to be kicked in the hurtfuls.'

Coverdale, part of the TCCB working party that helped Durham join first-class cricket, points out: 'If they had just struggled along for year after year they wouldn't have fulfilled some of the promises they gave us. Things developed after they came in which were unknown at the time – the whole history of Test grounds and the distribution of money. Durham in no sense can be faulted for the situation they found themselves in. They became unfortunate victims of changed arrangements they had no say in and no one could have foreseen.'

As the recriminations raged, coach Jon Lewis had to preserve what he could of his squad, and rebuild the rest. 'I was as shocked as anyone,' he says. 'I don't think anyone saw it being quite as severe as it was. I believed we were finding our way out of it. We had the end-of-year dinner on the Thursday night [29 September] and I saw David [Harker] as he left early because he had a meeting in London the next day with the ECB where we would find out what was happening. I was expecting some sort of points penalty, maybe some financial sanctions, maybe some impact on our international venue status.

'David phoned me Monday morning to say I'd better come in. He came straight out with it and explained what was going to happen, and that it was going to be announced in the next two hours. I said I needed to phone everybody. I spoke to everybody bar Keaton [Jennings], who was in an exam in South Africa, so I spoke to his dad. I spoke to the [coaching] staff as well. They were very short conversations because I had to get through 25 before it went public. I then went to the boardroom where they were discussing the wording of statements and basically ending their tenures – guys who had been supporting Durham in a variety of capacities for a long time. They knew when they walked out it would probably be for the last time.'

Jennings was sitting a bachelor of commerce exam in accounting sciences. 'The amount of work that goes into winning a four-day game is huge,' he explains. 'It's long hours, it's tough and you're buggered by the end of the four days, so to win a game first off and then to finish fourth in the league, it's massive. Rocky got a hundred in his final game... and a week later, it's ecstasy to that drop-off. It was a really tough week.

'It was only when we got to the end-of-season dinner that we started getting wind of what the sanctions could be. I walked out of an auditing exam and thought I'd failed and I had 25 missed calls. We'd been relegated, had points docked and walked into a snowstorm of sanctions and rulings. You're thinking, "How has this happened so quickly?" In a way it was quite cool to watch but quite terrifying to be part of.'

Chris Rushworth was at home the day before flying to Australia. 'When I put the phone down I was ranting and raving, I couldn't believe it,' he says. 'Ten, 15 minutes later it was on *Sky Sports News* and I realised it really had just happened.' Mark Stoneman was already in Australia having played his last game for Durham. 'I remember feeling very angry for the players and staff because we had done everything right that season to keep the club where it belonged not knowing what was going on in the background,' he reflects. 'That was a massive betrayal for some incredibly special and loyal people.'

Collingwood was in Bangladesh, working for the ECB on England's limited-overs coaching staff. 'I'd heard we were going to get relegated at the PCA dinner but when we heard about the points deduction I just thought, "You're kidding us!"' he says. 'I was having a game of golf with Straussy [England's director of cricket Andrew Strauss] and [ECB chief executive] Tom Harrison. They were saying we were in dire straits and they'd got a big-name chairman for us. They wanted us to move on as quickly as possible. I felt for the players more than anyone else because we'd been the only team in that first division such a long period of time. Straussy and Tom were giving us the harsh reality. We were seeing it from their point of view and thinking were we fortunate in many ways to be still going.'

Luckily this was 2016, and even from nearly 5,000 miles away Durham's captain was able to provide leadership with the help of Stokes and online messaging service WhatsApp. 'Colly was very good at calming the guys down and giving direction about what was actually happening,' Jennings reveals. 'When you've had ten years of international cricket I guess you learn a bit about pushing guys in the right direction and reassuring guys it will be okay – maybe not right now, but it will be okay. You don't really know what to make of it – are you angry with the ECB or angry with Durham or yourself?'

Collingwood and Stokes, also in Bangladesh, were important in channelling anger into a determination to rectify matters on the field. 'That's where Stokesey's really matured,' Collingwood comments. 'He wanted to lead and it was important he got his opinions across. Woody [Mark Wood] is very good too. All he wants to do is play for Durham and get us back to where we were. He hates that confrontation.'

Durham feared some players might exploit relegation to try to leave, while some of them were initially worried their contracts might be sold on, but Brydon Carse, James Weighell, Stuart Poynter, Barry McCarthy and Josh Coughlin signed contracts to add to those Stokes, Jennings, Collingwood and Coughlin's elder brother Paul agreed during the season. 'Durham have given me everything throughout my career and if they are going through a tough time I want to be there to try to help them out of it,' said Collingwood, whose pay cut was eased by a second benefit year in 2017. Former Durham University skipper Cameron Steel joined from Middlesex having impressed on a late-season trial.

It took until late October for Wood to agree a new deal. He stalled to see how things developed with Stoneman, Jennings and Scott Borthwick but a three-year contract 'was one of my main drivers… I wanted to make sure it just wasn't one year or if I came off my ECB contract people would question it [his future] again.' He received assurances from Strauss that playing Division Two cricket would not harm his Test chances. Second division batsman Ben Duckett made his Test debut in Bangladesh.

On 6 October, three days after the bombshell, Durham's board officially resigned. 'I couldn't work out why the club was getting into such a terrible mess,' says Sir Ian Botham. 'I got approached to ask if I would be interested in coming up to help. I said I would but I presumed they meant take over as chairman and they said yeah. It would have to be my board, not theirs.

'The approach came through a number of sources. I think a lot of people put their heads together and came to me. I was getting heavily involved before it was even announced [though his interest became public as soon as the punishment did]. I was basically feeling my way in and getting guided by David Harker, who was fantastic. I've known David ever since the club started [to play first-class cricket]; David and I have always got on well. He took me through the maze a little bit and then we started putting our own stuff together. My diary's full at least 18 months in advance so I've had to do a bit of juggling and shuffling and my days off have disappeared but that doesn't bother me in the slightest.'

Botham had left Durham on uncomfortable terms in 1993, but Hollins says: 'I think I was pretty well connected with the north east [as Durham's commercial manager] and when I start looking around at the people who could do the job and would be willing to – people like [former Northern Rock chief executive] Adam Applegarth and [businessman] Graham Wylie – it's a very small market. Durham is the youngest [first-class] county, with a relatively small population.

We didn't ask Ian to do it, he said, "I fancy doing that." The appeal to us was profile, being able to reignite the region and get some pride behind it, and the ability to open doors.'

Harker had no issues either. 'I don't think he ever had a difficult relationship with the club in terms of what the club stands for, or the members, or its position in the region,' he argues. 'It was a very difficult time because he was quite clearly at the end of his career so whether he'd been here or anywhere else, I suspect the sentiments might have been similar.'

Before Botham could take over, the ECB had to ensure there was something to be chairman of by addressing the £3.74m owed to Durham County Council. 'We said, "We can't do all [of Durham's debt] – we're struggling to do half of it, really. Can we both deal with it?"' Hollins explains. 'If the council had said no, I think that would have been it. We said, "OK, let's go 50-50," and we had a plan to get it back on its feet [by converting council loans into redeemable preference shares].'

'What was asked of us was how we were going to deal with that loan – are we going to write it off? I felt it was inappropriate,' council leader Simon Henig comments. 'It needed to be translated into some new arrangement which gave the flexibility to allow the club to continue. Never mind [losing] internationals and so on, there was a real threat of the club falling over, losing first-class status, and even though I wasn't there at the time I know how much effort went into that. The price of doing nothing and allowing that to happen was too great, given everything that had gone in, given that we still do have regular, annual international games, the only major sport that does in the north east.

'We're very proud to have first-class cricket and at various points Durham has had a basketball team in the top flight [the Wildcats, from 2011–15], we've got a women's football team that is defying gravity in a league [the Women's Championship] with Tottenham, Aston Villa, Manchester United, Millwall and so on. They're by far the highest-placed team in the women's pyramid not connected to any other sports franchise. It shows the enthusiasm for sport in Durham.'

Councillors were told if they did not agree to intervene there was a 'significant risk' of administration. The ECB promised a share of any 'special fee payments' due in the coming years – something the club would not get until clearing its debt to them. If the club folded, its Riverside home – which it leased from the council, and which also hosts concerts – would become a white elephant. The council estimated international cricket was worth £5m to the county's pubs and restaurants, and £500,000 to shops and hotels – enough to sustain 240 full-time jobs.

'As a council we were obviously aware of some of the difficulties,' says Henig. 'I'd had a number of conversations with them about their plans, partly because I'm a councillor for Chester-le-Street, so I was well aware of the plans to develop the ground further – the hotel and so on – to help the income position. We'd always been very encouraging of that. Whatever conversations they were having about their detailed financial situation, they were not necessarily sharing with us, certainly not with me, but there were elements of the plan I was aware of and we were trying to help. We wanted a strong club. Whatever happened it needed to be something that wouldn't chop the legs off the club. When we talked to the ECB we were all in agreement that this club needed to be sustainable.'

We are speaking three days after Oxfordshire-based insurance broker Stewart Donald agreed to buy League One football club Sunderland, and the contrast between elite football and cricket is uncomfortable. 'There is no fairy godmother out there and we're not an area that has a lot of rich people knocking around just waiting to bail out sports clubs,' Henig stresses. 'Even the football teams have struggled – clubs like Darlington and Hartlepool – and you look at the history of football in the north east. It's great that an individual not based in the north east is willing to put his money into Sunderland, and that Middlesbrough have a local guy in Steve Gibson who's been fantastic for them, but in general that's not the case.'

Part of the plan was for Durham to become a community interest company (CIC). 'It was David Harker's initiative and it was important to us and the council,' says Hollins. 'Two of Durham's assets are the strength of recreational cricket and its geographical location. We believe first-class counties should be as closely connected to their communities as they can be and it is healthier if the purpose of the county is serving the community. That was considered the right thing to do for the long-term sustainability. We could have taken a short-term view of, "Go find a billionaire."'

Harker explains: 'Being a CIC makes it harder to attract investment but you can still raise equity. You wouldn't have wanted it to come about in the way it did but I think the CIC model is a natural fit for where we are. We've been a members' club, we've been a company limited by guarantee, we've been a traditional private limited company and this is probably the best model for organisations like us where there's a degree of protection for the assets but still some freedom to try and raise funds.'

Henig represents the council on Botham's revamped board. 'Despite what some people think, it isn't my inclination to join lots of boards,' he stresses. 'However, having insisted we needed to [be represented] I thought it was quite important I did that as a statement, really. It's key that everyone's involved. I'm immaterial to this because I'm just an individual but the more I'm involved, the more important I realise it is. It's about partnerships and as soon as you move away from that, as we've seen in football and other things, the more you have problems. The more you're involved in your community at different levels, the stronger you are. I think there's an understanding of that now, not just from Durham County Cricket Club – where I think, to be fair, they had it from the start. Everything I do on the board will be to strengthen those links. That's how the cricket club will thrive and it's financially right for the cricket club and the council. Everything should flow in the same direction and everyone should benefit – in Chester-le-Street, in County Durham and the whole of the north east.'

Adding to Durham's sense of injustice was the fact they were by no means the only county in debt, or even the most heavily, and since the 2012 salary cap breach they had drawn their horns in. From then until 2016 their wage bill fell 32 per cent, and by 2014 it was the 13th biggest amongst the first-class counties and heading downwards.

It did not help the ECB's message that when Yorkshire were, in his words, '48 hours from being written off' in 2002, Colin Graves was their saviour, lending £18.9m. Although the loan was refinanced when he resigned as Yorkshire chairman to take up the equivalent ECB role, even the name of the new independently run lenders – the Graves Family Trust – jars. In 2015 Leeds City Council wrote off £1m of Yorkshire's debt, but the club had to borrow heavily again to replace the stand which bridges Headingley's rugby and cricket grounds. It added £18m to the 'core' debt which in March 2018 had been £24m. Yorkshire hope the 2019 Ashes Test and four World Cup games it had to be built for turn the tide.

In January 2012 Eastleigh Borough Council bought the Rose Bowl from Hampshire for £6.5m. Described as 'all but insolvent' when Rod Bransgrove came to their rescue in 2000, the county's financial situation was again perilous after being denied 2013 and 2015 Ashes Tests. Ironic, then, that Botham's friend Bransgrove led the charge against Durham. Warwickshire borrowed around £20m from Birmingham City Council to redevelop Edgbaston, and have taken a 'repayment holiday'. In 2018 their debts were £24m.

In 2015 Cardiff Council wrote off £4.4m of a £6.4m loan because, in the words of Welsh cabinet minister Graham Hinchley: 'It is imperative that this long-established sporting institution does not go into administration.' Close to bankruptcy in 2011, Lancashire's debts were £27m by 2018, Nottinghamshire's £7.5m. Even non-Test venues were suffering. In September 2016 Northamptonshire reformed as a limited company after severe financial trouble. In 2017 they borrowed £2m from their council and £475,000 from their directors to keep Wantage Road up to county standard.

'Debt's OK as long as you can service it,' Hollins insists. 'If you've got a benefactor or if, like Old Trafford, you've got a hotel, a matchday business, you're in a big city, you're near Old Trafford football ground for overflow hospitality, that's OK. The problem comes when you can't service the debt, as was the case with Durham. If I'm sitting in Manchester with Trafford Park shopping centre and Manchester United near me, I've got much more commercial opportunity than in Chester-le-Street. If you're earning £20,000 a year with a mortgage of £250,000 and I'm earning £50,000 with a mortgage of £300,000, I'm in a better place than you. Explaining that is sometimes difficult.'

At a time of austerity the ECB appeared to have an unsavoury solution to cricket debt. 'Quite a bit later [than the ECB's approach] we noticed there were a number of other cricket teams that were effectively being bailed out by [council] loans,' Henig comments. 'It almost feels like it's expected. At the time I didn't know of those other arrangements but when you discover the extent of this finance from other councils, it puts all of us in a very difficult position individually. I get some criticism for agreeing to our package of help but when you discover the amounts are even greater in some of those other places it certainly doesn't make it any easier. I think there's an issue of how appropriate that model was when we were already into an austerity situation for local government. In football nobody says, "Let's turn to Sunderland council" – it just doesn't happen. I haven't been around cricket management long enough to understand how we got to a position where it appeared to be fairly routine.

'Another thing we discovered afterwards was that some of those loans were written off, which is not the direction we want to go in. I do feel very strongly that we want to support sports teams. It's very good for the area to have a wide range, it shouldn't just be about football, but in a time of austerity I think it's only right that it has strings attached, and it was a loan we expected to be repaid. We still anticipate that funding will come back. I just don't think it's politically tenable otherwise. Durham is a robust council, we're not at the point of falling over financially, but we've had to save £215m since 2010.'

Harker 'always felt it [the debt] was a cricket problem, not a Durham problem. Quite clearly cricket's financial model was broken and that wasn't just Durham saying that, that was other counties saying that at various levels for a long period of time. Gloucestershire produced a paper about how it was all going wrong. But from an ECB point of view they'd seen what had happened at Glamorgan and elsewhere and wanted to be seen to be levering in support from other stakeholders rather than carrying the burden themselves.'

I asked Hollins if there was an ECB expectation local authorities would foot the bill when counties got into debt. 'There was no expectation but we were dealing with the council as the creditor,' he replies. 'If it had been a private individual we would have had a conversation with the private individual to try to find a joint solution. There was a hope that the council would see the benefits of cricket – recreational, first-class and international – to the north east and Durham in particular and they did. They were great, absolutely terrific, at a time when they were under extreme pressure financially.'

In 2016 it felt like the ECB had encouraged its clubs – at least those hosting international cricket – into reckless spending and expected the taxpayer to mop up any mess. That was not how they saw it. 'I was off the [ECB] board then but they would never be self-critical, never,' says Jackson. 'And that includes Colin.' Leaning on taxpayers would have been bad enough at the best of times but was particularly unpalatable because the ECB had reserves of £73m. They always argued they were very fluid depending to a large extent on the attractiveness of England's most recent tourists, and were partly to cover the cost of cancelled home series or other unexpected circumstances, and by early 2018 they were down to £8.6m.

Although Durham's councillors acquiesced, local MPs were less understanding. North Durham's Kevan Jones wrote to Tom Harrison asking 'why all other options were not explored before these incredibly harsh measures were imposed?' and how the ECB decided its sanctions. Blaydon MP and shadow cabinet member Dave Anderson complained: 'The weight of this punishment will only increase the chasm of inequality between our region and others.' City of Durham MP Roberta Blackman-Woods called the decision to remove Test cricket: 'Hugely short-sighted.'

Durham supporters Sylvia and Peter Savage set up an online petition which garnered nearly 2,000 signatures from across the country. In February 2017 their action group received a private visit from Hollins and ex-Durham bowler Simon Brown. 'Den and lions spring to mind!' says Hollins. 'But look, I thought we had to do it and I particularly had to do it because I knew some of the people in that room. The easiest thing to do was to hide in London but I thought it was right not just for the governing body but for Gordon Hollins to front up because the club means a lot to me. It wasn't the easiest two hours of my life but I think when I explained some of the history and the background there was a much better understanding by the end of it, albeit there was, and I'm sure there still is, real upset about the local club being hurt as badly as it was. That hurt me too. I didn't expect to come away from it thinking, "Oh, everybody's happy now," but I hope it helped increase awareness and understanding.' Sylvia Savage, who died later that year, told me: 'It did add flesh to the bones about how things had happened and we were very polite and courteous to one another… It was very interesting to hear but nothing actually changed our perspective. But it was good to meet the guy.'

It appears writing off £2m of Durham's debt was not an act of ECB clemency or an admission of complicity, but 'in exchange for waiving the right to be eligible to host Test matches in the future'. When Glamorgan released their annual accounts in 2018 they explained they had received compensation for not bidding to host Tests between 2020 and 2024. The policy was apparently agreed in principle at an ECB board teleconference in September 2016 but the revelation prompted Surrey chairman Richard Thompson and Somerset's Andy Nash to resign from the board. Compensation was set at £500,000 per year and the £2.5m payment pushed Glamorgan's profits up to £4.1m. Yet Durham's compensation, decided around the same time, was only £2m. I asked Hollins why. 'The template was formed out of Durham's situation,' he says. 'That principle was followed but time has moved since and the board felt £2.5m was the optimum number in the current market.'

It felt rather convenient Durham were wiped off the Test map when the ECB were creating an eight-team limited-overs franchise competition, but had nine major venues. The remaining eight became franchise hosts, but Hampshire – who refused to stop bidding – have since been ignored for future Tests. 'We've now got six venues staging Test matches from 2020, so this isn't a Durham witch-hunt,' Hollins insists. 'What we did with Durham was to say, "Let's try to make the landing as soft as possible," by £2m being a grant in return for relinquishing the right to stage Test matches.' Harker argues: 'That the ECB saw fit to pay compensation to Glamorgan reinforces the Durham view that significant Test cricket is an essential part of funding a Test-match venue. Without it, you can't make ends meet. It's unfortunate for us that the realisation came after our situation developed.'

There was, though, a sound argument for sanctions. Durham had managed their finances badly, and with combined debts across the first-class counties thought to exceed £150m, the ECB had to take a stand. The hope is that from 2020 a £1.1bn broadcast deal for the new 100-ball competition will be the silver bullet, but had things carried on as they were there would have been more Durhams. There still could be.

'We have to send a message about precedent,' explained Harrison in 2016, using a word echoed by Hollins. 'It's not the ECB's job to be a lender.' The ECB had rules about insolvency, but stepped in at Durham before it got to that. Only Division One counties can be relegated, so perhaps the next team to slip into unmanageable debt will also be docked 94 points? I ask Hollins what the precedent was.

'I don't think a precedent has been set,' he replies. 'I think the board would view each case on its merit and take a view of the individual circumstances if it happened again [to decide] whether or not they should intervene. The reason they intervened at Durham was strategic for the good of cricket in the north east and across the country. International player production and the prosperity of recreational cricket were important factors. It was a strategic decision, not a decision based on preserving all 18 [first-class counties] at all costs.'

18.

Minus 48

GRAHAM Onions had just fulfilled a long-held ambition, overtaking Simon Brown as Durham's leading first-class wicket-taker. Even though he failed to take the one more needed to beat Kent, the day before his 35th birthday ought to have been a time of great celebration.

After the drawn County Championship match, Onions spoke with great pride about what he had achieved for the local club that gave him his break, but with his contract up at the end of a 2017 season which had just two matches remaining, there were questions to be answered. His terse response hinted all was not well. 'Ask him,' Onions replied when BBC Radio Newcastle's Martin Emmerson asked if there had been any developments over a new contract. 'He' was coach Jon Lewis.

'I want to stay at the club and at this moment in time I'm still no better off if I'm being brutally honest,' said Onions. 'I feel as though I've got a lot to offer and hopefully the last few weeks have given the club enough indicators to say that I want to stay and I've still got the ability to take wickets.'

So we did ask him. The Riverside's home dressing room is just along from the dining room where Onions spoke, so we headed to it. 'We've made an offer,' Lewis explained. 'Graham has an agent so

I think it works more through him. He got an email two days ago — not just his agent but Graham as well. We made an offer based on red-ball cricket with more match payments for white-ball cricket... Hopefully we will get across the line.'

It was no surprise when it was announced Onions would join Lancashire for 2018. That the news came days after it was revealed Keaton Jennings and Paul Coughlin, Durham's 50- and 20-over captains, would trigger contract clauses to join Lancashire and Nottinghamshire respectively increased Durham's gloom. Amazingly, and to their immense credit, it was 1998 before Durham lost a player (Martin Saggers) to another first-class county, but with Mark Stoneman and Scott Borthwick now at Surrey the tide had turned. All but guaranteeing they would not win promotion in 2017, Durham's 48-point deduction initially felt like a two-year punishment — now Paul Collingwood sees it as more like four.

The harsh reality was all rather different from Sir Ian Botham's typically bullish optimism on his first official day as chairman. Very little was impossible for Botham the cricketer but now he was relying on mere mortals. In his eyes, starting the Championship 48 points back was 'pretty much a level playing field' and Durham did not fight the sanctions they had, after all, agreed to. 'I've got other things to do which are much more important than quibbling over that,' Botham explained.

The ECB's chief operating officer Gordon Hollins described the 48-point penalty as 'challenging for Durham to get back up but not impossible, so as to retain their ambition'. However, they had only won 200 points, finishing fourth in 2016's first division and that was a 16-game season — with the Championship stripped back to 14 matches in 2017, taking one of the two promotion spots looked a tall order. At least they were not the only county starting in the minuses — Leicestershire's persistent disciplinary problems saw them docked 16 points.

'I knew literally everything had to go our way,' says captain Collingwood. 'Beefy [Botham] was always saying, "It's only two wins," but I know how hard it is to get one point, never mind 48! It was always going to be a tough year but I still think a lot of good came out of it to give a lot of youngsters responsibility in key positions. We probably wouldn't have done that any other year.'

The challenge fuelled a real determination not just in Collingwood, Durham's top-scorer in 2017. For the first time in eight years, membership went up, from 3,310 to 4,067. 'My counterpart at Yorkshire rang me up and said, "I'm joining Durham,"' recalls Durham Cricket Board chairman Bob Jackson. 'He and one other joined as country members and that was mirrored by other people.' There were stories of fans from the opposite end of the country taking out memberships they had no intention of using out of solidarity.

As for the remaining players, 'The guys were a mixture of angry, hurt, sad, scared,' says Keaton Jennings. 'You don't really know at the time if this is real, can you fight it? Can you stop it? But the guys just pitched up at the gym the next day and got on with it. I think it took a couple of weeks for the realisation of what had happened and what we were facing to sink in.' Mark Wood urged his team-mates to 'show the north-east spirit and values we always carry of hard work, honesty and trusting each other'.

Lewis commented: 'I think we're officially everyone's second county now. I've been stopped in the street in Consett and one head coach emailed to say, "There's only one club that can get out of this and it's you."' With the benefit of hindsight he admits: 'I was probably a bit naïve. We had to say the right things and to a degree I believed we could achieve more than we did but the task was probably a bit bigger than even we thought.' Durham had just 15 full-time professionals (plus Wood and Ben Stokes when England allowed), compared to 26 for champions Middlesex, who loaned three out at the start of the season.

The fixture compilers did not help either. Despite Division Two having an even number of teams for the first time, Durham sat out its opening round so when they hosted title favourites Nottinghamshire, they were already 70 points behind. At least the new unbalanced second-division format spared them a trip to Trent Bridge. A defiant Good Friday crowd of 2,190 attended day one, which fell on the 25th anniversary of Durham's opening day of first-class cricket, but reality was quick to hit home. New Championship rules allowed visiting captains to forgo the toss and bowl first if they wished. At seamer-friendly Chester-le-Street in seamer-friendly April on a day when the floodlights were used throughout, Nottinghamshire's Chris Read was never going to do anything else. Jennings and Durham's overseas debutant Steven Cook emerged to roars of encouragement. 'The atmosphere when we came out to bat just showed the homeliness of the north east,' says Jennings. 'That for me highlights what the north-east people are about – there's trouble, but let's get through it together.'

Even so, Durham were bowled out in just 45.4 overs. Fourteen wickets fell on day one, five bowled, four lbw, the rest caught behind the stumps. Durham were 71/7 until a maiden first-class fifty for Stuart Poynter – their only player not born in the north east or South Africa – dragged the innings out to 162 – 38 short of a first point. That came when Alex Hales was lbw to reduce Nottinghamshire to 7/3 but by the end of the day they were more than halfway to parity on 96/4. Luke Fletcher equalled his career-best 92, making only his fourth Championship half-century and first for four years, adding 108 for the eighth wicket with James Pattinson (59). Even with Jennings carrying his bat for 102 second-time around, Durham lost by nine wickets. 'It was a bit of a reality check and a kick in the gut,' Jennings reflects. '[Nottinghamshire's] was a high-quality bowling line-up with Jake Ball, Patto [Pattinson], Fletch [Fletcher] and Harry [Gurney] on a tough Riverside wicket, so for a young side to turn them over would have been a hell of an effort. It made you realise this wasn't going to be as easy as we thought.'

'Easy' is not a word you would use to describe Durham's 2017. 'When we played at Gloucester [in the next game] and didn't get the win we deserved, I think we realised 48 points was a lot and getting promoted would be very, very tough,' admits Onions. The

Championship went on a month-long break for 50-over cricket with the Riversiders 97 points off the pace.

Initially, the change of scenery seemed to do Durham good as their top three cashed in on a batsman-friendly format. New one-day captain Jennings was continuing his 2016 form, hitting two centuries to average 57.5, and Michael Richardson (average 70.66) and Cook (45.66) – limited to six games because he had to fly back mid-competition to South Africa for fitness testing – one each. Overlooked for the opening two Championship matches, James Weighell also thrived, taking 18 wickets at 23.11. Only Surrey's Sam Curran took more 50-over scalps, and his 20 came from two extra games. The group winners automatically went into the semi-finals, with the second and third-place teams playing-off to face them. Durham had the northern group's third-best record but missed out because of their points deduction. 'I think the guys were a little bit angry,' Jennings comments. 'Once you go into those knockout stages, anything can happen. I suppose we were almost punch drunk that we should have qualified ahead of [eventual winners] Notts and that's probably where things unfolded.' Jennings's average collapsed from 65 in all formats to 12 after the disappointment, though there was more to it than just that.

Durham's desperation to play catch-up was proving costly. 'We tried to win games,' Jennings reflects. 'At Swansea we probably shouldn't have declared but we wanted to win. Against Northants we left 28mm of grass on the wicket because we wanted to win, knowing full well we were going to have to bat first. If we'd won those two, who knows what would have happened?'

Glamorgan's first Championship win of 2017 came at Durham's expense, by three wickets with three balls remaining after centurion Nick Selman struck sixes from the first two deliveries of the final over. The next game, at home to Northamptonshire, was equally thrilling and just as dispiriting. With three balls left, the Riversiders needed three wickets for victory, and although it was raining heavily the umpires could not really take the players off. Paul Coughlin took his second wicket of the over to leave Durham needing two from two balls, Northamptonshire one run. Nathan Buck swung at the next delivery, missed it, and ran a bye. Dropped catches on day two had cost Durham, who were bottom of Division Two after five games, and would have been even with 48 extra points.

'We were in July and we still didn't have a point,' Lewis explains. 'You don't look at the table every day but you're aware of that. That's not the easiest thing to deal with. Playing Notts first up wasn't ideal because they were one of only two sides I thought were better than us in 2017 – Notts and Sussex; Worcestershire were good when we played them in the last game but it was more to do with the confidence of a winning side against one that was struggling.

'There have been games or tournaments we've won where events conspired in our favour but [in 2017] the fixture schedule didn't help and when we were unable to win [against Gloucestershire] at Bristol we didn't get a Championship game for a month. We played some good 50-over cricket and Keats's captaincy was a step forward. We would have reached the knockout stages without the deduction but I was still hooked on the game against Worcestershire we should have won – the run-chase was comfortable and we butchered it.

'We went into Championship cricket and we twice had Kent nine wickets down, Colly was really aggressive with his declaration at Cardiff because of the rain and we lost by two wickets. We lost against Northants by two wickets. We were probably ahead going into the fourth innings but we only had three seamers standing, even if Coughlin was outstanding [taking the first two five-wicket hauls of his first-class career]. The reason we weren't more successful was because we weren't bowling teams out. That wasn't what we were expecting. Even at Bristol we should have bowled them out quicker and been chasing less than 100 with two sessions to go instead of 150 in under a session.'

Once Durham stopped chasing the improbable, their form improved. 'The guys are genuinely good people,' says Jennings. 'The smile's just permanently on Stuart Poynter's face and he just brings a warm, happy vibe. When you've got guys like that around it's very easy to continue a good feeling despite losing. Because things were going so poorly, the guys just went the other way. It's like when you get over-tired and you stop feeling tired – it almost got to that point where people just start enjoying it.'

The 5 June defeat to Northamptonshire was Durham's last in the Championship until 2017's final home game, although they were denied a first win by Kent's final-wicket pair in the next game, at Canterbury. Yasir Shah and Mitchell Claydon batted out the last 46 deliveries and, with Chris Rushworth off with a stiff back, Collingwood entrusted the final over to Matthew Potts, an 18-year-old debutant not yet on a professional contract. Even with six slips, two gullies and a short leg, he could not remove Yasir with his final delivery.

South African Cook arrived talking of the points deduction as 'a fantastic opportunity to make a difference', but despite his one-day form the opener found the Championship tough. His highest score in seven matches came in his final innings, where 89 not out secured Durham's first four-day win, over Glamorgan. Like Jennings, who also went to King Edward VII School (it is not just England who are over-reliant on private schools), the former South Africa A and Highveld Lions captain made a century on his Test debut but struggled to follow it up. He arrived at Durham having lost his Test place after three poor games in New Zealand and Sri Lanka and what was meant to be his acclimatisation for the England versus South Africa series cost him his place in it.

There were, though, some batting plusses. Graham Clark scored his maiden first-class century at home to Glamorgan having forced his way into the team with three consecutive second-team hundreds, and Cameron Steel took advantage of being caught off a no-ball on four to make his against Northamptonshire. Steel joined in the winter with six first-class appearances under his belt, three for Durham University against Durham in which he scored two half-centuries. Californian-born to English parents, he moved to Somerset aged three and Perth at 13 before coming to Durham City to study history and captain the university team. Released by Middlesex, he made 95 against them on trial with Durham in the 2016 Second XI Championship Final.

Lewis had called for five or six players to have 'their best season ever', adding, 'it's quite do-able', and in terms of Championship averages, Steel, Clark, Poynter, Ryan Pringle and Barry McCarthy obliged, as did Steel, Jennings, Weighell, Brydon Carse and Mark Wood with their weaker suits. Poynter's 20.69 batting average was not enough to stop his maiden season as first-choice wicketkeeper ending in early July.

As good as Durham had been in 50-over cricket, they were horrendous in Twenty20. With Jennings on England duty, Coughlin captained and, although he headed Durham's batting averages with 41.62 and was their leading wicket-taker with 13, he oversaw just three wins in 14 games and epitomised an extremely inexperienced team. Despite including Collingwood, the players who faced Lancashire in the opening game averaged 24 appearances in the competition. The 41-year-old became not only professional cricket's oldest Twenty20 centurion but Durham's first, yet his 108 not out against Worcestershire counted for nothing when Joe Clarke made an unbeaten 124. Cook's overseas replacement, New Zealander Tom Latham, was diagnosed with a stress fracture of the foot at the Champions Trophy and missed the first eight Twenty20 matches. He scored 88 not out on his debut as Durham beat Yorkshire by one run for their first win of 2017, finally reaching zero points.

Since appearing for Durham's junior teams in 2010, Latham had played 91 limited-overs internationals, plus 32 Tests after his second spell in 2013, so it was no surprise his experience made a difference. He marked his Durham Championship debut (he played for Kent in 2016) in early August with a century at Leicester in a 234-run stand with Steel, who hit 224 in the draw, and scored 382 runs in four Championship matches at 63.66.

Rain appeared to come to Durham's rescue at 1.56pm on 2017's final day of Riverside cricket with last pair Carse and Onions at the crease against Sussex, but when they returned two and a quarter hours later and lasted just six balls, the unbeaten Championship run ended. Durham finished ninth out of ten in Division Two, and 48 more points would only have nudged them up two places. The narrow early-season finishes did more damage. Twice Kent's tenth-wicket pair clung on for draws, and while it would be unrealistic to expect Durham to win both those games plus matches at Bristol, Swansea and at home to Northamptonshire, doing so would have been worth an extra 65 points on top of the 98 they finished with – plus significant self-belief. By September, matters off the field were again the concern.

Jennings and Coughlin's departures were announced during Sussex's visit. Like Mark Stoneman before them, they were being groomed to succeed Collingwood having been given captaincy roles on the back of new contracts towards the end of the 2016 season. Sunderland-born Coughlin captained Durham against Sri Lanka A in June 2016 – a match his brother Josh made his first-class debut in. Paul's performances on his Championship debut, in the 2014 One-Day Cup Final and as Twenty20 captain, showed he could rise to the occasion. Unable to bowl in the 2016 Second XI Championship Final, he scored 231 and was chosen for England's winter Pace Performance Programme. While Jennings left on good terms, Sir Ian Botham was furious at Coughlin's exit.

'I respect Paul's right to move clubs and understand players at certain times in their careers may want to move on,' said Botham, who played for three counties. 'However, it's without question our second-division status, points penalties and difficult financial situation has created an opportunity for rival counties and intermediaries to unsettle players with promises of first-division cricket, greater England opportunities and immediate financial reward. It concerns me the current arrangements within cricket do not reward counties who invest in academies and produce exciting young English players. The ECB... need to introduce a transfer or similar system of compensation, to remove the potential for conflict of interest by preventing serving directors of cricket acting as selectors, and to better regulate the behaviour of agents.' Having taken over as chief executive midway through the 2018 campaign, Tim Bostock says: 'I have been surprised how many calls I've received from agents. I didn't ever think of cricket as being like soccer, and while the money's different the intent's the same with player movement.'

Although under-contract players switching clubs is becoming more common, county cricket does not yet have a transfer system. The £50,000 compensation Yorkshire paid Northamptonshire for David Willey in 2015 was seen as a first step and Durham received £20,000 for Coughlin. In 2014 Nottinghamshire's director of cricket Mick Newell and his Middlesex counterpart Angus Fraser became England selectors, an uncomfortable and impractical situation finally ended in 2018.

'When Coggers [Coughlin] signed his three-year deal in 2016 he was very close to going to Warwickshire but ended up making the decision to stay at Durham,' explains his agent, James Welch. 'We were told by another county he should wait because something was going to happen over a points deduction. We spoke to [Durham] and they said they weren't aware of anything, and Coggers wanted to stay so he signed. We then went back to the club [after the points deduction] and said we were pretty sure they must have known what was going to happen so we got them to insert a clause in the contract with a buy-out. They set the value. Other clubs, including Warwickshire and Nottinghamshire, were aware of that.

'After the [2017] season Coggers had, and discussions with people around the set-up, it was clear the ECB do want players playing in Division One, and with the new 100-ball competition I think you will see more and more players moving to counties who are going to host games. When we saw what Notts were offering I thought it was a great opportunity for Coggers. Paul was still seen by a lot of people as a young player but he was approaching 25 and I don't think he could afford to risk another year or two at Durham.

'We had chats about who they were hoping to bring in and I thought they were still going to struggle finance-wise for a while. Initially everyone was pretty angry because they saw him as a key part of the team in all formats and someone they could build a team around. I can understand Botham's points about how Durham are not rewarded enough for developing players, but when he took over he maybe thought it would be an easier job than it was to convince players to come to Durham and to keep them, but players have to think about their own careers. Paul had the opportunity to leave a couple of times [previously] and didn't. The only way he was going to leave was if he genuinely believed it was going to develop his cricket sufficiently. If Durham hadn't had the points deduction and had been competing [for silverware] it might have been different.'

In 2016 Jennings also negotiated a release clause which could only be activated if Durham were in Championship Division Two. 'I'm not a selector so I don't know what importance they put on [Division One status] but I want to test myself against the best,' argues Jennings. 'Vernon Philander was so much better than me in June/July 2017 [when Jennings played for England against South Africa] but I want to know the next time I meet him I can compete against the best to know where I am, and if I'm not good enough, that's cool. If Division One is the best quality [county] cricket I can play, I want to try it.'

'When I signed [a four-year Durham contract in 2016] there was a lot of uncertainty about whether other guys like Woody and Stokesey were going to sign and I think we were still second or third in the table, but it was more if things didn't go well were my three points [outlined in chapter 16] going to remain if we didn't keep our firepower?' Jennings continues. 'The clause couldn't be activated for a year [contrary to rumours in the winter of 2016/17 he would trigger it]. I'm not a half-in-the-boat person, I'm all in or all out, so it was quite tough to be part of something when you didn't really know what was going on. At that stage there were only six or seven guys who were definitely staying because a lot were into their final year [of contracts].'

The 2017 season was difficult for Jennings. After Durham's One-Day Cup exit he only passed 50 twice, both for England Lions versus South Africa A to cement his place for the Test series between the seniors. He struggled badly in it, scoring 127 in four matches and losing his place to Stoneman for the home games against the West Indies. 'There was a lot going on,' he points out. 'My father was diagnosed with cancer so you start dealing with personal issues at a time your performances haven't been great. It was a tough time for me but through them you grow and hopefully I won't make the same mistakes again. There was a lot more to the two halves of my season than just performance but I wouldn't change it. I learnt so much from doing the [contract] negotiations myself. I made good contacts and had tough conversations.

'It was a strange time to balance your own career with a new [Durham] chairman and my England career, and work out how you were going to manage this process. My dad was a key person in guiding me and so was Sir Ian, who was awesome and a massive influence in helping me when I wanted to use that clause to leave. He was fantastic in the way he engaged with me. I'm happy with the decisions I've made. Durham will always have a special place in my heart. They gave me an opportunity and, although I got called a Judas when I walked away, it's a fantastic place. I hold it in such high regard because of the way they treated me, which made moving away so much harder. It's even tougher for a guy like Coughlin, a home-grown Mackem lad who loves home and loves the place but wanted to pursue his career, and you can't hold that against him.'

Collingwood made it known how unhappy he was at the 'disloyalty'. 'It hurts me,' he admits. 'The whole reason why this place was built and all that time, effort and money went into getting first-class [status] was to give local people the opportunity to play first-class cricket and to play for England so for people brought up in this area to want to leave, it's like losing a member of the family. I still don't understand it. I'm hoping it's simply money, but if it's not that hurts me even more.' Chris Rushworth is more phlegmatic. 'It's sad when your friends and team-mates leave but it's professional sport,' he says. 'Not everyone shares the same drives, opinions and ambitions. If people feel they have to move on to progress their career that's up to them but you want to keep all your best players. Circumstances haven't always allowed that in the last few years.'

I asked Jennings if he felt any guilt at leaving at the most difficult time in Durham's first-class history. 'You've got to look at it terms of it being how you put bread on your plate,' he replies. 'I'm very blessed that I've grown up with my mates since we were in the academy together and we've forged strong relationships which can continue regardless of what walk of life we choose. You're walking away from 10, 12 best mates and when you have to tell them you're leaving you think, "How am I actually going to do this?" It was tough telling them essentially you don't want to play with them anymore. Before the Worcester game [Durham's last of 2017] I had a chat with everybody individually. You've got to park your emotions and ask what is best for you at that moment of your career. JJ [Lewis] said to me it was a business call and he may not agree with me, but it was a call I felt I needed to make.'

A transfer system would theoretically make it easier for richer counties to circumvent the contracts of other clubs' players, but Durham director David Harker argues it is happening anyway. 'Contracts don't really matter,' he says. 'I've never known anyone held to a contract who didn't want to be there. It would seem two-division cricket is making it harder for second-division clubs to keep their squads together, I'm sure the recruiting counties use that. I was never in a position where a player came to me and said, "I would be quite happy to stay but in all honesty they're offering me so much more money, I really fancy that." I would never blame any individual who says, "You've made me your best offer but these guys are going to pay more and I've got a short career and a family. I'm going for the money." I might not like it but it's a perfectly legitimate reason to move. But no one's ever actually moved for money in all the time I've been involved!'

During the 2018 season it was announced Zak Chappell, Joe Clarke, Aneurin Donald, Ben Duckett, James Fuller, Craig Miles, Liam Norwell, Josh Poysden and Ben Slater would be leaving Division Two sides to play in the first division, either immediately or at the end of the season. All joined counties hosting the new 100-ball competition, as did Richard Gleeson, who left Northamptonshire to fight Lancashire's unsuccessful battle against relegation. Jennings and Coughlin's departures were a direct result of Durham not winning 2017 promotion, which arguably could be traced back to the 48-point deduction. 'It was career development which I could argue with but I can at least respect why they did it,' Lewis reflects. 'If the best players want to play for England they want to play Division One so that can be a factor. The difference between Div One and Two is not to be denied but the difference between Div One and Test cricket is massive.'

Jennings was back into England's Test team for the 2018 season as the new selectors continued where their predecessors had in flailing around for Andrew Strauss's long-term successor, but Lancashire were relegated from Division One. The first summer of Coughlin's three-year Trent Bridge contract was a washout. He dislocated his shoulder playing for England Lions in the winter of 2017/18, and his only first-team appearances came in three Twenty20 games, where he scored 13 runs and did not bowl.

That, as well as representing Coughlin and Stoneman, Welch was also Onions's agent probably did not help the bowler. 'Since I was 19 I'd negotiated all my contracts,' Onions explains. 'I had an agent but I wanted to do it and as a rule I got what I wanted through talking with the club, building that respect, and then knowing I had to produce the performances to back it up. But in the final year I didn't have that relationship anymore and I didn't really understand why.'

Onions had back and side problems in 2014, a pre-season knee injury in 2015, followed by a 'minor knee' and chest problem, but was a Championship ever-present in 2016, taking 54 wickets. 'I got injured at Sussex [in May 2017] and was out for four weeks and I think they were thinking that was me done, and I can understand that but I'm determined, I wanted to play two more years,' he says. 'I didn't play in the one-day team but I played in the second team and took [ten] wickets, bowled loads of overs [102] and I'd proved myself well before the last game of the season, so I don't know why it took them until then to say yes or no.'

To his undisguised frustration, Onions only made two one-day appearances in his final three seasons, plus two Twenty20 games in his last four years. 'In 2017 I thought it was going to be my last year, without a doubt,' he says. 'I had an idea that Sussex was going to be my last home game but I couldn't say anything. It infuriated me that such a long career ended in a slightly bitter way. At the beginning of the game I was offered a contract but it was poor – it was a one-year deal and the money side was bad, and I said, "Thanks for the offer, but you need to improve it." There were no opportunities to get involved in the coaching side either, and Lancs gave me that. We played the game out and to be honest I felt as though they were waiting for me to break down [injured].

'Jon should have just said, "We're in the process of negotiating a new deal." It might have made people think I didn't want to stay but I categorically said to everybody I did not want to leave Durham. Why on earth would I? It's my club and I love it. Hopefully my situation highlights some of the things that need to be better but it reached the stage where I needed to look after Emma, my wife, and my kids Oliver and Esmé.

'To be brutally honest a little bit of how I was treated by England was taken out on Durham because I was thinking, "No, I've been an unbelievable servant for the club and I think I deserve to go out the way I want to." I'd like to think my bowling performances were good enough for people to say, "Actually, he was just determined to be as good as he possibly could be."'

Onions accepted Lancashire's two-year offer and was replaced by Nathan Rimmington, an Australian with a British passport. Two months younger, he was also on a contract until 2019. Rimmington took 11 second-division wickets in the 2018 Championship, compared to 57 for Onions in Division One, although he was the country's fourth-highest Twenty20 wicket-taker, with 22 victims.

Compounding the loss of three key players was the stupidity of one of their most promising talents. Jack Burnham had played for Durham's junior teams since the age of nine and showed he had something special on his senior debut. When Collingwood suffered a back injury at Scarborough, the 18-year-old batsman from Esh Winning starred in front of the Championship's biggest crowd of 2015. He was bowled for a four-ball duck by the best ball of the match in his first innings but, against an attack where the reliable Steven Patterson supplemented internationals Ryan Sidebottom, Tim Bresnan, Liam Plunkett, Adil Rashid and Glenn Maxwell, Burnham's second-innings half-century was Durham's only one in the 183-run defeat. He was last out trying to smash a fired-up Plunkett for six. Three centuries in six games made him the top scorer at the 2016 Under-19 World Cup, passing Alastair Cook's English record. Only Pakistan's Hasan Mohsin had a higher average and Burnham hit 15 sixes when no one else managed double figures. At The Oval that summer he followed Nicky Peng and Ben Stokes as Durham's third-youngest Championship centurion.

Lewis was joking when he said of the teenager in April 2016: 'He's a very, very talented cricketer, not very talented when it comes to life skills!' But 12 months later Burnham failed a second drugs test of his career, and at the end of the season he failed another. A month after agreeing a new two-year contract and a week after Stokes was arrested following a fracas outside a nightclub while with England, it was terrible timing. Durham decided against sacking Burnham but the ECB handed him the standard 12-month ban, during which time he underwent an approved rehabilitation programme including education, counselling and treatment, while working as a labourer. Counties are not informed of a first offence, and the second was kept quiet because his 21-day ban coincided with a broken thumb, but a fourth violation would see him banned for three years. It perhaps explained Burnham's poor 2017, scoring just one Championship and one Twenty20 half-century. He was 14th in Durham's Championship batting averages with 24.77 from seven matches.

There were new contracts for Ryan Pringle and Stuart Poynter, although Adam Hickey was released when a shoulder injury left him one match short of automatically triggering a new deal. Popular former captain Will Smith's return from Hampshire was announced hours after Jennings's departure.

'We lost a quarter of our team, and you would have to say the best players,' Collingwood reflects. 'So the whole impact probably put us back four years. Now we've got to wait for the next generation to get up to the level Rocky, Scotty [Borthwick] and Keats were at. We'll regrow. These players will become big players themselves because everyone gets replaced.'

19.

One Step Forward, Two Steps Back

THERE was excitement in the cold Chester-le-Street air as a youthful crowd awaited Durham's first home Twenty20 quarter-final in a decade. A couple of hours later, their 2018 season was effectively over a month early.

Although the Riversiders took an unexpected step forward in Twenty20, their 50-over form was dismal and Championship results little better. There were hints of better things to come – the signings of Alex Lees and Ben Raine were coups, as was retaining Brydon Carse, and for the second time in three years Durham were second XI champions. A new chief executive and director of cricket offered fresh thinking to a structure which had changed little for years, but with Paul Collingwood's retirement taking more experience from a squad which had lost so much since 2016, there was much to do.

The previous two seasons could barely have offered more contrasting evidence as to whether Durham were finally getting to grips with Twenty20. In 2016 they hit on a winning formula at Chester-le-Street, where only Lancashire beat them. With five of their first six games away, as the 14-game northern group reached its conclusion, they built momentum that carried them to their first final.

The perceived wisdom about 20-over cricket is that supporters want to see as many sixes as possible, so as bats and batsmen have become bigger and white balls less responsive, boundary ropes have been pulled in. Durham prioritised wins by making the Riverside outfield as big as possible. It emphasised different skills, favouring running between the wickets and athletic fielders, as opposed to what then-Northamptonshire coach David Ripley referred to as 'big chubsters' who could clear short boundaries with mishits. It worked – just – as Durham's lithe players squeezed into the quarter-finals.

They had been slow out of the blocks – hammered by 38 runs in their opener at Worcester, and by nine wickets at Edgbaston – but recovered to head into their final group game, against Derbyshire at Chester-le-Street, needing home wins there and at Old Trafford, where holders Lancashire entertained Birmingham. When, early in the 16th over, Birmingham had chalked off 80 of the 125 runs needed for the loss of four wickets, it seemed Durham's dream had died; somehow, though, they collapsed to 94/8 off 20 overs. Durham still needed to do their job, and owed their 13-run win to players making final Twenty20 appearances for them at the Riverside. Mark Stoneman had announced he was leaving for Surrey, while, as a limited-overs specialist yet to make a half-century in 2016, Calum MacLeod's chances of a new contract looked slim. Stoneman scored 82 not out from 55 deliveries, MacLeod 83 from 50, as Durham posted 193/2 – their highest score of 2016 – and defended it thanks to Scott Borthwick's 3-33.

By finishing fourth in the north, Durham – whose only away win came at Old Trafford in May – secured a quarter-final in the tighter surroundings of Bristol's County Ground. 'We'd been really good at home on big, big parks and everywhere we'd gone away we'd struggled,' coach Jon Lewis reflects. 'We got 180 (for five) – which felt big for us because games here were more 165 scores. Mark Wood was a key component [taking 2-28] and his Twenty20 performances that season were unbelievable. His first couple of overs knocked the back out of them, then Rushy [Chris Rushworth] and Richo [Michael Richardson] combined to get rid of [Michael] Klinger, which was massive. Richo took a ridiculously good catch standing up, which deflated them a lot, and we had two direct-hit run-outs which were probably our only two all season!' Seven of Durham's ten run-outs in the 2016 competition came in the knockout stages, four at Bristol.

Victory set up a semi-final against a Yorkshire side including six current England Twenty20 internationals and former world champion Tim Bresnan. Gareth Breese appreciated the significance. 'I felt like I was playing because it was the only thing we hadn't won in an 11-year span, so I was thinking, "Come on, do this and it would be a dream,"' he says. Lewis's starting point was more prosaic: 'Our previous experience of Finals Day [in 2008] was rubbish, we didn't even turn up at the Rose Bowl, so we were keen to avoid that.'

The rain which delayed the first semi-final took Durham's batsmen off twice in the second game as Ben Stokes's 56 helped them to 156. With two sixes in his 17, Jack Burnham scored more than in his entire domestic Twenty20 career to date – less impressive when you consider he had only played twice, but that made his selection ahead of Gordon Muchall a show of faith.

'Yorkshire had all their stars and it really felt like we were supposedly turning up to let them get through to the final, but we put in one of our best games in the field,' says Lewis. After conceding 12 runs in his first over, Wood removed Jonny Bairstow, Gary Ballance, Bresnan and Liam Plunkett to take 4-25. His best work came in his second over, when according to Joe Root: 'He made me look as if I was batting with my hands and feet on backwards.' Wood was cute as well as quick. 'Woody had a great plan to Rooty which we'd spent about a week trying to develop with everybody you could think of because he was in a bit of form,' says Lewis. 'It was also a good plan to bowl Bresnan with a slower ball. A lot of things we'd planned came together – it doesn't always work that way but it feels pretty good when it does. It [victory] felt more comfortable than seven runs.'

Both last-four games were played in full, but after the weather interruptions something had to give. The mascot race took priority over cricket, so by the time the second semi-final finished, there were just 32 minutes before Durham faced Northamptonshire. Sky only had time for an advert break and an interview with man-of-the-match Wood before the toss; Collingwood did not have the chance to fill out a team-sheet. 'In hindsight we picked the wrong side,' Lewis admits. 'There was an argument for playing [Paul] Coughlin as the extra seam bowler we didn't need against Yorkshire, but with 25 minutes between games I can't honestly say I was thinking about that. The turnaround was bloody hard.'

Burnham was not Durham's only Twenty20 novice. Keaton Jennings had played a little more in the format, but as a bowler until Phil Mustard's departure three weeks earlier catapulted him to limited-overs opener. Jennings began 2016 with a career-best Twenty20 score of one not out but started Finals Day week as the first batsman in England to 1,000 first-class runs. He had shown what he was capable of in June's One-Day Cup game at home to Nottinghamshire when, batting at nine, he hit the final two scheduled balls for six and four to clinch victory.

Jennings's 88 from 58 deliveries, more than double his previous best, was the highest score at a Twenty20 Finals Day, but Stokes (18) and Borthwick (10) were his only team-mates into double figures. Although Durham's 153/8 was only three fewer than against Yorkshire, it never felt enough. Wood, Rushworth and a Borthwick run-out reduced Northamptonshire to 9/3 but captain Alex Wakeley made 43 from 39 deliveries in his second century stand that day, and Josh Cobb 80 not out as the 2015 runners-up cantered to the trophy.

Only six of Durham's finalists made more than four appearances for them in 2017 and their inexperience showed in ten defeats from 14 games. Even captain Coughlin had only played 16 Twenty20 games. They addressed that for 2018, bringing Will Smith back from Hampshire and signing Indian Premier League, Big Bash and Champions League veteran Nathan Rimmington. Having missed all but four games in 2017, Tom Latham returned as Durham's ever-present captain and his fellow overseas player was one of the world's best Twenty20 bowlers. Leg-spinner Imran Tahir had played 20-over cricket for Delhi Daredevils, Rising Pune Supergiant, Chennai Super Kings, Highveld Lions, Lahore Lions, Gauteng Titans, Hampshire, Warwickshire, Natal Dolphins, Nottinghamshire, Derbyshire, Multan Sultans and South Africa. In February 2017 Tahir was ranked the world's top Twenty20 (and 50-over) bowler, and joining Durham equalled Marcus North's record of playing for six counties. A less experienced side might not have shrugged off two defeats to Yorkshire in their opening three games, particularly with two daunting fixtures to come.

'We suddenly had Rimmo [Rimmington], Immy [Tahir], Smudge [Smith], Tom and Colly playing the majority of games and whether their numbers were stellar wasn't the whole thing, they understood the game a little bit better,' Lewis argues. 'I thought a good start was going to be important. We started the first game well but the last seven overs of Yorkshire's innings got out of hand and they scored 100 so we ended up chasing 201 when it looked more like being 170.' Leicestershire were beaten by 33 runs before Yorkshire completed a double. Next were 2017 finalists Birmingham and Nottinghamshire.

'I was thinking we could easily be one win from five because they are two of the toughest places to go,' Lewis admits. 'Birmingham was important, because we won that without Immy, really. He had his only bad game – or [Colin] de Grandhomme had a really good game, you can look at it whichever way you want [de Grandhomme was 63 not out, Tahir conceded 0-53]. It was one of the best pitches we played on all year with a short boundary – it was brutal. We won because with the short leg-side boundary, [James] Weighell and Rimmington went for 12 runs in total [for two Weighell wickets] from overs 17 and 19, where they really needed 20 from each. Tom played one of the best innings I've ever seen at Nottingham [98 not out from 55 deliveries]. The scores don't make it look like a poor pitch but it was really difficult and we got 184. They won the powerplay by 15 runs, and we still knew we had too much because once we got out of the powerplay Immy would be able to work on a slow, low, turning pitch. Because we'd picked up a couple of wickets, I was still really confident we'd win and we closed it out comfortably.' Collingwood compared the victories to 'beating Man U at Old Trafford'.

Durham went on a run of eight wins from nine matches, including comfortably beating holders Nottinghamshire again and the team who would succeed them, Worcestershire. 'We got on a roll and nobody thought too much about it,' says Smith. The only defeat was the reverse game at Worcester which Tahir, travelling separately so he could fly to the Caribbean Premier League afterwards, missed after badly misjudging the Friday-afternoon traffic.

Tahir finished second in the competition's bowling averages and, importantly for an overseas player, his contribution outlasted him. 'We didn't play the wrist-spinner in the 50s [the 50-over One-Day Cup] because Ben [Whitehead] was only just making his reintroduction to the club,' Lewis explains. 'He'd now gone through another couple of months in the second team, where he'd been the most successful spinner. When we got Immy on board, knowing he'd only be here for the first bit, we said, "Let's just put Ben with him for a month." Ben took every opportunity to learn from him and when his chance came, he made a really good fist of it.'

Cumbrian off-spinner Liam Trevaskis took centre stage in the first post-Tahir game, at Old Trafford, where Lancashire needed six off the final over with four wickets in hand – a formality in Twenty20. The 19-year-old, picked more for his batting having taken only one wicket in seven previous appearances, claimed 3-1 from his final over for figures of 4-16. 'How much of a pressure situation was that?' marvels Smith. 'It took him a bit by surprise [to be asked to bowl the final over], which probably helped. He was just going to bowl one over to fill in but he bowled that so well and the next one so well, he kept going [for four straight overs].' James Faulkner was caught at long-on, Danny Lamb stumped, and Matthew Parkinson held by Smith at deep midwicket. 'Tom didn't say much, just "Back yourself,"' Trevaskis revealed. 'I'd bowled a touch full in the few overs I'd bowled, so I dragged my length back.'

Without Tahir, Durham limped to the line. Lancashire bowled them out for 78 – their lowest Twenty20 score – at the Riverside, and the final group game at home to Derbyshire was abandoned without a ball bowled. 'The signs that we were running out of gas with the batting were there towards the end of the group stage,' Lewis admits. 'Should we have changed a couple of the batters going into the last two or three? We only made one fifty in the last six games [Latham's 52 at home to Leicestershire], and only had one fifty partnership [Latham and Collingwood at Northampton]. You think you've got to keep faith with the guys who have got you here.'

Focussed on negating Sussex's fearsome pace attack of Tymal Mills, Jofra Archer, Chris Jordan and David Wiese, Durham came unstuck in their home quarter-final. Once Ben Stokes – initially denied permission to play by England, then told he could appear only as a batsman – was out for 34, they were choked by spinners Danny Briggs and Will Beer, going ten overs without a boundary. Sussex comfortably chased Durham's 140/7 to win by five wickets. 'Sussex played better than we did,' says Lewis. 'The pitch was dead and the boundaries were big and they'd got three 90mph bowlers [Mills, Archer and Jordan]. I thought we nullified them really well, we just didn't adapt to how well their spinners did. There wasn't a lot of turn but there was no pace. Apart from Stokesey, no one looked particularly fluent.'

Defeat punctured the optimism building at the Riverside. Earlier that week, Alex Lees and Axar Patel made promising debuts in an innings-and-30-run Championship win in Cardiff. Indian Patel made 95 not out in his debut innings, leading a recovery from 144/5 to 295 – a 141-run advantage – and was said to look 'crestfallen' when Michael Hogan bowled Rushworth to end the innings. With 18 wickets at 13.05 in four matches, Patel's bowling impressed too. 'I've never seen as good a left-arm spinner – his control and skill were like no other I've ever seen,' Smith gushes.

Patel, though, was a short-term fix. Lees, who made 69 in Cardiff, was a long-term signing, his loan the precursor to a three-year contract. In 2015 a 22-year-old Lees became Yorkshire's first specialist limited-overs captain the season after being the Cricket Writers' Club's young player of the year. He had lost his way since. 'Having discussed it at length with him, I think it's generally felt by Alex and us that for his future career it's probably the right move,' said former Durham coach Martyn Moxon, now Yorkshire's director of cricket. 'I fully expect him to excel.'

If signing Lees was a signal Durham were again becoming competitive in the market for players, so was Brydon Carse's three-year contract. Injury stopped the South African-born all-rounder playing in 2018, but Collingwood tipped him as a future England player and a number of Championship Division One clubs were interested in signing him when his contract expired in the winter. Following the loss of academy graduates Mark Stoneman, Scott Borthwick, Keaton Jennings and Paul Coughlin, retaining Carse was a much-needed vote of confidence.

More controversially, Durham signed Cameron Bancroft as their 2019 overseas player. The Australian had been guilty of rubbing sandpaper on to the ball in a Test against South Africa. He was banned from Australian international and domestic cricket for nine months, as opposed to a year for vice-captain David Warner and captain Steve Smith. Former Gloucestershire opener Bancroft had been due to join Somerset for 2018, and although his ban did not apply to county cricket they wisely cancelled. Durham chairman Sir Ian Botham was quite happy to offer the then-25-year-old a second chance once his ban expired.

'What do these people want?' he asks of those uncomfortable with that. 'Should we just ban him for life? I would say to those people grow up and get a life. I didn't realise we had so many people up for sainthood in this country. They can go and polish their halos somewhere else. The guy made a mistake, he's a young man, he's admitted that, he hasn't played in the Caribbean League or the

Canadian league [unlike Smith and Warner], he's stayed at home, done his community service and worked with junior clubs. Half the people whingeing about it are doing it because they didn't think of it. He's served his time and the boys here are very excited about having him in the team and I think you'll find the public will take to him very well.'

Tim Bostock believes: 'He's a really good guy who probably made the biggest mistake of his young life so far but everybody deserves another crack. I spoke to people in the cricket world, here and in Australia, to ask what sort of character he was and even the England players who played against him that winter said he was a really good kid and they were really, really surprised he got involved in something like that. We thought he was going to be really hungry to succeed and really grateful to be given the opportunity. I think we're going to get 150 per cent out of him. Whilst we've had one or two of the usual, "I'm not going to renew my membership," overwhelmingly it's been extremely positive because I think supporters realise what was happening behind the scenes and that he should be a good fit for us.'

Having taken over as chief executive in July, Bostock was himself part of Botham's revamp. A former Cheshire batsman who played first-class cricket in Zimbabwe, he had been a senior executive with National Australia Bank and the New South Wales government. David Harker became a non-executive director, while former Olympic 400m runner Allison Curbishley also joined the board, adding to the 2017 additions – marketing consultant Phil Collins, commercial lawyer Naynesh Desai and Paul Woolston, who worked on Durham's first-class business plan for Price Waterhouse.

'David Harker was fantastic when I first got here and guided me through a lot of stuff,' says Botham. 'But David had been here a long time and I knew he was itching to move on a bit. I went to Australia and found my old mate Tim Bostock, who I've known for years. You don't run banks around the world and banking institutes unless you know what you're doing. He'd been abroad for 14 years and I sat him down under Sydney Harbour Bridge, we had a bottle of wine and some oysters and at the end of that he said, "OK, I'd be quite interested." He came here on a massive pay drop and he's been a breath of fresh air, working with me and Phil Collins, another very successful businessman. There's a bit of tinkering to be done but we've pretty much got the [boardroom] team we need.'

Bostock succumbed to Botham's powers of persuasion. 'Cricket's pretty much been in my blood since I've been old enough to know what cricket was,' he says. 'When I finished playing pro cricket in my late teens, early 20s, my ideal job would have been in sport but I decided a career in banking was likely to be more lucrative and it allowed me to play minor counties cricket.

'Botham was doing a Q&A for a charity function on Sydney Harbour in November 2017 and I was a trustee of the foundation. I had a friend at Worcestershire who had asked if I would consider coming back to the UK to take on the Worcester job. Whilst I'm from Liverpool, I'd lived in Worcestershire for 15 years. I'd sort of said I wasn't thinking of coming back but if I did it would be to a job like that. That evening the guy who'd asked me was speaking to Botham and he spoke to me afterwards and said if I was thinking of coming back, it should be to Durham – a bigger job, more opportunity and a bigger challenge. It planted the seed. He got me excited, understanding some of the history of where Durham had been, particularly in recent times. I thought it was a great opportunity to make a difference over the next three or four years. He texted me around Christmas time from New Zealand and said he hoped I'd still be interested. I flew back, met the board, had some Skype interviews and I was offered the job.'

Fifty-over cricket was a struggle from the start for Durham, losing their opening games against Yorkshire and Lancashire by a combined 334 runs, then a four-wicket defeat at Derbyshire with only two deliveries remaining. This time there would be no 2014-style revival, winning two of eight matches to finish bottom of the northern group. 'I was disappointed because we played it well the year before,' Lewis reflects. 'Keats [Jennings] was captain in 2017 and did a good job,

Tom's not a dissimilar captain. Rimmo's white-ball bowling was a positive but we only scored two hundreds and one of them was Richo, who we lost to a thigh injury early on. I was frustrated with the top order, which was our real strength in 2017. In 2018 we didn't get a single fifty from the top two. We had Tom at four, arguably our best player, but we never really set up the innings well enough. We were always five down after 30, which doesn't allow you to hit the last 20 well enough. Clarky [Graham Clark] couldn't find his 2017 form [averaging 39 in 2017, 16 in 2018]; Colly opened a couple of times, which was a bit of a left-field one to try to keep the fires lit under him by giving him new challenges, but his body was creaking a touch. Cam [Steel] played four games, but he'd only played seven List A games in his life.'

Batting was also the major problem in the Championship. Points are awarded for every 50 first-innings runs from 200–400 and Durham claimed two from their floodlit pink-ball match at home to Warwickshire, but their 297 was still way behind the opposition's 424, which featured 170 from Jonathan Trott. Not until the final game, versus Middlesex, did Durham claim any against the red ball at the Riverside, amassing 310. Dismissed for under 100 against Kent and Derbyshire, Durham trumped it in their final away match, at Leicester. Unable to cope with the class of strongly wind-assisted Pakistan seamer Mohammad Abbas, they were bowled out twice in a day, for 61 and 66. Their previous lowest first-class score was 67, against Middlesex at Lord's in 1996. Of the five second-innings wickets Abbas took to add to five in the first, four were bowled. 'It was embarrassing, and that's not a word I've had to use before,' said Lewis in the aftermath.

Durham led at the end of the first innings of only three 2018 Championship matches. The experiment, started in 2017, of giving away captains the option of bowling first did not help the most northerly team in a competition largely pushed to the margins of the season to prioritise limited-overs cricket. Leicestershire in May and Warwickshire in June's day-nighter tossed up at the Riverside but

Middlesex surprisingly batted first in September because they won a game of rock, paper, scissors – Collingwood had got out of the habit of bringing a coin to the toss. 'Because of the [uncontested toss] rule everyone's trying to produce a pitch which would require a toss, so if they're still not capable of it, you've got to say everyone needs a 50-50 chance of first use of it,' Lewis argues.

Perhaps, as in the Riverside's early days, Durham's batsmen found the confidence lost playing regularly on such bowler-friendly pitches difficult to recover on their travels. Steel top-scored with 638 runs and his average of 29 was the highest of any Durham batsman to play five or more matches. 'The first thing you have to say is we didn't play well enough,' stresses Lewis. 'Any cricketer needs resilience because there are difficult days and if you carry them around with you, when things are in your favour you miss out. Later in the season a lot of our batsmen had a lot of baggage. Pre-season was a nightmare, we didn't practise on grass. We had nine days of matchplay scheduled and played one. We didn't have a grass net – the bowlers were on grass, the batsmen were on a mat with snow all around.

'We got blown away by Matt Henry in our first game [the Kent bowler took 12-73] and didn't realise he was going to do that to everyone,' says Lewis. 'Then we went to Northants for our second game and didn't bowl a ball for four days. In our third Championship game the batsmen were still looking for their first runs. We should have dealt better with some difficult circumstances.'

Durham's batting struggles mirrored those nationally, even at Test level, despite a mid-season heatwave. Middlesex, Gloucestershire, Northamptonshire and Glamorgan recorded fewer batting points than Durham's 16 (no one in Division One did), and Kent were promoted with the same number. Surrey's Rory Burns (1,359), Somerset's James Hildreth (1,089), Warwickshire's Ian Bell (1,027), Derbyshire/Nottinghamshire's Ben Slater (1,025) and Wayne Madsen of Derbyshire (1,016) were the only players to score 1,000-plus Championship runs and just 12 averaged over 40 from double-figure appearances. The 19 instances of teams bowled out for less than 100 was the third highest in 40 years. 'I think the balls did more,' says Smith, who averaged 21 in nine matches. 'I remember in the Sussex game here being thrown the ball and just thinking, "The seam's massive!" I'd never thought that at any stage in my career or any other time that year. I wouldn't want to use it as a massive excuse but the scores were down everywhere bar [champions] Surrey.'

Lewis insists that does not tell the full story. 'It doesn't mean there hasn't been progression from the players, it just means it hasn't yet translated itself into the numbers,' he argues. 'That is probably indicated by our batsman of the year being Tom Latham, who only played four Championship games but made as many scores above 50 as anyone bar Cameron Steel [Latham three, Steel five]. We had 11 players averaging 20–29. For some of the bowlers that's OK, but you can't have your entire frontline batting line-up doing that and expect to do well. But there wasn't a visiting batsman who scored a hundred at the Riverside in red-ball cricket, yet we scored three. Over the course of a season we only conceded four hundreds and scored six.

'We'd like to have achieved promotion and we didn't get that close but I still think we finished a better side than we started, even though we ran out of gas and a couple of the late results weren't great. I don't think we were as far off as the final position looks.' Eighth in the ten-team Division Two with four wins, Durham's 130 points were only 32 more than in 2017 after their 48-point deduction.

Matt Dixon, an Australian with a British passport, took five wickets in nine one-day matches on loan from Essex in May/June, but was not retained for the resumption of Championship cricket. He was replaced by ex-Essex and Hampshire seamer Matt Salisbury, who took 44 wickets in ten Championship appearances. 'Salisbury was outstanding from the moment he came in and Rushy was outstanding in all three formats [taking a combined 80 wickets] – his powerplay bowling in the [Twenty]20s was a big part of our season – but nobody else took 20 [Championship] wickets,' Lewis points out.

It did not help that injury restricted James Weighell to just three Championship appearances, Matty Potts to two, and Brydon Carse none. Wood only played four games. 'Injuries are a part of life, even more so for young fast bowlers,' says Lewis. 'To have lost [Paul] Coughlin was one of the more frustrating aspects because he'd had three years of stress fractures and finally got to the point where he could get through a season. We just didn't have many new-ball options without Coughlin and [Graham] Onions.'

At times, Durham showed good character with their backs to the wall. Following on 256 behind in their third Championship game, they beat Leicestershire by 46 runs. Weighell's 38 helped set the visitors 148 to win after Aiden Markram's 94, Steel's 86 and Smith's 74. Rushworth took three early wickets, then limped off with a groin injury. 'It inspired me because I knew I had the job of bowling them out,' said Weighell, who did so with a career-best 7-32.

Smith feels the dressing-room mindset helped. 'I've been amazed with the minimum level of fuss,' he comments. 'At Hampshire in periods of up or down there would be people who were equally up and down but the younger guys here seem pretty level about it and approach each day in a very consistent fashion, which can help you deal with the bad times but also the good times. That's why we probably did so well in Twenty20 – we got on a roll but no one got too giddy.'

However, Lewis cautions: 'You've got to be careful when you say a team has shown great character from bad situations because if you've really shown great character, you'll make sure the next time you won't be in that situation.' As Smith says: 'The challenge to become a force again is to do it from ball one and not be reactive to situations.'

In September, Durham fought off Warwickshire's interest to re-sign Ben Raine for 2019. Released in 2012 after one first-class and one one-day appearance, Sunderland-born Raine reinvented himself at Leicestershire from a batsman who bowled to a new-ball bowler capable of important batting contributions. He took 207 first-class wickets for the Foxes and made a Twenty20 century in 2018, but they released him a year early because of 'changed personal circumstances'. Along with Smith, Raine was the second English player to re-join

Durham since the 2016 semi-bailout – third if you include Ben Whitehead, let go before playing for the first XI. Like Smith, Steel captained Durham University, and even Latham and Tahir played second-team cricket for the Riversiders in their youth.

'To have sustained success you have to have a core backbone of values and ideals true to that particular club,' Smith argues. 'A lot of Surrey's [2018] Championship-winning team were home-grown players alongside world-class players. It was very similar when we had success. Ben Raine's a local lad, a competitor who will step forward before anyone else. He'll want to be dominant in a game early on.

'The fabric of the place and a lot of the people around the club, the people that are the heartbeat of it, from Lesley and Dorothy on reception to the catering staff and most of the coaching staff, are just the same as when I left [in 2013], which is fantastic. There's still those core beliefs. But equally the squad is so different in terms of how many are proven players – most of the guys are in the first half of their career. It's incredibly exciting to be involved in something like that.'

Lewis says Smith was signed to add much-needed experience and Raine to add quality, rather than for their backgrounds. 'We're more looking to sign players we believe can play for England again,' he stresses. 'All the players who have come through our system, you want them to believe that being successful for Durham is a stepping stone. Leesy [Lees] can play for England and stranger things have happened than players of Ben's type doing it. He has to get better but he's got so much better over the last two or three years. It's an added bonus that Ben's a local lad.

'The identity of the club is really important and that's about production of players – ideally from the north east – and success on the field, but if Cameron Steel becomes a top player there's no downside to the fact he was born in California. It is important they are thinking about going higher and if they fall short, we still have excellent players.'

The off-field changes continued, with ex-Australia batsman Marcus North returning to the club he played for in 2004 as director of cricket to replace the retiring Geoff Cook. North will be much more involved at senior level than Cook, who was sidelined after stepping down as coach.

That, along with the new and changed coaching roles in the structure North created marginalised Lewis's role to the point where when the existing staff were invited to reapply for their jobs, he decided to leave instead.

Raine was Durham's 14th external post-semi-bailout signing, as opposed to ten from 2010–16. Increased recruitment was always going to be necessary after the 2016–17 exodus, but what does it say about the production line? Durham's second XI reached their Twenty20 semi-finals in 2018, beaten by Essex in a game reduced to five overs a side by rain, but won their Championship after drawing with them in the final at Chester-le-Street.

This time the weather worked in Durham's favour. They bowled Essex out for 130, then posted 263 with wicketkeeper Ryan Davies, another 2018 signing, top-scoring with 83. Second-innings centuries from Aaron Beard (124) and Feroze Khushi (123) set the hosts 247 to win, and they closed day three in trouble on 90/7, but the rain that brought them off early that afternoon allowed only 27 final-day overs. When last-wicket pair Whitehead and Chris McBride batted out 42 deliveries to secure a draw, the title went to Durham because they led after the first innings.

With only one fifty all season – in Twenty20 cricket – and 17 wickets, it was no surprise Collingwood retired aged 42. Had he done so 12 months earlier it would have felt like abandoning a sinking ship, but now he was much more confident about the future. 'The T20 campaign was a very positive season for us and we nearly got to Finals Day, but in the Championship we just weren't able to get any rhythm with the bat and post many big scores,' he says. 'We always seemed to be trying to drag our way back into games. It was a season where I think everyone in the dressing room was disappointed, but we recruited really well and I think there are real positive signs we will move in the right direction.'

20.

Recreating the Magic

THE 2018 appointments of Tim Bostock and Marcus North heralded the start of a new chapter in the history of Durham County Cricket Club. David Harker had been chief executive for 18 years, while Geoff Cook had driven the cricketing side throughout Durham's first-class life. The challenge for Harker's replacement Bostock and Cook's successor North will be adding fresh ideas without damaging what made the club so successful.

'The future has to look brighter – it can't be darker – but you could bring the greatest business brains in the country in to run this place; there's no silver bullet,' insists Bostock.

Things have to change, though. 'Because the base of the squad is very different to a few years ago, you can't keep doing the same thing,' argues North. He has been here before. The Australian, then an uncapped 24-year-old, played for Durham in 2004. They finished bottom of Championship Division Two, one-from-bottom in the Twenty20 northern group, sixth in the 45-over National League's second division, and were knocked out of the 50-over Cheltenham and Gloucester Trophy at the first attempt; yet Liam Plunkett, Phil Mustard and Graham Onions became England internationals, and Paul Collingwood and Kyle Coetzer captained their countries; Gordon Muchall retired as one of Durham's top-five first-class century-makers, and Mark Davies with the best average of bowlers to take more than 50 wickets.

'After 2004 there was a pretty clear moment to really look at what they did and there was some important recruitment,' North reflects. 'You have these natural cycles as a club, and not very often do you get an opportunity to stop and look at how we do things and have a real clear understanding of how we move forward. Durham's in that stage. The same outcome would be great but it's hard to get another Michael Hussey, because there isn't another one.'

Jon Lewis became the first victim of North's re-evaluation, choosing to leave in December 2018 after 21 years at the Riverside when his head coach's job was effectively downgraded.

After Durham, North played county cricket for Lancashire, Derbyshire, Gloucestershire, Hampshire and Glamorgan, as well as wearing the baggy green cap of Australia. Having married a Gateshead girl, he returned to the north east in 2015 as South Northumberland's chief executive, and has been a Durham supporter ever since. Supporting is how he sees his director of cricket job. 'You've got directors of cricket in a suit, guys more in a tracksuit, and guys who do a bit of both,' he says. 'I've got to give it some time and get some understanding of how I'd be best utilised. If there are times to use my experience as a coach or a mentor or a player, that's a given, it will happen naturally; but my job's probably going to be more balanced towards the administrative side. It's about getting a really good support group for the players, then challenging the coaches to look at ways to get better, to get the team better. Initially I'll be looking more at producing a really good high-performance team which then leads the show, but we're merging with the Durham Cricket Board [who organise recreational cricket in the county] and my role is to have an influence on the pathway too, so over time I'll put more energy into that.

'It's about how we create the best learning environment to develop these guys – not quickly, but with intent to show progression straight away. We've got a group of guys, many of whom are still establishing themselves as consistent first-class players. We've seen Surrey win the [2018] Championship after a cycle of being in and out of the first division, then bringing through some good academy players and recruiting some really good international mentors into an environment where the majority of them have been together. We can do that here. The successful teams all have very similar philosophies, it's not rocket science. The magic is how you create that environment.'

Durham have the same invaluable base as in 2004/05. 'Our pathways and our academy have been a great foundation,' North reflects. 'So many players have come through the system that have become extremely good first-class players or, even better, internationals. Of those internationals, all but Paul Collingwood [who pre-dated it] have come through the academy, which obviously shows we're doing something right. People will, and always have, looked at Durham and how they do that. That's great credit to John Windows, heavily mentored and influenced by Geoff Cook.

'The challenge is to keep evolving and challenging that environment to get better. We've got some really good catchment areas – Cumbria, Northumberland, Durham, Scotland – but it's not a given that we have a pool of talent that just rightfully comes through. John and his team work really hard at talent identification and developing them in the right way. I think young people, certainly in Durham terms, are craving to learn. We don't have an environment where the group is happy to be satisfactory.'

Keaton Jennings and Neil Killeen had that mindset as Durham players. 'The guys are going to get an opportunity to learn as I did in 2012 and 2013, and make a life out of playing cricket, which is fantastic,' says England international Jennings. Killeen recalls: 'It was almost a bit of a sink-or-swim environment when we came through, and we're not far off that point again where you have a few seasoned pros but the majority of the team is pretty young. Whilst we're still in the second division, we can look to put youngsters into that side. We may have missed that opportunity a little bit in our first couple of seasons, but if the second-teamers keep knocking on the door with 150s and five-wicket hauls, that's what it's about.'

There is little doubt, though, after losing the core of their side in 2016/17, outside help is needed. 'I had so many young Durham players say to me when I left, "Who am I going to speak to now?"' Graham Onions reveals. 'When I was coming through I had six or seven experienced bowlers around me and you could just see what they do – not necessarily talk to them, just see how they prepare, how they try to win games in certain situations.'

For Durham's recruits, 'Strong character is absolutely key,' according to North. 'We need people we are very confident will buy into the Durham spirit and add to it. Their skillset has to be of high quality, but it's not just about performances, it's the character of the person. Over the years we've had some really, really good players come in from overseas, but people like Callum Thorp and Gareth Breese are really, really good people too. Gareth might not have been the first name on everyone's lips when you talk about key players, but if you ask the blokes in the dressing room they would say he was for what he did, on and off the field. Callum Thorp was an outstanding bowler but also a great character.

'Alex Lees had a quiet period at Yorkshire, but he brought up his 5,000th first-class run [against Sussex in September 2018]. He's got a lot of cricket to play, and it wasn't long ago he was in the England Lions set-up. Michael Hussey is known as Mr Cricket and I grew up with Cameron Bancroft in Western Australia at the back end of my career; and that tag got aligned to him as well. He's extremely competitive and will be a great addition. Ben Raine has been a seasoned campaigner. They're all good characters. We want players who can perform, but they've got to be the right people to help create an environment where the players are a bit more challenging of themselves, but with support. It's easy to create a challenging environment, but if you don't support them you don't get that learning and that buy-in.'

Largely left to Jon Lewis and Collingwood between 2013 and 2018, recruitment will become a more collegiate process in the new coaching structure designed to spread expertise throughout the club now they have left. 'I'll certainly have influence,' North promises. 'I'm not a believer in one bloke being responsible for everything. We've got blokes like Neil Killeen, Alan Walker and John Windows who have been on the ground for a long time and they've got an eye for talent. We need to not be reactive, looking at the strengths of the squad, the ages, to see when players might retire and move on so we can look two to three years ahead.'

It will be a lot easier back in Division One. 'We've got a great culture built by Geoff Cook and his team over the last 15 years of real success at the top of the English pyramid, producing brilliant players for England,' North comments. 'That gives Durham's members, supporters, cricket followers in the north east and, more importantly, us as a club high expectations. We're not a club to stay still, we want to be competing. We're a first-division club and we want to get back there to represent the north east in the top flight again.'

Chairman Sir Ian Botham is typically confident that will happen quickly. 'I'll certainly be having a punt on us [to win promotion in 2019],' he says. 'We have more right to be in Division One than any other county on present-day form and the players we've produced. Other clubs can't whinge because you can't produce England players if you've got Kolpaks and overseas players, although every club might need one or two to compete. Once you get into the top tier you can be winning it the next season if not that season.'

Attracting players of the calibre of Lees, Bancroft and Raine was a significant step forward, says former coach Lewis. 'If you want a player to join you, you've got to sell him something,' he argues. 'In terms of pay, I don't think we were way behind everyone but I'm pretty confident we offered less to those who chose to join us, so they had to be thinking there was something other than money they were coming for. Durham want to be successful and produce players, and I think people want to be involved in that type of club.

'The connection between the club and the region is different at Durham. I've only played at one other county 20-odd years ago, and Essex is a really well-run club I really enjoyed playing for, but you cannot say the connection is the same. Everybody thinks they've got a really good dressing room when they're winning, but we had a good dressing room when we didn't win as well. We had one of our lowest points of 2018 at Leicester. Ben Raine was telling me when they lost against us here they couldn't keep the team together, they were all wanting to get off. When we lost at Leicester we couldn't get the bus home because the driver had done too many hours, so we were staying for the night and we made a conscious effort to keep the whole side together for the whole evening. There wasn't a moment's question. That can serve Durham well at times, and comes across to opposing players too. Because it's been there doesn't mean it will always be there, but so long as they maintain the identity they've had throughout our first-class history, they should be in good shape.'

North believes it extends beyond the club and even the sport. 'The club has a unique and special spirit,' he claims. 'I experienced it in 2004, I've seen it over the last four years as a supporter and I've spoken to a lot of people who have played against Durham and visited here. Even in 2018, the thing that stood out was the spirit. The team was very inconsistent, sometimes losing heavily in the Championship but bouncing back and winning against some top teams, and without a strong spirit and culture that probably wouldn't be the outcome. A lot of that is to do with the people before but also it's a special place, the north east. We see that in our football clubs, in Newcastle Falcons [rugby union side], Newcastle Eagles [basketball club] – there's a great spirit and a great support for sport in the north east.'

Will Smith, not born in the region but lured back twice after graduating from Durham University in 2005, sees it too. 'A lot of counties will have their own idiosyncrasies which make them feel special, but the people who come here build an instant affinity, which is a credit to what has been built here over the last 20, 25 years,' he says. 'People feel a slight difference to any other place.'

North will measure progress in much the way David Boon did. 'It's easy to say we want to win all competitions, everyone does, I'm more worried about the process to get into a position to do that,' he stresses. 'In the next two to three years it's important we can look back at the end of each season to say this team has progressed, it's getting more consistent and we're seeing players establish themselves as very good first-class cricketers and beyond. We want people putting themselves into [England] Lions contention. If we're getting people picked for higher honours, we know we're doing things right here from a structure and a professionalism point of view.'

Despite their financial troubles, Durham have pressed ahead with a project Tom Moffat was raising funds for more than a decade earlier – to build a nursery ground just behind the Riverside to be used by schools, clubs and the academy. 'If you'd asked when they built the ground if you could ever outgrow the facilities, I bet no one would have foreseen that,' says Windows. 'The majority of clubs in the region that would be up to hosting second XI or academy cricket are maxed out with junior teams, three senior teams, and we're asking them to start women's sections. Groundsmen can't find space on the ground to service 16 grass nets; there's just not the facilities. It will be a training base for the junior teams and provide nets. Initially it was hoped we would have a ground the same size as the Riverside but the cost of that is in the millions, not the £150,000 we managed to raise.'

Having crowdfunded £52,150 in 2015, Durham finally sowed the seeds on the ground in 2018, although a wet winter and hot summer delayed its opening. 'It's massive for the club,' says Bob Jackson. 'We've been very well looked after by the clubs but we need our own place now. The development of the women's academy is massive, and that's increased the demand for pitches. I'm sure the boys, particularly the 13- and 14-year-olds, will be excited to play so close to the county ground. Durham will never lose that vision to develop young players. It's not what we've achieved that I'm most proud of, it's that we've done it the right way.'

Given its importance to Durham, supporting league cricket is critical. 'The standards have dipped a little bit and clubs are struggling financially and for players,' Neil Killeen warns. 'Clubs are struggling to turn out two teams on the same day so I'd love us to go to purely first XI cricket on a Saturday and move second XI cricket to Sundays, with third XI midweek to take off the pressure of having to turn out 22 players, for volunteers and umpires. We've got to get the quality on the field as good as it can be, whether that be players, pitches or umpires.'

The nursery ground brings together the two strands Botham intends to rebuild Durham on – the continued production of youngsters, and stronger community links. 'This club is going to be accessible to everyone,' he promises. 'In the winter we want club sides to use the facilities, in the summer we want kids coming into the ground from teatime onwards for no charge. That's how we start the growth again. The club was dying on its feet. It's a rebirth.'

It is something Simon Henig is keen to push now his council is on the board. 'The strong relationships we're building with the whole community need to persist,' he says. 'The way the board's now populated it's not just about cricket, it's about lots of other things – it's about the community and the sporting community, as shown by having [athlete-turned-commentator] Allison Curbishley there. I think it's in a stronger position.

'I want to see a well-functioning community body in Chester-le-Street that puts on lots of events and isn't actually just about cricket. The concerts the Riverside hosts are great for the local community and I want to see it develop as a real community hub, working with everyone else in Chester-le-Street, because it puts the town, the county and the region on the map, and that fantastic view of Lumley Castle on its own dispels myths about the north east; that's massive publicity for us. We should all be proud every time we see any international game at the Riverside showing off a vibrant, full stadium and that lovely view of Lumley Castle and showing people, "This is the north east." We've got to try and preserve that in the most sustainable way we can.'

Henig is determined the council will be supportive, but not exploited. 'They knew we were not going to call in the loan [in 2016],' he says. 'From what I understand, that's what [usually] sends football clubs into administration. Potentially we wouldn't have got a penny back. I just don't understand why some people would think that was the right way to go, to lose everything that had been done over the previous 25 years. It was important that the terms were always a loan, though. I'm constantly aware that we're living in a period of austerity that is clearly very difficult for the council. Council services are under a lot of strain and a lot of other organisations outside the council are, so it was entirely right for ourselves and the LEP [local enterprise partnership] that it was done in that way. It's probably more likely that the council will get that resource back now.'

Tim Bostock explains: 'We've got ten years to pay off the council debt but we're committed to putting big holes in that in the next three or four. We've got a debt with the LEP which will be paid off in 2019. The ECB are not rushing for us to pay them back but they fund us anyway, so if they were there are ways for them to get it back. I don't think that's a major concern, albeit we'd like to clear it. We could do it within a relatively short period but it would leave us with no money to grow the business, so you've got to take a sensible five-to-seven-year approach. With that amount of debt, if we rushed to pay it off in two to three years, we'd be back to square one.'

The 2019 World Cup ought to provide extra revenue, with the Riverside hosting three matches, and the ECB are introducing compensation for clubs with centrally-contracted players at the Indian Premier League. Given that it will be based on earnings, Ben Stokes's county could be the biggest beneficiaries. From 2020, the plan is for The Hundred to raise much-needed funds for county cricket. 'In two years we'll be as solvent as any club in the country. There are a lot of clubs financially far worse off than we are,' Botham insists. Bostock stresses: 'This is a small business in terms of turnover even though it's massively high profile. You don't need millions to make a difference. If you create an additional revenue stream to provide £250,000, £300,000 a year, that's often all you need.'

After more than a decade of trying, Durham are still hoping a 140- or 150-room Riverside hotel could be what David Harker calls 'a game-changer'. 'Every time we get a game here teams stay in

Newcastle,' Botham complains. 'We could have a hotel just there [he says, pointing to the north-east corner of the Riverside]. We'll be open all year round with restaurants, gymnasium and what have you. We'd create probably 100 jobs for this area – or more – and then you've got the spin-offs. You speak to people before and it was always, "We couldn't do this, we couldn't do that," but now you're going to have your hotel. We'll take a little bit out of the book of the Ageas [formerly Rose] Bowl because [Hampshire chairman] Rod Bransgrove's a very good friend of mine, and I've picked his brains a bit about how the hotel works – and it's making a killing. There's stuff that should have been done that hasn't been. I know certain people said in the past, "We're not doing it unless it's as good as they've got," but the north east is slightly different to the south coast or London.'

It is not quite that straightforward. 'Part of the development would be in a flood plain,' Harker cautions. 'There are issues around that and raising the money with land values in the north east, but if we could do it, it would give us great confidence around our ability to invest in cricket around the region, in particular in terms of facilities for women's and girls' cricket.'

Bostock believes the hotel project highlights why lingering resentment towards English cricket's governing body needs to be let go. 'I've had a few meetings with the ECB and I think our relationship's really good,' he says. 'They want Durham to succeed without any doubt whatsoever. We absolutely have to bring the ECB along on the journey because one of the restrictions they placed on us was a first charge on the ground, so they had line of sight over anything we planned to do in terms of development. That's absolutely fair enough. When we get to the final proposal I'll go down to Lord's and speak to the guys there to sign off on it. If they're happy with it, they'll remove the charge and a bank will be more liable to get involved and there's a whole circle of relationships affected.'

That area of the ground is one Bostock has designs on. 'If you take a real long-term view, I'd like to make the north-east terrace look much prettier with picket fences and marquees,' he says. 'We want to reinvest in the ground because, whilst it's a very nice ground, it's tired. In a perfect world we'd like to be starting after the World Cup matches with a view to finishing it in 2021 to supply us with an additional revenue stream. As well as the hotel, there's going to be a conference centre and banqueting centre, we're going to revamp the bar in the Don Robson Pavilion, and there's a restaurant chain interested so that should create more of an experience.'

Could Chester-le-Street one day become a Test venue again? 'Durham would need to demonstrate clearly that Test-match cricket was a vitally important part of their business model, and have a sustainable business to get back in,' Gordon Hollins replies. 'International cricket has to be there for a very specific reason.' Bostock is more interested in the Riverside forcing its way on to The Hundred map after being overlooked as a venue. 'I can't see The Hundred only playing its [north-eastern] games in Leeds, I think they'll end up playing a game here,' he believes. 'Either that or they will increase the number of teams to ten and have an extra team here and in the south west. But first they'll want to get the eight up and running.'

So much for the future, but what about the past? Before we even start our interview, Botham makes it clear he does not want to think about it. 'Those days are gone, they're history,' he insists. 'It's done, it's dusted, it's water under the bridge. What happens here is from this day on. That's all I'm interested in.' If Durham – if anyone in county cricket – ignore their mistakes, they risk repeating them.

It took huge ambition to break into the closed shop of English first-class cricket and once Durham were in they were not going to be satisfied with making up the numbers. It was both their strength and their undoing. 'All clubs are encouraged to maximise their ambitions,' Cook argues. 'Durham wanted international cricket – and the ultimate is an Ashes match. All the things that are required of county cricket – such as producing your own players and international players – Durham fulfilled those in spades. The aspirations were wonderful and did credit to the people involved and the Durham cricketing people because it was all for them, really.

'If Clive [Leach] was guilty of anything it was that the club wanted overtly to be successful, not just in terms of claiming international cricket, but winning trophies. The players to do that were getting better and demanded a bit more dosh, so the club paid out some decent wages and breached the salary cap. I think that brought resentment from other clubs which manifested itself in varying ways – that's my interpretation, anyway. I think the ECB should have advised better, not necessarily given financial help or exclusions or whatever, but a better steer would have been beneficial.'

Harker asks: 'Could we have muddled on, found a way through, found a better solution? I think we were at a point where enough was enough; it had to be sorted. Even if cost-cutting made arithmetic sense, we wouldn't have been able to contribute in anything like the same way and it was made clear to us that the ECB wanted to preserve Durham; they appreciated what had been achieved.'

As one of those who led Durham into first-class cricket, Tom Moffat has no regrets. 'I cannot think of anything I was involved with that I would have done differently,' he insists. 'A lot of people say we bought trophies but I think that stems a bit from jealousy. I always believe our success was largely down to having the infrastructure right.'

'You'd think there are bound to be lots of things you would have done differently with the benefit of hindsight,' adds Harker, 'but honestly, if you look at it, could we have raised more income elsewhere? In terms of our trading income, we did as well as most. On the back of the success we had on the playing field we pulled in Emirates [as sponsors]. What you can always do is cut more costs, but the amount you would have had to have taken out of the business, which was pretty lean to start with, would have decimated the business and the playing side. If you'd have done that – and you'd have to have sustained that for a number of years – what would we have achieved in terms of producing England players and success on the field? If we aren't producing England players and we aren't competitive on the field, why would the ECB or anyone else want to support you? We genuinely tried everything we could to bring in private investment. That's where we failed.

'The only thing I can think of that we might have done differently is that very early in the piece we should have said to the ECB: "This isn't going to work." Pre-2007 we should have said, "The model's broken, the bidding thing [to host internationals] is going to cripple us, so unless we can find a solution then we're going to have to close the gates." But of course the attitude has always been, "Let's give it a go, let's do what we can, let's be positive and try and make it work." We're a club that has punched above its weight despite the financial limitations, rather than because we've indulged in over-spending. The biggest difference between us and the other larger venues is that we've not had the same share of international cricket.'

Their close brush with extinction has done nothing to quell Durham's ambition – not with Botham as chairman. Just as in 1992, he has brought new energy. 'I've never known a chairman with more passion,' comments Paul Collingwood. Although Botham does not spend much time at the Riverside, when he appears, 'It gives people a bit of a shot in the arm,' says Harker. Within hours of his first day, a sponsorship deal with Royal Caribbean was announced. 'I haven't been able to spend as much time here as I would have liked but that will change in 2019 because my diary fills up 18 months in advance,' Botham explains. 'But my job's not really to sit here watching cricket, my job is to go out there, source certain deals – to really generate interest, and hopefully income, for Durham County Cricket Club.

'I'm really enjoying it. I wouldn't do it if I didn't. I don't take a single penny out of the club; I'm doing it because I believe in it. That rather shoots people down straight away. When I come to games I bring my family and my mates along. Why do you think someone like Ben Stokes stays here, why does Woody? Why do you think if they aren't playing for England, they're here in the dressing room? It's simple – because this is a family. That's what we want to build it back as. It was certainly a family for many years and then they lost a few members but we've got to move on, there's no point harping on about it.

'This is a bit of an evolution and it's great to be part of it. We're not going to sit back and wait for things to happen, we're going to do our utmost to make them happen. That's the way I did it as a player, that's how I like to think I do it when I'm commentating – I always want to go forwards, not backwards – and it's very much the same attitude as chairman of Durham County Cricket Club. We don't want to take a backward step, we've done all that. Now that we're on the front foot, we're going to stay on the front foot.'

Harker thinks Botham is right to talk about evolution, not revolution. 'If you look at the building blocks of a successful club, all of them are in place,' he argues. 'Sometimes it sounds as if the whole place was trashed [in 2016] and we had to build it up from scratch. The academy's still there, we've probably got the strongest off-field staff we've had because we've been able to invest a bit in that, so the rebuilding is more about replacing playing talent. All of the other bits and pieces either had never gone away or are in better shape.'

Whatever the future holds, Cook is sure Durham will be England's last new first-class county. 'Without a shadow of a doubt,' he says. 'It's like heresy for me to say it but you look at Durham County Cricket Club and I don't know how many people we employ or what the turnover is, but to replicate that 18 times – is that the right thing for English cricket really? I'm a real believer in the best playing the best and, if that means regional cricket at four-day level or T20 level or whatever, that will improve the standard of domestic English players. It's a compromise to keep 18 counties happy and I think a nettle has to be grasped. It will take a very brave man to do that, or a couple of counties – as Durham nearly did – to disappear but the ECB exists for those 18 counties, it's in their constitution.'

It is something Gordon Hollins may have to wrestle with at some point. 'The question I get asked the most is: "Are there too many first-class counties?"' he admits. 'My answer is always the same: "We need as many good first-class counties as we can get." If 24's the right number, we should have 24. If 18's the right number, or 12, that's how many we should have. The game's job is to get the maximum return from all 39 counties [in England] for the good of cricket in this country, whatever the best way of doing that might be.

'Cheshire is the tenth-biggest cricket county in the country in terms of clubs and players; half of Lancashire's team are from Cheshire. It works, so why touch it? Our job [at the ECB] is to give the support and direction for counties to be the best they can. If you let someone like Derbyshire go, I don't think cricket's better for that. You probably wouldn't start from here – you'd probably have Cheshire as a first-class county but it's not the way it is and it doesn't need to be different – as long as it works.'

County cricket constantly seems to be in a state of self-analysis, seeking to improve attendances and, when they are not going well, England's results. The turn-of-the-millennium solution was splitting the Championship into divisions, but Durham are now finding how vulnerable it leaves those Division Two clubs producing quality players. Bob Jackson was as frustrated as anyone at seeing Paul Coughlin picked off by Nottinghamshire in 2017, yet he insists: 'I'm a strong two-division man – the best play the best and I think it's better to produce strong international cricketers. The sad thing is, they're not allowed to play for their counties sufficiently. I think if we'd won promotion, Coughlin would have stayed, but that was never going to happen.' Bostock blames 'the yo-yoing between Divisions One and Two' for some of the damaging short-termism at other counties.

Get mired in Division Two for too long and the danger is Durham might effectively become a feeder club to richer, Test-hosting counties higher up the food chain. Even though he made the jump to one of the 'haves' in the winter of 2016/17, Surrey's former Durham captain Mark Stoneman cannot see that happening. 'If the business model is there to support the work done in the academy and keep the production line going while enabling the growth of players to international standard and recruiting accordingly, of course Durham can get back to winning ways,' he says. 'It won't happen overnight, and any success needs many factors to come together, but there's no question Durham will always remain a key player in a successful English county system.'

In the early years of the 21st century the Riversiders set standards Bostock, North and those at other counties aspire to. It could not have happened without great vision, talent, dedication and ambition. 'I'm proud to have been involved,' says Cook. 'It was a privilege really to help bring a lot of satisfaction to the north east.' It has been a remarkable story but it is not over yet.

'As for what happens in the next couple of years, it could be anything, which is exciting,' says Will Smith, 'but hopefully things happen a bit more as a natural course of time and performance. I'm sure there are so many people who will try to understand how it went from 2009–2013 to where it is now, but the only way is up in certain respects. Why couldn't that happen again? We're at a starting point with much more infrastructure and experience than in 1992. Why can't this be the start of something incredible again – but maybe with a slightly more gradual rise this time?'

Whatever the future holds for Durham, it will do well to match the drama of their first quarter of a century as a first-class county.

Select Bibliography

Books

Graeme Fowler, *Absolutely Foxed*, Simon and Schuster, 2016

Simon Hughes, *A Lot of Hard Yakka*, Headline, 1997

Ian Botham with Peter Hayter, *Botham: My Autobiography*, Collins Willow, 1994

Michael Vaughan with Martin Hardy, *Calling the Shots*, Hodder and Stoughton, 2005

Andrew Strauss, *Coming Into Play*, Hodder and Stoughton, 2006

Jack Bannister and David Graveney, *Durham CCC: Past, Present and Future,* Queen Anne Press, 1993

Simon Hughes, *From Minor to Major*, Hodder and Stoughton, 1992

Simon Wilde, *Ian Botham: The Power and the Glory*, Simon and Schuster, 2011

Tom Moffat, *The Impossible Dream… Come True*, FPO Print, 2009

Ben Stokes with Richard Gibson, *Firestarter: Me, Cricket and the Heat of the Moment*, Headline, 2016

Stephen Harmison, *Speed Demons*, Sport Media, 2017

Tim Wellock, *Summers With Durham*, Caboodle Books, 2009

Michael Hussey, *Underneath the Southern Cross*, Hardie Grant, 2013

Newspapers, magazines and periodicals (various editions)

All Out Cricket magazine

The Cricketer magazine

The Cricketer's Who's Who

The Cricket Paper

Daily Express
Daily Mail
Daily Mirror
Daily Telegraph
Durham CCC Yearbook
The Guardian
i
The Independent
The Journal
Manchester Evening News
Newcastle Chronicle/Evening Chronicle/Football Pink
Northern Echo
Nottingham Evening Post
The Observer
The Sun
Sunderland Echo
Sunday Sun
Sunday Telegraph
The Times
Wisden Cricketers' Almanack
Wisden Cricket Monthly

Websites
BBC.co.uk
Cricket Archive
CricketWorld.com
DurhamCCC.co.uk
ESPN Cricinfo
MindTheWindows.com
You Tube

Index

349